Public Management in
an Interconnected World

Recent Titles in
Contributions in Political Science

Public Management in an Interconnected World

Essays in the Minnowbrook Tradition

Edited by
Mary Timney Bailey
and
Richard T. Mayer

Contributions in Political Science, Number 293

GREENWOOD PRESS
New York • Westport, Connecticut • London

Library of Congress Cataloging-in-Publication Data

Public management in an interconnected world : essays in the
  Minnowbrook tradition / edited by Mary Timney Bailey and Richard T.
  Mayer.
      p. cm.—(Contributions in political science, ISSN 0147-1066
  ; no. 293)
    Includes bibliographical references and index.
    ISBN 0-313-27457-6 (alk. paper)
    1. Public administration. I. Bailey, Mary Timney. II. Mayer,
  Richard T. III. Series.
  JF1351.P828 1992
  350—dc20   91-34160

British Library Cataloguing in Publication Data is available.

Library of Congress Catalog Card Number: 91-34160
ISBN: 0-313-27457-6
ISSN: 0147-1066

First published in 1992

Greenwood Press, 88 Post Road West, Westport, CT 06881
An imprint of Greenwood Publishing Group, Inc.

Printed in the United States of America

The paper used in this book complies with the
Permanent Paper Standard issued by the National
Information Standards Organization (Z39.48-1984).

10 9 8 7 6 5 4 3 2 1

Contents

Preface

This volume came out of the experience that the two of us had at the second Minnowbrook Conference in 1988. Though as old in years as some of the participants of the first Minnowbrook Conference, which had been held in 1968, we were both relatively new to the academic world of what Dwight Waldo likes to denote as Public Administration when we attended the second conference. We both had—in the interim since 1968—raised families and gone back to school, we both cut our academic teeth on Frank Marini's (1971) presentation of the first conference's proceedings, and we both had spent years as practitioners.

Minnowbrook II was frustrating for both of us: there seemed to be little recognition in either the written materials or most of the discussion that American public administration—and the American polity—is playing in an entirely new game. Despite declarations during the 1980s that entrepreneurial selfishness is the key to American society's future, the rules of this new game are very different from the dominating, masculine-style, short-sighted requirements of competition and efficiency that governed the old game.

The process of Minnowbrook II, however, shaped the work in this volume. Papers prepared for Minnowbrook II had been sent to the participants. Because most participants had read most of these papers before arriving, we agreed to a one-day session in which only critiques of the papers were presented, along with short responses from the authors. After this, for the next two and a half days, we followed an ad hoc agenda.

One morning, we in the 1980s cohort insisted on having our own session separate from the 1960s people. In a brainstorming discussion, we identified those conditions we saw as fundamentally different from those in the 1960s. Most prominent among these were interdependence and interconnectedness of policy issues, private-public organizations, nation-states, and so forth; and cultural diversity in a variety of forms—the workforce, the public, the world. Public administration, it seemed to us, faces significant challenges and opportunities in such conditions.

First, we saw the impossibility of ever achieving solutions for public problems. In our world, in contrast to the 1960s world of Minnowbrook I, interconnected problems can never be solved but can only be *ameliorated*. Second, we saw the public administrator as the central actor in an interconnected world. Public administration is the only sector that intersects with all others—private, political, social, and so forth. In this central position, the public administrator can take several new roles beyond efficient and effective administrator, including facilitator, negotiator, and ameliorator.

The difficulty we were left with, and the impetus behind the current collection of essays, is that public administration theory at present does not address situations of interconnectedness. Thus, we agreed, there was a need for new theory to address fundamentally different conditions than those assumed by earlier public administration scholars and theorists.

The essays in this volume represent the efforts by some of the 1980s cohort to address this need for new theory. They are original, having never been presented anywhere, at least in their present form, and they have a strong link with Minnowbrook II, because the project was essentially drawn out of that experience and the interaction of participants there. If the Minnowbrook II conference was intended to be a means of identifying new directions in the field, then this book represents a product of that effort.

Minnowbrook itself has become a metaphor for thinking about where the field is going, which is why we invited Dwight Waldo and Frank Marini to contribute to the volume. The contributions, then, represent a continuum of public administration thought in the context of what we are calling the "Minnowbrook tradition."

The interconnectedness, this interdependency of the social fabric—both within the United States and between the United States and the rest of the world—requires a new paradigm, a new world view, a new orientation. This multiversalist paradigm would be a perspective that understood the rules of empowerment, of collegiality, and of working with, toward, and through. These new rules require a dialogue between all parties, one that has regularity, trust, and honest difference of opinion and value.

The theme of interconnectedness is not original with us nor is it foreign to practitioners and theorists in the field and other management fields. Indeed, none other than Thomas Peters discusses the impact of interconnectedness on business management. Jeff S. Luke has published several articles on the same basic theme, one coauthored with Gerald Caiden in James L. Perry's *Handbook of Public Administration* (1989). At the 1990 American Society for Public Administration Conference in Los Angeles, Mary Timney Bailey convened a roundtable panel discussion that presented the basic ideas articulated above. The audience, a good mix of practitioners and academics, produced lively and productive discussion. The practitioners seemed to understand the concepts better than did the academics—it seems they operate in an interconnected world.

This collection is meant neither to be definitive nor to provide concrete directions on how to manage in an interconnected fashion. Rather, its purpose is to begin the discussion and the search for sources of new theory. Feminist theory is one place to look, but not the only one. Clearly, there are lessons to be taken from cultural and ethnic theories of diversity, environmental ethics, and others. They are not included in this volume because, unfortunately, they were not discussed in any depth at Minnowbrook II. We hope that others will add those pieces to the literature as a result of this collection.

Our "revolution" at Minnowbrook II was very similar to that of the original conference except in tone and time. Because the 1960s were different from the 1980s, we were much more genteel than they were, possibly because so many of us were women and middle-aged at that.

To help the coherence of this multiversalist paradigm develop—and develop it will—we have brought together this set of essays. We offer them to the reader in the spirit of the new game in town: will you join us in the conversation?

We would like to thank George Frederickson, as well as the godfather and the Boswell of the first Minnowbrook Conference—Dwight Waldo and Frank Marini, respectively—for their encouragement in this endeavor. Mary Ellen Guy, in addition to providing a fine contribution to this volume, was central to its creation; she arranged and coordinated several blind reviews of all the essays in the volume while they were still in manuscript form. We want to thank those reviewers for their assistance: Robert Cunningham, University of Tennessee; Robert B. Denhardt, University of Central Florida; Georgia Duerst-Lahti, Beloit College; Gerald Gabris, Northern Illinois University; Mary M. Hale, Texas Tech University; Ralph Hambrick, Virginia Commonwealth University; Larry O' Toole, Auburn University; Edward T. Jennings, Jr., University of Kentucky; Ruth Hoogland deHoog, University of North Carolina; and Mylon Winn, Indiana University.

Finally, we want to thank the other authors—it was a real pleasure learning from you.

Introduction
Frank Marini

This book has its origins directly in the second Minnowbrook Conference held in September 1988. Indirectly, it has origins in the first Minnowbrook Conference held in September 1968, the phenomena and arguments that are usually referred to as the New Public Administration, and related ideas of the last two decades. Thus—as is clear in the chapters that follow—the relationship of Minnowbrook I to Minnowbrook II is something of a subtext of this volume. I would like to comment on this relationship, on the special status of the themes of this book as an outgrowth of the Minnowbrook tradition, and on the contributions that I believe the present volume makes to public administration.

As a participant in both conferences—and especially as one who has tried on several occasions to present a critical summary of Minnowbrook I and its contributions—it was perhaps inevitable that I would experience the 1988 conference continually against the backdrop of my experience of the 1968 conference.

There were many similarities between Minnowbrook I and Minnowbrook II. Somewhat surprisingly, both conferences had few minority participants, though Minnowbrook II improved ever so slightly upon the record of Minnowbrook in this regard.[1] Both conferences exhibited:

- Deep commitment to public administration and its future;
- Profound concern for our society and its problems;
- Overall optimism that public administration can creatively contribute to a better future (as well as a sense that a dark, dreary, dangerous future could result if public administration and our society fail to cope effectively with their challenges and responsibilities);

- Concern about the epistemology and ontology of public administration and about appropriate values and our field's approach to values;
- Serious respect for social theory; and
- Emphasis upon authenticity for public administration and its practitioners and scholars.

The sense of crisis in our society was neither less nor more intense in 1988 than in 1968 (though there were differences that I will comment upon below), and the perspectives on the crises were not strikingly dissimilar.

Both meetings were concerned about the circumstances and future of minorities in the United States. Both were concerned about poverty. Both were anxious that the perception that changes are needed in our society not be weakened or diverted by inertia, uncritical acceptance of the status quo, or reactionary sentiments. Both meetings took more or less predictable sides on perennial issues:

- Democracy is good, more democracy is better;
- Bureaucracy can develop rigidities and dysfunctional aspects, and we should work against this;
- Humane phenomena, actions, ideas, and approaches are preferred to their alternatives and should be fostered;
- Public service should stand for the enlightened interest and welfare of the citizenry;
- Simplistic methodological assumptions and approaches should be eschewed for sophisticated and sound alternatives;
- Values should not be ignored by public administration, and intellectual orientations that hold otherwise are unlikely to be helpful to our field;
- Our society should be kept as open and free as possible, and we should work against any aspects that threaten to create a permanent underclass or permanent exclusions to full participation; and
- Public administration should be in the service of the people, with justice and equity among its cherished goals.

The two conferences also had some similarities in style of dialogue and participant interaction: both meetings were characterized by frank, open give-and-take, and both meetings were characterized by very cordial and collegial interactions among participants.

There were also dissimilarities between Minnowbrook I and Minnowbrook II, and it is principally in these, of course, that Minnowbrook II and its products will make new contributions to the field. The most striking and, in retrospect, the most shocking (and perhaps in some ways the most important) difference between the two conferences was in the demographics of participants. It is very embarrassing to recall that there were *no* female invitees to Minnowbrook I (whereas fifteen of the sixty-eight participants in Minnowbrook II were women). Almost as interesting a difference is that, in attempting to identify some new voices for the field, the conveners of the 1968 conference set an *age* limit, while the conveners of the 1988 conference considered date of completion of degree or comparable professional threshold event. At the 1988 conference, many—if not most—of the 1980s group had received their terminal degrees or comparable professional achievement in the 1980s but were not twenty years younger than the conference participants in the 1960s group. Perhaps we should find comfort and evidence of progress in the fact that certain characteristics of participant selection that seemed unobjectionable in 1968 seemed embarrassing in 1988. This is especially so since the conveners of the two conferences were, in the main, the same individuals.

There were some differences in style and intellectual orientation between the two conferences. No doubt the state of society and our field in 1968 and 1988, as well as the participant groups of the two meetings, help account for these differences. It seemed to me that there was considerably less heat (with no loss of light) in the discussions of Minnowbrook II than at Minnowbrook I. I heard a greater consensus about public administration's state, mission, and merit at the more recent conference. Partly this seemed to be rooted in a more practitioner and midcareer training emphasis than had been true of the 1968 conference. Partly, also, it had to do with the events of the past twenty years and the salient issues of public administration in the 1980s. The participants' sense of the state of public administration and its challenges at the 1988 meeting seemed to be a factor unifying the conferees, whereas at the 1968 meeting this had tended to be a factor dividing the group. In some ways, the 1988 group seemed to have a greater confidence in the security of public administration as a field and a greater identity with public administration as their field than seemed true in 1968. Somewhat paradoxically, this may have been partly a product of fifteen years or more of denigration of public servants and public service at the federal level. (There was much reference to "bureaucrat bashing.") Not to put too fine a point on it, but to sum it up: the 1988 meeting seemed to me to be more inside public administration and empathetic toward the dilemmas of the practitioner than the 1968 meeting.

Certain structural aspects of the 1988 meeting probably encouraged the perception that it was a meeting of two different generations. As indicated, insofar as the Minnowbrook II conference conveners organized a meeting with a generational division, it was a division of those who completed their education in the 1960s and those who completed their education in the 1980s. (Even this distinction does not fit the facts, strictly speaking, but it is close enough for present purposes.) At the conference itself there were some breakout sessions where the 1960s and the 1980s people met separately, and there were other aspects of the conference program that kept some such distinction alive in the discussions and perceptions of certainly some participants. Whether or not such a distinction makes sense in understanding Minnowbrook II, the papers presented and discussed there, and the impact of those papers and the conference upon the future of public administration, will be answered elsewhere over time.[2]

The question of generational cohort, whether relevant or not to under-standing Minnowbrook II and its contributions more generally, *is* relevant to understanding and appreciating the present volume. Some of the Min-nowbrook II participants from the 1980s group have united in this project because of their conviction that they have something new to say. This book was conceived in the later hours of the conference and formulated and implemented as a post-Minnowbrook II project. Its authors clearly believe they have something to add to the works discussed at the conference.

Moreover, that they clearly believe that, while agreeing substantially and significantly with the products of Minnowbrook I—usually called the New Public Administration—their statements are an addition to and a modification of the New Public Administration. This view is well founded. To be sure, one could question whether the view of the New Public Administration in this volume is accurate. With the exception of Jay D. White's essay, for example, most of the description of the New Public Administration seems to assume that it was totally contained in the idea of social equity and in a concern for normative theory and values. Perhaps more strikingly, there is a repeated indication that the New Public Admini-stration failed to carry out a paradigm shift; I believe that little if any evidence exists that a paradigm shift was attempted, intended, or perhaps even believed possible. Other examples could be offered, but this is not the place to pursue this question. In any case, I believe it fair to say that these authors have gone beyond the New Public Administration, no matter how one defines it.

In the last two decades, there have been intellectual developments in public administration and in the fields upon which we draw that have influenced the authors of this book and that were absent or imperceptible at Minnowbrook I. These developments have occurred in our usual sources such as the social sciences, but also in less frequent sources such as the natural sciences and philosophy, and in rare sources such as linguistics, literary criticism, and literature generally identified as feminist. Many of these intellectual developments are given admirable expression in this volume, and their relevance to the future of public administration is, in the main, cogently and eloquently stated.

While individual chapters make separate arguments and unique points, a set of themes also wends its way through the various essays. Among the salient themes are: the interconnectedness of phenomena that have not always been viewed as connected, and the fundamental importance of this; alienation; socialization; technicism; bureaucracy; democracy; deconstructionism; epistemology; methodology; paradigmatic views and the nature of theory; feminism; and sexism and its paradigmatic effects. These are not necessarily all of the same importance or prominence in the discussions, and they are accompanied by many more textual and subtextual themes than I can recognize here.

A characteristic of the present volume is a concern with paradigms, a contention that among its other shortcomings the New Public Administration failed to accomplish a paradigm shift, a sense that a new, multiversalist paradigm may be forming, and that the emerging new paradigm will incorporate an appreciation of the interconnectedness of everything. The understanding of paradigm and its related notions is, I think, not advanced beyond the understanding of the participants of Minnowbrook I, but the sense of direct, conscious participation in paradigm recognition or construction *is* different from Minnowbrook I (though perhaps not from all of the New Public Administration), and the aspects of the allegedly emerging paradigm *do* go beyond Minnowbrook I. As is usual in arguments from the paradigm perspective, other kinds and levels of theory and their status enter into the discussion. Those enamored with Kuhnian perspectives will presumably find this characteristic congenial and important; those who have been "paradigmed out" may nonetheless profit from the theoretical discussion.

Deconstructionism is a thread running through these essays, sometimes less obviously than at other times. What would normally emerge as a methodological or epistemological discussion has a richer and more varied texture here, partly because of the influence of deconstructionism— though the influences of Carl Jung, Marshall McCluhan, Edmund Husserl,

Juergen Habermas, and others are also apparent. The interplay in these essays of the concepts of paradigm, metaphor, voice, text, subtext, oral rhetoric and written rhetoric, among others, is interesting and fertile. None would pretend that all questions raised about deconstruction and related concepts are resolved here. Such is not the purpose of their introduction into the discussion. Rather, these essays do show how such concepts may help illuminate perplexing issues of concern to us all.

Feminism is important in much of the discussion, and its presence and influence are important even when feminism is not explicitly under discussion. It cannot be said that all the statements and implications about feminism are consistent in this book—indeed, there seem to be some specifically contradictory interpretations—but there is the consistent view that women, and also feminism, can contribute much to public administration and its future. The general tenor of the voice of interconnectedness is inclusive, and a sensitivity to what women and feminism may offer is consistently evident.

Although the inclusiveness of the essays obviously is meant additionally to be sensitive and hospitable to the entire ethnic and racial pluralism of our society, it cannot be said that the special perspectives of ethnicity and racial identity are given effective voice in these essays. This is partly due, no doubt, to the fact that none of the authors (as far as one can tell) are of ethnic or racial minorities, which, in turn, is a reflection of the surprisingly few minority participants at Minnowbrook II.

The chapters are also sensitive to the other aspects of pluralism in American society and have contributions to make about pluralist democracy and its relationship to complex organizations, government, and administration. As one would expect, the relationship of bureaucracy to democracy is a thread woven through much of the discussion.

This volume will undoubtedly be received, as are all such efforts, with mixed emotions. Some will agree with this, others with that; some will find insight and relevance here, others will not; some will see important innovations for the field, others will see "more of the same"; some will find here the makings of a "newer" public administration, others will doubt this. All students of public administration should, I think, find these essays interesting and worth serious consideration and reflection.

These chapters, and the other products of Minnowbrook II, are likely to revive some of the questions of "generations" stimulated by Minnowbrook I. Are the Minnowbrook conferences the disciplinary manifestation of the idea that about every twenty years each generation must set out its own course? Although those who favor such a view surely will find support for it in this volume, I think the matter is more complicated. For one thing (as has been frequently noted), people are not produced in twenty-year increments, generation-by-generation, though we sometimes find it convenient to think they do. For another, the question of whether Minnowbrook II participants, the 1980s group, and the "interconnected" subgroup all represent "generational" elements is complex. Considered from the point of view of chronological age, the 1980s group at Minnowbrook II (and its interconnected subgroup) is not, by and large, a different generation from the 1960s group made up partly of Minnowbrook I participants. Whether the roughly two decades separating the dates when members of the two groups received their terminal degrees can be said to constitute them as separate intellectual generations, although they may not constitute neat chronological generations, may be an interesting question. The most significant difficulty with interpreting the 1960s group and the 1980s group as representing different ideas, though, is that in the discussions at Minnowbrook II and, I believe, in the essays emanating from that meeting, significant variance is hard to attribute to the ideas of the two groups. Thus, insofar as Minnowbrook II represents a criticism or reformulation of Minnowbrook I, those members of Minnowbrook I also in attendance at Minnowbrook II (all Minnowbrook I participants were invited and twelve of the original thirty-three attended) seemed a part of this criticism or reformulation. Minnowbrook II seemed to represent the New Public Administration twenty years later, rather than something fundamentally different from or in opposition to the New Public Administration that came out of Minnowbrook I.

Whatever may be said of the second Minnowbrook, however, the chapters in this book frequently do have a tone of correction to the New Public Administration similar to the posture that the New Public Administration frequently took toward what it defined as the "Old Public Administration." This is clearest in the repeated assertion that the New Public Administration failed (failed to accomplish a paradigm switch, failed to effect sufficient reform, and perhaps failed to understand things now obvious or emerging). It is apparent also in the occasional unfortunate implication that insights new to the field over the last twenty years are being brought to the field solely by those who are recent products of graduate school. (It should be admitted that the New Public Administration group of twenty years ago frequently demonstrated this same attitude.) Perhaps this is only further evidence that "what goes around, comes around."

It is probably important to keep in mind something of the genesis of the present volume. The chapters in this volume were not among the manuscripts presented and discussed at Minnowbrook II. The book is, strictly speaking, a post-Minnowbrook II work, and it may be to a certain extent as much a product of arguments unaccommodated by Minnowbrook II as it is a product of the second Minnowbrook Conference. The idea for this book was partly stimulated by the sense that the second Minnowbrook Conference and its papers had neglected, or at least underappreciated, important issues.

Mary Timney Bailey wrote soon after the conference that "conferees left Minnowbrook in 1988 with a sense of incompleteness," and she asked "was this the best that could be done?" (Frederickson and Mayer 1989, 224). This sense of incompleteness gave birth to the present volume, and the chapters were born out of a desire to add significant contributions, not only to those of Minnowbrook I, but also to those of Minnowbrook II. It was decided that "interconnectedness" was an appropriate rubric under which to present these chapters. But, more perhaps even than by the concept of interconnectedness, the chapters seem defined by a set of themes:

- The view that contemporary public administration has not escaped the problems and rigidities to which the New Public Administration had called attention;

- A sense that public administration needs and is ready for an intellectual breakthrough, and that such a breakthrough is at hand;

- An ecological view of earth and all the activities of earth's lifeforms;

- A pluralist view of our society and public administration;

- A somewhat eclectic, postpositivist, humanist, and avant-garde epistemological and methodological orientation;

- A generous assessment of what feminism has to offer to the theory and practice of public administration and a reminder that the exclusion of women is indefensible and excludes half the talent and intellect available;

- A general and theoretical rather than a nuts-and-bolts orientation; and

- The familiar attitude that the present time is unlike any ever known before, but that there are presented here ideas that may provide a new way of dealing with the unprecedented realities.

The book's subtitle—*Essays in the Minnowbrook Tradition*—in some ways fits my sense of the unity of these chapters better than does the title. While these statements are intended to be beyond the New Public Administration in important respects, the subtitle indicates that the authors perceive them also to be within "the Minnowbrook tradition." My view is that this book *is* in the Minnowbrook tradition; that it will help continue a dialogue that is very important to the future of public administration; and that it has things to say that are significant, stimulating, and beyond the perspective of Minnowbrook I. It is my hope that when Minnowbrook III is convened, the general view will be that this volume was useful.

NOTES

1. To the best of my memory: Minnowbrook I had one African-American participant and no other participants of U.S. minority groups; Minnowbrook II had three African-American and two Asian-American participants, but none of these were in the 1980s group.

2. Early impressions will probably be formed by reactions to this volume, as well as to the other publications coming out of the conference. So far, two works, in addition to the present volume, are outcomes of the conference: Frederickson and Mayer (1989) and a two-volume collection of the papers and discussions at the conference to be published as *Public Administration and Democracy: The Minnowbrook Perspective II* and *Public Policy and Administration: The Minnowbrook Perspective II*.

PART 1

The Implications of Interconnectedness for Public Managers

The chapters in this book are presented as a beginning to what we hope will be a long-term project in the field of public administration. We do not intend this collection to provide answers or solutions to the complex problems entangled in the web of interconnectedness. Rather, we present to public administration scholars and practitioners a set of hypotheses as a place from which to embark on a quest for new theories and practices to guide the future of the field.

The chapters in Part 1 provide a vision of public administration dramatically different from that described by the founders of the field, who saw a world that could be reduced to its elements, a la POSDCORB, and addressed through simple rational decision models. In contrast, as Jeff S. Luke describes, we now see a world of complexity wherein everything—problems, policies, nations, public organizations—connects to everything else.

Luke describes the conditions of this complex environment for public managers. While some have argued that change and uncertainty are the conditions with which managers must learn to cope, Luke argues that the fundamental factors are interconnectedness and interdependence. These conditions demand more than coping mechanisms; rather, different types of management, policy analysis, and leadership styles are necessary to manage successfully in the interconnected world. He proposes a focus on substantive organizational learning, development of policy ethics, and catalytic leadership skills as means to transform the role of public administrators for interconnectedness.

Mary Timney Bailey extends this discussion to an examination of the basic decision methods of managers and the economic system. She argues that the Rational Model, which has governed the field since its beginnings, is no longer effective in conditions of interconnectedness. A fundamental assumption of the Rational Model is that individual decisionmakers, problems, and organizations are all independent. When such independence does not, in fact, exist, the model produces ineffectual solutions that may even exacerbate problems.

Bailey proposes a new model of decisionmaking—SupraRationality— to overcome the anomalies presented by interconnectedness. As a tool for Luke's catalytic public managers, SupraRationality aids the development of ameliorative policies, while lessening the impact of unintended consequences outside the decision problem.

Camilla Stivers examines public administration through the lens of feminist theory. Like Luke and Bailey, she sees the fundamental focus of the field as an effort by individual managers to control presumably discrete problems and situations. Feminist theory offers, in addition, an understanding of the separated self—the masculine premise—as the base of traditional public administration theory. Because of its emphasis on control and simplification of complexity, masculine theory is unable to operate effectively in the interconnected world.

Feminist theory offers the insight of replacing the separated self with a relational and altruisticly oriented self, one better able to deal with interdependencies and uncertainty. As a guide to the public administrator, feminist theory provides a means to reconcile scientific rigor with relevance, a necessary skill for Luke's catalytic manager.

In the concluding piece in this set, Carol J. Edlund offers feminine leadership style as an approach to managing in the realm of interconnectedness. In contrast to masculine leadership style, which favors domination and control, Edlund's ideal manager values relationships and cooperation. Feminine leaders also use intuition in problemsolving and emphasize equity rather than uniformity in dealing with employees and clientele.

Although feminine leadership style is derived from an understanding of women's life experience, it can be incorporated by both male and female managers in accord with Jungian concepts of the masculine and feminine that present themselves in all human beings. Edlund finds that currently the feminine style is subjugated in organizations by the masculine style, which can lead to dehumanized organizations and an alienated workforce. Edlund hypothesizes that, as women's numbers in management increase, feminine leadership style will ultimately be accepted by all managers, a hypothesis challenged by the findings of Mary Ellen Guy's work in Part 2 of this volume.

1

Managing Interconnectedness: The New Challenge for Public Administration
Jeff S. Luke

Public-sector leaders and managers now operate in a complex environmental context that is considered beyond the bounds of even the most-brilliant minds (Mosher 1980). Public-sector officials regularly lament the increasing complexity and turbulence in which they are forced to manage and lead. Unfortunately, this concern, and even preoccupation, with turbulence and complexity has overshadowed a more fundamental emerging pattern: the crystallization of interconnectedness. Since the 1960s, this pattern has represented a very significant change in the United States.

Several social scientists have recognized this underlying pattern and are turning their scholarly attention increasingly toward the dynamics of interdependence and interconnectedness.[1] Frederick Wakeman, Jr., president of the prestigious Social Science Research Council, noted that a renewed focus on interconnectedness "is partly a result of the dramatic globalization of networks of all kinds that has taken place during the last decade" (1988, 85), such as with international banking, trading and market networks, labor and political migrations, and energy and technology flows. The global concern toward issues of interconnectedness, he emphasized, is equally a result of the considerable ecological and climatological impacts of the natural-resource, political, and economic interdependencies. Public administration scholars must now focus on these developments.

What the United States has witnessed in the last decades is analogous to what evolutionary biologists call anagenesis: a rather sudden, qualitative shift in evolutionary development. In this case, the anagenesis was the

rapid formation of global and local interdependencies, creating invisible—
yet tangible—intersocietal and interorganizational webs that now encircle
the planet (Luke and Caiden 1989). These interconnections and interdependencies did not develop slowly in a linear fashion, one step at a time
(Rosenau 1980). Rather, their emergence was similar to the crystallizing
of rock candy, which, at the right moment, suddenly forms on the string
hung in the liquid sugar and water. Similarly, networks were instantaneously formed to link historically separate and autonomous agencies,
organizations, and institutions. An intergovernmental and intersectoral
network emerged, converging around interdependencies among the polity,
the economy, and the biosphere. As a result, the historical nature of public
policy and management has changed fundamentally at the local, state,
federal, and global levels, leaving little resemblance to the public administration context that had existed during the first two hundred years of
American history.

The problems faced by public leaders today have become so interconnected that now, more than ever, public managers need an expanded
perspective—a multiversalist paradigm, as Bailey calls it in the next
chapter—in order to grasp the interdependencies, make sense of them, and
use them to more effectively manage in the public interest. Although much
of the administrative and political rhetoric of interconnectedness has been
adopted, policy strategies, managerial skills, and values for dealing with
that interconnectedness have not emerged as quickly.

FROM TURBULENCE TO INTERCONNECTEDNESS

Many argue that continuously accelerating change is the crucial factor
in contemporary management. The environment has become more complex at an increasing rate, this argument goes, with a concomitant increase
in uncertainty and unpredictability. Everything seems in motion. Constant
change—and its extreme form, *turbulence*—became the rallying concept
for much of the education and training of managers in the last decade (see,
for example, Waldo 1971 and Drucker 1980). Indeed, one could argue that
a theology has been spun around the notion of turbulence.

Others see *uncertainty* and *complexity* as the dominant forces, forcing
managers to learn to cope with ambiguity. Many writers suggest that
uncertainty in the environment is the major contextual factor for managers.
H. George Frederickson (following James D. Thompson), for example,
emphasizes that "uncertainty is the fundamental problem for complex
organizations and coping with uncertainty is the essence of the administrative process" (1982, 505).

This preoccupation with change, uncertainty, and complexity, however, has overshadowed the more-fundamental underlying patterns that have been emerging. The metaphor of turbulence, which brings forth an environment full of uncertain, muddy, swirling forces, has actually clouded the thinking about these issues, obscuring more than it clarifies. Interconnectedness—not change, turbulence, or complexity—is the essential feature in the environmental context of public administration that has replaced uncertainty as the fundamental problem of complex organizations (Luke 1986b). Managing interconnectedness, in other words, will be the greatest challenge to public-sector leaders in the remaining years of the twentieth century.

Complexity and uncertainty are certainly major issues; nonetheless, continued focus on them, to the exclusion of interconnectedness, keeps attention prematurely fastened to managing the symptoms while ignoring the causes. Turbulence and complexity are symptoms of, and caused by, the underlying interdependencies and interconnections. At the same time, however, turbulence is not an inevitable result of interconnectedness. It is increasingly clear that interconnected environments can also create increasing stability as expanding webs of stakeholders spread power widely, resulting in more people having the ability to prevent action from occurring (Bryson and Einsweiller 1991).

The Shrinking World and Public Administration

The world of government and public administration is shrinking. This world is best described by the spreading networks of subtle and direct interconnections and interdependencies that enmesh public administrators from one part of the planet to another (Luke and Caiden 1989). Essentially, these interdependencies and interconnections, characterized by reciprocal effects among public executives, involve mutual dependence, in which the actions of one individual or agency both influence and are constrained by the actions of another.[2]

There is widespread evidence of increasing interdependence. Intricate networks of interdependencies, first noted in the economic sphere after World War II, are now spreading to a wide variety of other public policy areas such as immigration, law enforcement (drugs), energy consumption, natural resources, environmental degradation, and public health (AIDS). Three fundamental changes created this new context:

- Communications, computer technology, and a global infostructure,

- Economics and the internationalization of trade, finance, and technology transfer, and
- Natural resource interdependencies in the biosphere.

The Global Infostructure

Advances in transportation technology and the steady decline in costs of transporting people and goods have been instrumental in stimulating and facilitating global interdependence; however, the exponential rate of development in computer technology continues to accelerate the global information exchange. Computers are steadily becoming smaller, quicker, and cheaper. The information power of a large computer in the 1960s is now compressed into a silicon chip the size of a fingernail. Miniaturization continues; as the machinery gets smaller and smaller there is a computer implosion, with predictions that the next step is the bio-chip, an organic compound the general size of a large molecule.[3]

In addition, communications technology has lessened geographic and social distance, dramatically shrinking international space. The world is being rendered smaller and smaller, and countries are linked in such an interlocking system that actions in another country can have both immediate and delayed effects on American states and communities. Distance has been rendered less relevant as the new infostructure makes it electronically possible to reach anywhere almost instantaneously (Luke and Caiden 1989, 84).

Economics and Internationalization

The most significant impact of the new global infostructure is that it stimulated the emergence of a truly global economy that goes well beyond mere international trade. Two critical aspects have emerged. First, the global integration of capital markets, one of the byproducts of the communications revolution, has eased the movement of capital to less-developed countries, speeding their entry into the world economy. Second, worldwide industrial development has also been reinforced by the increasingly rapid diffusions of technology. It took Japan two decades to develop its auto industry, for example, but just a few years for Korea and Singapore to build consumer electronics and computer industries, essentially from scratch (CSPA 1989, 3).

Natural Resource Interdependencies

A third unifying force is the increased relevance of natural-resource interdependencies in the biosphere. Environmental issues of the 1990s, unlike those of earlier decades, are essentially global issues, with significant natural resource and climatological ripple effects. The greenhouse effect is caused by a combination of the emissions of carbon dioxide, fossil-fuel combustion, and deforestation; it is now forcing state and local governments to analyze the potential impacts on their jurisdictions. Acid rain is a more tangible example; industrial emissions of sulfur dioxide mix in the atmosphere to create rain that is toxic to plants and damaging to buildings and cars. Acid rain in Canada, for example, causes at least $1 billion in damages annually; at least 50 percent of that rain originates in the United States, creating a transborder environmental and economic problem (Burney 1989). This is the type of interconnected policy problem that public executives increasingly face.

Every government—local, regional, national—now functions in a situation of resource interconnectedness. No jurisdiction is immune from global environmental problems; none is insulated from the outside world. Furthermore, there is a growing sensitivity to the interdependence of natural resources, such as the connections between natural life-support systems on the planet and the need to protect such basic elements of the biosphere as the ozone layer, equatorial forests, and phytoplankton in the oceans. This ecological consciousness has increased to such a degree that business leaders are calling the environment the key issue of the 1990s and are expecting environmentalism to be a movement of global force (Kirkpatrick 1990).

Fundamentally new skills and approaches are now required. There is little resemblance to organizational contexts that have existed during the last two hundred years of American history. Nothing so interconnected on such a scale has existed before. Continuing as if nothing significant has changed ultimately leads to the ineffective policies, policy inertia, and policy paralysis that seem to dominate so many government agencies.

Impacts on Public Policymaking

Global infostructure, international economic fabric, and biological ecosystems create a web of overlapping interconnections that reduce separateness (Luke and Caiden 1986). This has three general effects. In the first, the interdependencies cross jurisdictional boundaries, thus creating *geographic interconnections*. Actions taken in one part of the state, country, or globe have consequences for other geographical areas. At the same time,

> the costs and benefits of any action are not evenly distributed. Turning Brazilian jungles into orange groves may be good news for the food processor in Sao Paulo, the Dutch company that owns the tank ships, the juice distributor in Newark, the Tokyo banker who financed the project, and those of us who like cheap OJ; but it is bad news for the Brazilian Indians, Florida orange growers, and environmentalists. (CSPA 1989, 6)

Second, a *functional interdependence* now exists among policymaking, administration, and judicial activities, resulting in a noticeable blurring of the historical separation of governmental functions. As a result, it is very difficult—if not impossible—to separate administration from politics; public administrators do make, and influence, public policy. In addition, the joining of the polity and the economy expands the sphere of intergovernmental relations horizontally into the private sector at the national, state, and local levels, creating issues of intersectoral relations.

Third, and perhaps more difficult to grasp, is that generations of human beings are now interdependent. A *temporal interconnectedness* ties together the past, present, and future. Decisions made by earlier generations directly shape the policy issues faced today, while policy choices made today can have significant influences on future generations' quality of life and capacity to govern.

Interconnectedness and interdependence have thus emerged as *the* essential features in the environmental context of public administration. Managing in the public interest is increasingly handicapped by five conditions of interconnectedness that require new policy strategies, skills, and perspectives:

- Public action occurs in expanding and crowded policy environments in which everything depends on everything else and power is dispersed and shared by a multiplicity of public and private actors (Bryson and Einsweiller 1991).

- There is a significantly reduced capacity for any single governmental jurisdiction, administrator, or politician to effectively act unilaterally (Kirlin 1979). Participants within the intergovernmental and intersectoral system cannot safely act without taking others' needs into account; this forces the invention of new collaborative mechanisms and collective strategies.

- An enlarging ring of often unforeseen, unintended, or indirect consequences increases vulnerability and openness to outside influences, making public managers increasingly dependent on individuals and organizations outside of the managers' view (J.D. Thompson 1973).

- Public policy formulation and implementation moves forward very slowly (unless, on rare occasions, it is somehow stimulated by a major crisis), leading to an increase in slow-acting remedies to important policy issues. This increases a public manager's need to use strategic opportunism in solving nagging public problems such as low-income housing and unemployment.

- The consequences of policy choices and public action are often far-ranging and delayed, and have indirect or hidden costs beyond the "normal" externalities. Because desirable and undesirable consequences are difficult to separate, important and often critical second- and third-order effects of enacted policy choices can go unnoticed (C. Stone 1985). In other words, managers and policymakers have difficulties achieving the outcomes they want and have trouble avoiding the outcomes they do not intend (Scott 1982).

MANAGING INTERCONNECTEDNESS

Interdependence and interconnectedness require multiple policy strategies that are smaller and incremental in nature. Similarly, new interpersonal and analytical skills are required of the individual leader and administrator in order to manage in the public interest.

Policy Strategies

In an environmental context of interconnectedness, public policies often have dispersed, nonlocal, and unintended consequences. In such an environment, urban and social problems easily piggyback on one another; each problem becomes linked to every other problem, interweaving and causing unpredicted new problems. Each new public policy typically interacts with other policies, thereby exponentially increasing the probability of unanticipated outcomes. Unintended consequences in crowded, shared environments tend to take on a life all their own, with the results not always positive.

This suggests that large-scale policies can easily create more problems than they solve, generating ripple effects that unpredictably extend far into the future (temporal dimension), cross jurisdictional boundaries (geographic dimension), and interfere with other governmental functions and programs (functional dimension). Wildavsky (1979) notes that as large public programs are developed and implemented,

> they begin to exert strong effects on each other, increasing reciprocal relations and mutual causation; policy A affects B, B has this effect on C, and C back on A and B. An immediate effect of new large programs amid this increased interdependence is that their consequences are more numerous, varied, and indirect, and thereby more difficult to predict. (p. 64)

This leads to the Law of Large Solutions: large policies aimed at dealing with large problems become their own worst problem, with impacts spreading unpredictably into other, entirely new policy realms (p. 63).

Policy actors—out of fear of stimulating uncontrollable or unpalatable ripple effects or in order to avoid creating actual outcomes that deviate from the intended—may contract their sphere of action. This leads inevitably to segmented and limited policy action, policy inertia, or, worse yet, to policy paralysis.

A more appropriate policy strategy would be to generate multiple smaller, less-grand programs and policy initiatives that are based on some longer-term goal or vision agreed upon collectively by the governmental and nongovernmental actors inhabiting the particular policy domain. One now-common example is to use economic-development initiatives in stimulating a multiplicity of small business enterprises (i.e., "business incubators") versus implementing the large solution of recruiting a big firm or industry to relocate in a community (i.e., "smokestack chasing"). Public policy for providing affordable housing and helping the homeless provides another example where multiple, smaller, interconnected public policies and programs are more likely to succeed. As compared to either a single solution or a comprehensive housing plan by one jurisdiction, a smorgasbord of separate but related policy initiatives for providing and financing affordable housing and related social services is likely to have more positive impact.

Such a strategy involving multiple minisolutions through several jurisdictions, agencies, and enterprises entails mobilizing interorganizational resources and formulating action based on a shared interest in certain policy outcomes.[4] This, of course, requires greater skills on the part of the public manager. Three in particular stand out: the capacity to stimulate substantive organizational learning, the ability to assess the ethics of public choices, and catalytic leadership skills.

Instrumental to Substantive Organizational Learning

The notion of organizational learning is now in common currency (Schon 1983). A review of existing research and theory on organizational learning reveals that the typical instrumental focus is inappropriate for public administrators caught in a web of interconnections and interdependencies. Instrumental organizational learning is typically a process of detecting and correcting errors in an organization's decisionmaking processes.[5] In general, *instrumental* organizational learning features some or all of the following characteristics (Ventriss and Luke 1988, 347-48):

- A preoccupation with organizational adjustment, the monitoring of individual and organizational performance, and the necessary adjustments of action in order to reach established organizational goals and objectives.

- A goal of learning new techniques and processes that contribute to the more efficient or effective achievement of existing organizational goals, i.e., an emphasis on organizational means to larger organizational ends typically assumed as given.

- A focus on managerial processes for guiding or motivating individual behavior for organizational purposes of organizational efficiency, effectiveness, or adaptation.

- A predominant focus on the immediate moment; on immediate organizational needs, predicaments or errors of immediate practical interest; or on ensuring organizational survival in its immediate environment.

Contrary to this orientation, a substantive, rather than an instrumental, focus is required in the present interconnected context where public administrators are looking outward more and inward less. *Substantive* organizational learning does not center on issues of efficiency, adaptation, organizational maintenance, or other intra-organizational issues. Rather, it is a process of improving policy choices by critically examining the normative implications of the multiple intended and unintended outcomes of public policies. It is more a process of continuously analyzing the environmental context in which one exists (Freire 1968), engaging in a reflexive learning process (Habermas 1973) where public administrators are more "concerned with meaningful choices about larger social purposes or societal ends" (Denhardt and Denhardt 1979, 109).

This substantive learning is increasingly critical in the intergovernmental and intersectoral web in which public action now takes place. Such learning is essentially a normative process of personal learning that involves critical reflection and subsequent reformulation of organizational goals and policy choices (see Ventriss and Luke 1988). It includes the following characteristics:

- Substantive organizational learning assumes that public organizations are more than mere technical instruments to produce goods and services; they also provide a larger mechanism for making policy choices in a context characterized by interdependencies among the economy, the polity, and the biosphere.

- Although organizations themselves are no more than means to ends, substantive organizational learning requires critical analysis of the substantive ends and outcomes of organizational action.

- Substantive organizational learning, by focusing on social values, seeks critical and reflective awareness by individual organizational members in order to identify unintended and indirect geographical, functional, or temporal outcomes.

- Substantive organizational learning focuses on past, present, and future policy choices for the purpose of human betterment, rather than developing administrative means to implement enacted policy. As such, it is value-*creating*, rather than value-*conserving*.

From Behavioral Ethics to Policy Ethics

With public action increasingly intertwined throughout intergovernmental and intersectoral activity, public administrators must not only account for the immediate consequences and visible costs of policy choices, they must also consider the delayed consequences and the less-visible costs borne by the organization and passed on to others who may not have any direct recourse (C. Stone 1985). The crystallization of interconnectedness raises moral and ethical issues that contemporary discussions of governmental ethics fall far short in addressing.

Current debates regarding governmental ethics are unfortunately pre-occupied with the behavioral ethics of personal conduct, typically empha-sizing such issues as standards of individual conduct, accountability for administrative discretion, professional codes of conduct, and conflict of interest. The common thread of the contemporary dialogue on governmen-tal ethics is that the discussion focuses on individual behavioral choices and the potential for using one's position or office for personal gain; this is the perennial tension between *self*-interest and *public* interest. The focus of governmental ethics must instead extend beyond the narrow constraints of intra-organizational accountability, personal codes of conduct, and the administrative functioning of separate independent actors.

Policy leaders now have larger time horizons (see Jaques 1976 and 1989; Neustadt and May 1986), and because of the anagenesis of a highly interconnected environmental context in which policies are formulated and implemented, they also now have an expanded set of ethical obliga-tions. In their regard for quality of life and the wellbeing of society, public executives, both elected and appointed, must consider the *ethical* and *normative* implications of public policies and must pay attention to the long-term consequences and externalities of those policies. As a result, ethics in public administration involves not merely the avoidance of dishonorable behavior or the pursuit of virtuous behavior by an individual manager, it also involves principles of action to guide them in making ethical policy decisions in an interconnected global society (Luke 1991).

The need for such policy ethics has not gone unnoticed by all policy leaders. For example, in a recent public statement, Richard Darman, director of the U.S. Office of Management and Budget, argued that the federal deficit is unethical. The public debt, he noted, was approximately $3 trillion in fiscal year 1989-90 and interest payments had risen to nearly $180 billion, 15 percent of the federal budget. This significantly inhibits federal spending and soaks up private savings. "Collectively," Darman emphasized, "we are engaged in a massive backward Robin Hood trans-action: robbing the future to give to the present."

The increasing internationalization, combined with the longer-term consequences of environmental problems, provides a more-poignant illus-tration. Unlike the environmental issues of the 1970s, current environ-mental problems are best characterized as global and interrelated: regional air pollution, ozone depletion, the greenhouse effect, transportation and storage of hazardous wastes, expansion of existing deserts, deforestation, and extinction of species (and threats to biodiversity). Unfortunately, giving consideration to the long-term ethical issues of policy choices is often very difficult. William Ruckelshaus (1989), former director of the U.S. Environmental Protection Agency, warns that it is hard for people to change their policies "in order to avert threats that will otherwise affect a world most of them will not be alive to see." Although it is a difficult endeavor, assessing the ethics of policy choices in terms of the long-term, normative impacts of policy decisions can no longer be avoided. A source of guidance for doing this is the field of environmental ethics. Underlying environmental ethics are two assumptions:

- Scientific discoveries have created new opportunities *and* perils that result in potential side effects on the interconnected systems of nature. (Jonas 1984)
- The potential effects of today's actions and deeds on future people, as well as other species, require policymakers to be more explicit about responsibility for those effects. (Attfield 1983)

As a result, an environmental ethic is critical, although there are several divergent schools of thought today. They range from radical biotic egalitarianism to the ecology movement. The former argues that there is no more value in human than in nonhuman lives and that all animals are of equal significance, whatever their species. The latter is more narrowly preoccupied with the problems of pollution and natural-resource depletion as they currently affect developed countries (Attfield 1983).

Nevertheless, the diverse schools of thought in environmental ethics all agree that a policy ethic heightening awareness of obligations to posterity is needed and that moral horizons have to be broadened (Attfield 1983).

Interdependence and interconnectedness among the polity, the economy, and the biosphere do not automatically create a moral relationship. There is, therefore, no *a priori* moral or ethical obligation among any independent individuals, agencies, or jurisdictions. In an interconnected policy context, however, two preliminary values can illuminate potential ethical obligations in policy choices: stewardship and intergenerational ethics.[6]

The ethic of *stewardship* is a major part of current moral thought and tradition, emerging historically from the ancient and continuing Jewish and Christian traditions, and is currently considered an ethical obligation in public administration. In general, stewardship acknowledges that "people are the custodians and stewards of a precious natural order and have a creative role in enhancing it as well as being among its participants" (Attfield 1983, 63). The notion of stewardship is also firmly rooted in the fiduciary role of public administrators, and as Cooper states, "Since public service is a fiduciary role, such employment is ultimately bound by an obligation to the public of that jurisdiction" (1982, 35). This fiduciary relationship assumes that public administrators and leaders act on behalf of clients or citizens who lack expertise or time to undertake an important task themselves.

In addition to the concern for stewardship of the existing biosphere, ethical considerations must be expanded to include *intergenerational equity*—responsibility toward future generations—because, in an interconnected and technological world, it is increasingly within the power of those living today to affect seriously the quality of life of those yet unborn (Jonas 1984).

An emerging issue revolving around intergenerational equity is aging policy (Neugarten and Neugarten 1989). Some argue that an aging society is being unfair to younger generations by allocating disproportionate resources and advantages for older people (Longman 1987). Another, more dramatic example of intergenerational inequity is the production and storage of highly toxic nuclear wastes that are radioactive for 1,000 to 500,000 years when there is no known, completely safe way to package and store them. This has a significant intergenerational impact, one that implies ethical obligations to nearly 30,000 generations (Routley and Routley 1978). A third, more local, but equally emotional issue is providing tax breaks to attract industrial firms to relocate into a community or state. Such tax breaks reduce the local fiscal capacity and tax revenue for twenty to thirty years. Although tax incentives may have immediate effects on job generation (and there is considerable debate on the efficacy of this approach), the long-term impacts of the education in future revenue-generating capacity is often ignored.

From Charismatic to Catalytic Leadership

In an interconnected environment, managers and policymakers have difficulty achieving the results they want and have trouble avoiding outcomes they do not intend. Insofar as public administrators recognize that large problems cannot be solved by large solutions, they will pursue strategies of amelioration. This focus on amelioration entails a shift from *problem solving* to *solution building*. Solutions—and most often they are

Exhibit 1.1   Strategic Thinking Skills

- Anticipating future policy windows in order to seize them as opportunities.

- Thinking about how future problems will render current solutions obsolete.

- Detecting interrelationships and assessing the importance of their linkages.

- Anticipating what the future will demand of the public agency for it to be seen as successful and accountable by the wider interconnected web.

- Thinking systematically—seeing the whole as well as its parts and seeing multiple, rather than single, causes and effects.

- Thinking in terms of a web of strategies that can be constantly updated and refined.

- Reflecting on ultimate outcomes and second-order and unintended consequences of policy choices.

- Considering the broadest possible set of stakeholders—include the intersectoral as well as the intergovernmental arena.

Source: Luke, 1986b; Mitroff and Kilmann, 1984; Botkin *et al.*, 1979; Luke and Caiden, 1989.

only partial solutions—are built strategically and incrementally with the commitment and ingenuity of a broad range of stakeholders.

Strategic thinking[7] becomes the critical conceptual skill, and strategic opportunism the derivative behavior (see Exhibit 1.1). Unfortunately, strategic, future-oriented policy thinking is not necessarily an easy process, and identifying future consequences of policy choices can be difficult. Extrapolations from present trends can be misleading. The seriousness and intensity of existing problems tend to filter perceptions of future issues. In addition, people's capability to gaze into the future is constrained by limits in their capacity for higher levels of abstraction.[8]

Not only is a conceptual capacity for strategic thinking required, but an increased emphasis on certain interpersonal skills is necessary for public administrators in a context of interconnectedness. More attention must be concentrated on the in-between relations of public managers and key stakeholder groups: citizens, private-sector executives and entrepreneurs, nonprofit executives, and other intergovernmental and intersectoral actors. The decisionmaking process in the new managerial context requires specific skills to generate movement and action among these interdependent entities: this means collaboration, facilitation, negotiation, and mediation.

Today's public administrator seeking to influence specific public policy arenas must learn how to stimulate and manage cooperative efforts in three arenas:

- *Intersectoral*—the public, private, and nonprofit sectors,
- *Civic*—citizens, advocacy groups, and neighborhood associations, as well as
- *Intergovernmental*—local, state, federal, and international levels of government.

Policy formulation and implementation are most often interorganizational, multilateral, and collective. Interconnected policy arenas are thus more accurately characterized by shared power and require empowering strategies that stimulate stakeholder movement toward a desired policy outcome.

Managers who intend to influence a particular policy outcome must therefore recognize the existence of shared power and avoid depowering other policy actors. This assumes a broader conception of power, one where power is defined as the collective, not just unilateral, production of intended effect. Power thus becomes catalytic, not commanding, and facilitative, rather than dominating. In this context, successful public managers need to feel a personal responsibility for the situation as a whole, but also realize that they are only partly responsible for the general outcome of their efforts.

Interconnectedness also creates new opportunities for joint action. In an environmental context characterized by shared power and crowded, dense policy arenas, administrators must develop and refine their skills in collaboration, networking, bargaining, and negotiation. These skills are not new to public administrators, but they are now fundamental for developing the necessary joint-task orientation and collective strategies increasingly required in interconnected policy systems. Interdependence, as well as the expanding diversity in the public sector, provides opportunities for highly creative and innovative policies and services if administrators assume a facilitative posture. Diversity and interdependence can generate and nurture creative and original policies if pursued synergistically, and not adversarially.

As interdependencies in the environment increase, so do the requisite levels of coordination *and* the potential for conflict. Incentives for collaborative action already may exist in some policy arenas because of the shared stake individuals may have in solving a particular problem; however, successful administrators must have the skills to further stimulate, nurture, and maintain adequate levels of collective action outside their organizational boundaries. The requisite set of interpersonal skills shifts depending on (a) whether a public manager is dealing with multiple actors or a single individual and (b) whether conflict over values, goals, and means is low or high in pursuing a particular policy or strategy (see Exhibit 1.2).

CATALYTIC LEADERSHIP

The essential requirement of public administrators in the 1990s is a new type of leadership. In an interconnected context, a leader is one who can stimulate collective action toward a particular goal or vision. Bass argues that effective management today requires a transformational leadership style based predominantly on charisma: "Charisma is one of the elements separating the ordinary manager from the true leader in organization settings" (1985, 34). Charismatic leaders, he concludes, have the ability to motivate others to action through inspiration. A charismatic leader can stimulate collective action in an interconnected web only by virtue of his or her referent power (French and Raven 1968).

Charismatic leaders with their individual visions, however, are just not powerful enough to move the web of government and nongovernment actors in a particular policy direction. In an interconnected context, catalytic leaders are required who engage in strategic thinking and facilitate the development of a shared vision and collaborative goals. Unlike charismatic leaders, who persuade individuals to follow their vision by means of emotions and exhortation, catalytic leaders are able to facilitate development of a critical mass of diverse policy actors motivated by a goal or vision created collectively.

Public-sector organizations—national, state, county, and city—are typically communications nexus. Because government, unlike the private or nonprofit sectors, has this characteristic of being a node in the middle of information and social networks (Hood 1983), public managers and elected officials are uniquely positioned to establish roles as catalysts. The relevant catalytic skills are both conceptual and interpersonal in nature. They include (1) the capacity to be a strategic thinker for planning and a catalyst for action; (2) the capacity to pull together crucial stakeholders in a common effort; (3) the ability to assess correctly the differences and

Exhibit 1.2   Requisite Interpersonal Skills

<table>
<tr><td></td><td colspan="2" align="center">Level of Conflict</td></tr>
<tr><td></td><td align="center">Low</td><td align="center">High</td></tr>
<tr><td>Bilateral
(2 individuals
  or agencies)</td><td align="center">collaboration</td><td align="center">negotiation</td></tr>
<tr><td>Multilateral
(network of indi-
  viduals or
  agencies)</td><td align="center">facilitation
and
networking</td><td align="center">mediation</td></tr>
</table>

similarities among key policy actors in terms of goals, values, perspectives, and roles; and (4) the conceptual skill to see the subtle interdependencies among these individuals. Generally, the dynamic processes of catalytic leadership require a combination of:

- Identifying where the relevant policy actors and stakeholders exist, including both the subtle and nearly invisible and the more explicit obvious;

- Assessing who among these policy actors may support and who may resist collaborative efforts and how strongly; and

- Developing networks with these individuals or agencies to facilitate the analysis, negotiation, or experimentation required to stimulate policy action.

THE METAPHOR OF INTERCONNECTEDNESS

Not only has the preoccupation with complexity, uncertainty, and turbulence monopolized attention, it has also overshadowed the recent crystallization of intersectoral and intergovernmental connection and the anagenesis of an expanding web of stakeholders. Even more troublesome in terms of deflecting an understanding of the world's interconnectedness are the internalized assumptions about separation that abound in traditional American public administration thinking.

Public administration has unfortunately been plagued by the notion of separation since its beginnings. The assumption of separation expressed in the U.S. Constitution and its underlying political theories are rooted deeply in English law and in the political philosophies of Locke, Hobbes, and Montesquieu. One distinguishing feature of these Enlightenment philosophers, but one that today appears inappropriate, is their conception of human beings as separate from, rather than part of, nature.[9]

Governmental jurisdictions certainly have their own separate and distinct identities. Each has its own unique internal governance structure, processes, and procedures that emerge from their legal, constitutional, and jurisdictional bounds. The pressing social and economic problems confronting these legally separate agencies, however, are more ambiguous, less contained, and defy boundaries. Separation is no longer the appropriate metaphor for governmental action because public agencies are no longer totally autonomous, self-reliant entities separated from each other and their citizenry.

Major changes are now required in the most basic premises, because a fundamental incongruence now exists between present interdependencies and the predominant metaphors and assumptions about separation. Separation was a concept created for analytical purposes, but it now reinforces false distinctions. Data from the macrosocietal level down to the micro analyses of quantum physics and the depth psychology of Carl Jung clearly indicate the existence of interconnections in most, if not all, levels of personal and social interaction. Viewing organizations through the metaphor of interconnectedness creates a new lens that helps one see public agencies in ways that escape the older administrative perspective.

The metaphor of interconnectedness is a more accurate assumption or fundamental premise on which to base public action. Such a generative metaphor makes explicit relations that too often go unnoticed; in addition, it cuts through the surface detail and welter of information to see what is fundamental.[10]

SUMMARY: FUNDAMENTAL SHIFTS IN PERSPECTIVE

In many ways, the world of public administration is profoundly different than it has been at any other time in human history. The number and intensity of interdependencies and interconnections are growing at a fast pace, creating a major theoretical and managerial challenge for the future. The problems faced by public-sector administrators and leaders today have become so interconnected that what is needed more than ever is a metaphor or perspective—a multiversalist paradigm—to help managers grasp the resulting interdependencies, to make sense of them, and to utilize them.

Five specific shifts in conceptualizing that would be part of a multiversalist paradigm are:

- From focusing on turbulence to focusing on interconnectedness;

- From instrumental organizational learning to substantive organizational learning;

- From behavioral ethics to policy ethics;

- From unilateral (charismatic) action to collective (catalytic) action; and

- From the notion of separation and autonomy to the metaphor of interconnectedness.

Although much of the rhetoric of interconnectedness has been adapted, public administration training and education has not. It could be that interdependencies have expanded so quickly that Americans just cannot keep up.[11] Nevertheless, the basic assumptions still imply the notion of separation: that one organization is separate from every other organization and that governmental action is separate from nongovernmental action.

This preoccupation with autonomy and independence and the near-total neglect of interconnectedness, feminist scholars suggest, is the result of the male-centeredness (androcentrism) of science in general (see E. Keller 1985), and public administration in particular. Considerable evidence today indicates that the focus on independence and self-reliance is peculiarly male in its origins, with women typically more relationship- or connectedness-oriented (see, especially, Chodorow 1978 and Gilligan 1982). This sense of separateness and independence has become embedded in the American value system (e.g., frontier individualism), has shaped administrative thinking and language, and has been the underlying principle guiding most administrative strategies. This value framework—the self-contained, the autonomous, the separate—has subtly become an institutionalized thought structure for the public administrator. Mayer refers to this as technological modes of thinking-and-acting (see Chapter 6). Instead, new metaphors are required to guide investigations, new language and concepts to map the world, and new skills provide leadership in economic, political, and organizational systems that are globally interconnected.

The core of the problem may be aversion to the metaphor of interconnectedness. Shifting one's perspective from seeing separateness to truly perceiving interconnectedness is not easy. If Chodorow (1978) and Gilligan (1982) are correct (and there is ample evidence to suggest they are), this shift will be much more difficult for men than women.[12] Louis Gawthrop also suggests that "viewing our democratic polity as a seamless garment can easily be dismissed as metaphysical nonsense" (1989, 196). The notion that everybody is connected may threaten or be discounted by many individuals. Old intellectual baggage, no matter how outdated, often feels lighter to carry than baggage that promises more accuracy. John Stuart Mill once noted that every age has held opinions that subsequent generations found not only false but absurd. Contemporary public administration appears to have reached this threshold.

NOTES

1. For example, see Keohane and Nye (1977) and Rosenau (1980) in the field of international relations and such feminist scholarship as Chodorow (1978) and Gilligan (1982), as well as Bailey in Chapter 2 and Stivers in Chapter 3.

2. Interdependencies—the high-cost, very important, mutual dependencies—can further be distinguished from interconnectedness. The latter describes low-cost, relatively unimportant, mutual dependencies (Keohane and Nye 1977). Although the two can be differentiated empirically, the terms "interdependence" and "interconnectedness" are used interchangeably in this essay.

3. See Luke (1986a) for a discussion of the impact of this implosion on local government.

4. See Luke *et al.* (1988) for examples of minisolutions in economic development.

5. Instrumental organizational learning originated initially as a laboratory approach and moved to organization development (Golembiewski 1971); later, it was delineated by Argyris and Schon (1978) and Bennis and Nanus (1985).

6. See Luke (1991) for a more detailed discussion.

7. See Luke and Caiden (1989).

8. For an excellent discussion of this point, see Jaques (1976 and 1989).

9. For discussions on such uses of metaphors, see Schon (1979), Morgan (1983), and Gulick (1984).

10. For an intriguing exegesis of the separation of *man* from nature, see Stivers in Chapter 3; for an analysis of the philosophical consequences, see White, in Chapter 7.

11. An alternative explanation is that narrow, technological modes of thinking-and-acting, which predominate in some quarters as *the* orientation to the world, significantly inhibit any rapid conceptual change; see Mayer in Chapter 6.

12. Except, see Guy in Chapter 5 on the ways in which, at least at present, organizational arrangements seem to have much stronger effects than does gender on attitudes and orientations in the workplace.

2

Beyond Rationality: Decisionmaking in an Interconnected World
Mary Timney Bailey

As the world enters the last decade of the twentieth century, it is now clear that we human beings live in an interconnected world. We see it in our economies, in our political systems, and in our natural environment. As formerly simple distinctions between public and private activities in the United States have become increasingly blurred, organizations have become interconnected, too.

Public administrators in the United States face this newly recognized world with tools developed in a far-different environment. Theory and practice derived from scientifically rational models of administration and decisionmaking depend on a reality of separate, independent administrators and policy systems. When that reality changes, the same old methods no longer apply. Public administrators are inhabiting an essentially different existence and must therefore seek a new theoretical base for the discipline. Because public administration has experienced anagenesis—a rather sudden, qualitative shift in evolutionary development—we who study and practice it must address the new problems with more than modifications in the old equipment.

What we are seeing, in my view, is the emergence of an environment for human social systems fundamentally different from that which we have understood up to now. It is so different, in fact, that many basic assumptions about human society are being transformed and, thus, theories and practice of social processes developed earlier no longer address modern problems. Both theory and practice are, in fact, obsolete. As Jeff S. Luke argues so eloquently in Chapter 1, public administrators must develop new ways of thinking about themselves and their roles in the interconnected world.

This new reality requires a new paradigm, a new way of thinking and acting in the world. As Jay D. White argues in Chapter 7, the stories of science, society, and government need to be rewritten. And, indeed, they will be rewritten and this new paradigm will, consciously or not, as human beings grapple with the world that reality presents them. Although the outlines are not completely clear, the result will clearly be a multiversalist paradigm in which the effectiveness of decisions is only meaningfully measured in the context of the whole, one in which terms such as amelioration and facilitation have more currency than do managing and control.

Other chapters in this volume define and explore portions of the multiversalist paradigm. In this chapter, I argue that to perform effectively within the interconnected environment, both public administrators and society must also develop a decision theory appropriate for interconnectedness and for the multiversalist paradigm. The Rational Model that to date has governed organizing, decisionmaking, and policy analysis is inherently incapable of solving problems or developing viable policies in the interconnected world. A decision theory—a SupraRational Model—is needed that reaches beyond the narrowness of instrumental rationality to incorporate within the decision calculus the side effects and values of interconnected problems.

What follows is an examination of these two approaches to decisionmaking—the Rational Model and the SupraRational Model—in relation to the challenges presented by interconnectedness and interdependency.

MODELS OF PUBLIC ADMINISTRATION

Public administration, on one hand, has long utilized the Rational Model of decisionmaking. At its heart is the concept of independence or separation. Human beings, nation-states, public organizations, agencies, and departments are all seen in this model as separate units whose actions and policies can be individually developed in isolation from other considerations.[1]

Interdependence, on the other hand, is at the heart of the SupraRational Model; all units are seen as interconnected. This means a decision or policy that is good for one is good for all or, at worst, neutral; conversely, if one is hurt, all suffer as well. An example of such a policy decision would be nuclear war. It must be clear that there would be no winners in such an encounter. Even if it could be contained to one part of the world, the fallout—radioactive, political, social, and economic—would be experienced universally.

In the Rational Model, conversely, nuclear war is a natural progression of conventional warfare and is, in theory, an acceptable means of conflict resolution between nation-states. From the perspective of the SupraRational Model, war itself becomes impossible, since to engage in any conflict is to risk the possibility of nuclear war. Whereas conventional war could be isolated to small areas and losses would presumably also be localized, nuclear war creates losses everywhere. With the SupraRational Model, we now see that where we inflict hurt on others, we are hurting ourselves as well. We can no longer assume that losses will be contained and, since nuclear war remains in the natural progression of Rational Model decisionmaking, we can no longer validate the use of war as a means of conflict resolution.[2]

Operating from within the Rational Model, American public administration—and, indeed, all organizations and political systems in the U.S.—have developed to date as independent and unconnected units. Policy initiatives, management models, and decision systems have been designed to address narrowly defined problems, usually without reference to problems or factors outside (Etzioni 1988, 1). Research models and theories based on the Rational Model require that problems be treated in isolation. Interdependence is lately emerging as the challenge for the field. Administrators at all levels of government are urged to develop skills in strategic planning (Reagen 1989) and managing global interdependence (Luke and Caiden 1989). What has not been discussed extensively to date, however, is the inherent conflict for managers and politicians when they apply rational methods to interconnected problems. Interdependence represents an anomaly for the Rational Model because it introduces complexity beyond the borders of individually rational problems.

The SupraRational Model better addresses the reality of interconnected worlds and interdependent public administrators. For social systems, the intellectual upheaval required by interconnectedness is equivalent to the epistemological and theoretical changes brought about in astronomy by the Copernican Revolution. For centuries, astronomers subscribed to the theories of Ptolemy, the basic premise of which was that the planets and the sun revolve around the earth. Once scientists, because of Copernicus's work, recognized that the planets revolve around the sun, it was no longer possible for astronomers to persist in their former science; it was necessary to develop a new epistemology for the newly recognized reality.[3] Similarly, once there is recognition of the interconnections and interdependencies, it is no longer possible to design policies and organizations as if they were isolated units.

The reality defined by interconnectedness requires public administrators—scholars and practitioners—to make revolutionary adjustments in their thinking about theories and their applications. Astronomers were forced to develop a whole new epistemology for research and practice once they accepted the reality that the sun, rather than the earth, defines the universe. In the same fashion, once the reality of interconnectedness is accepted, the former ways of organizing and of making policy become outmoded. The unitary model no longer fits for creating human organizations, making decisions, and implementing policies in the interconnected world.

THE RATIONAL AND
THE SUPRARATIONAL MODELS

The Rational Model of decisionmaking is based on assumptions of welfare economics about human nature, the fundamental one of which is that individual decisionmakers—whether a single manager, an agency, or a nation-state—will make decisions that maximize their own welfare. Self-interest, narrowly defined, produces the best decisions and, added together, all self-interested decisions result in the maximum welfare for the entire society.[4]

Because the Rational Model is derived from economics theory, it works best when all components in the decision problem can be expressed in terms of market values. Policy values that are not traded on the market, such as clean air or saving human lives, are given surrogate market values. Decisions in the Rational Model are taken principally to achieve short-term benefits in the form of profits or efficiencies that reduce costs or other individual goals. Future benefits and costs are discounted to their present value, and any effect that can be projected to occur more than ten years into the future will have virtually no value to the present decision, depending on the interest rate chosen for the calculation.[5] This means, *ipso facto*, that intergenerational effects of decisions are irrelevant. Externalities—costs imposed on individuals or the entire system outside the decisionmaker's frame of reference—are generally ignored.

Policy decisions in which numerous individual costs and benefits are involved could present a problem for the Rational Model because rational voters would not choose policies that would disadvantage them. Public choice theorists overcome this problem through the test of Pareto optimality or the Kaldor criterion. Pareto optimality is obtained when it can be shown that at least one party is made better and none are made worse. The Kaldor criterion assumes rationality if it can be shown that hypothetically the winners *could* compensate the losers, although this rarely happens in practice (Mikesell 1986, 6). These choices are further modified through the application of risk assessment in which costs or individual losses are evaluated in terms of their probability of occurrence, and decisions are based on the lowest probable cost or risk.

The Rational Model focuses principally on efficiency, which generally means reducing costs of inputs in order to maximize the market value of outputs. In the case of public activities that do not have a market value, efficiency generally means only reducing the costs of inputs with the assumption that this will result in maximum output value.

Decisions taken and policies developed within the Rational Model must conform to strict requirements in order to produce valid outcomes.[6] First, there must be a clearly defined problem; this almost always requires demonstrating that a cause-and-effect relationship exists. Thus, in order to develop policies to reduce acid deposition caused by acid rain in the Northeast, for instance, it is first necessary to *prove* that (a) there is a detrimental effect in the forests caused by acid deposition and (b) the acid deposition is being generated by an identifiable source. Since there may be a considerable lag time and distance between the generation of acid deposition at its source and the development of noticeable effects in the forests, meeting the cause-effect requirement is problematic. Additionally, it may be difficult to isolate the cause from intervening variables, such as insect infestations and weather. Problems of this nature are typically referred to one or more study committees in an effort to prove, or disprove, the relationship. Because of the complexities these studies usually can establish only a probabilistic relationship, which then engenders more studies.[7]

The second requirement of the Rational Model is that the decisionmaker is presumed to have access to complete information. This requirement presents serious difficulties because decisionmakers have limited time and resources to develop all pertinent data. Moreover, decisionmakers can mentally handle only a limited amount of information at any one time. Herbert Simon identified this phenomenon as bounded rationality and argued that because of it, the outcomes of all decisions can only be suboptimal (Huber 1980, 25). Even when bounded rationality is accepted intellectually, however, this requirement of the Rational Model pushes in the direction of gathering more data as the means for getting better decisions. Yet, with the most sophisticated forecasting methodologies, the most important information needed to make accurate decisions—the future variables—is unavailable. This inherently forces the analyst to assume (at least implicitly) that the future will mirror the past or, in other words, that the environment is static and unchanging.

The third basic requirement for the Rational Model is that problems must be well structured. Too many variables create too much complexity for the model. As a result, decisionmakers tend to break down complex problems into simpler, more manageable pieces. This leads to the development of solutions for each part, which may in sum either fall short of solving the whole problem or even worsen the situation. Huber summarizes the consequences of the psychological and situational difficulties of decisionmakers as (1980, 29):

- Limits on rationality lead to the use of simplistic strategies and inadequate models.
- Use of simplistic strategies and inadequate models leads to savings in time and other resources, at least in the short run.
- Use of simplistic strategies and inadequate models leads to solutions that tend to be of less than maximum quality.
- Use of simplistic strategies and inadequate models is increased when time and other resources are decreased and when stress-producing factors are increased.

Or, as the great Anon. has observed: For every complex problem there is a simple solution—and it is wrong.[8]

These difficulties can be overcome with the use of the SupraRational Mode of decisionmaking, in which self-interest is defined in relation to the whole.[9] In this model, decisionmakers focus on the achievement of long-term, collective values or benefits. Costs and benefits are examined in relation to multiversalist effects rather than merely individual gain. In a reversal of the welfare-economics model, the SupraRational Model assumes that if a decision is good for the entire society then individual welfare is also maximized.

SupraRationality incorporates externalities and intergenerational costs into the decision calculus and seeks to ameliorate the effect of present policies on both outside entities and future generations, as well as the self. In place of the test of cause and effect, SupraRationality accepts uncertainty as given. This means that, in the face of a probabilistic relationship, it not only incorporates the costs and other impacts of a decision or policy potentially facing the decision unit; it also incorporates the costs and impacts potentially facing those outside the decision unit.

In the Rational Model, complex systems must be broken down into parts, decisions made for each part, and then the parts symbolically recombined. Maximum social welfare is presumed to be the product of the sum of the parts. While simplifying complexity, this method also loses the information contained in the interstices of the system. As a result, when the system is reconstructed, the sum of the parts is actually less than the whole.

In the SupraRational Model, parts cannot be addressed except in the context of the whole. Interconnectedness is incorporated into the decision focus, even though the cost of decisionmaking might be higher and, thus, efficiency (as the Rational Model defines it) would be reduced. The measure of success in the SupraRational Model is social and organizational effectiveness. Impacts of decisions, regardless of how low their short-term costs might be, are the principal concern because the effects of interaction, if ignored, create much greater long-term costs.

Another aspect of problemsolving in the SupraRational Model is the recognition that problems are constantly changing and not static. This means accepting the likelihood both that policies might be effective for only short terms and that policies themselves might alter the problems at which they were directed or create entirely new problems. From within the SupraRational Model, in other words, one recognizes that problems cannot be solved, only, at best, ameliorated.

SupraRationality goes beyond simple cost-benefit analysis to base decisions on consideration of consequences and externalities, even when those are relatively small, rather than excluding them. The sum of externalities from hundreds of individually rational decisions can be a collective negative that no individual would rationally choose.

For example, this type of irrational outcome of Rational-Model decisionmaking can be seen in the case of global climate change, which is the product of the Rational Model insofar as it represents the sum of the externalities of hundreds of thousands of individual rational decisions, each of which doubtless had a favorable benefit-to-cost ratio. The cost of the externalities was probably immeasurable individually, yet those externalities combined to create effects that may ultimately make the planet uninhabitable. It would now be possible to solve this problem within the Rational Model only if it could be determined exactly when the (individually summed) collective costs would become higher than the (individually summed) collective benefits.[10]

SupraRationality addresses the problem of global climate change by developing ameliorating policies—reforestation and energy conservation, for example—that are implemented in anticipation of possible dire outcomes. SupraRationality accepts uncertainty, taking action to ensure the best outcome for the system rather than only for individual decision units. SupraRationality also takes the risk that the dire outcome might not ever happen, either because of the interventions taken or because the effects were not properly understood by the decisionmakers. Despite the absence of the projected outcome, the decision to intervene was still the more rational because the worst possible outcome was avoided. Avoiding the probable negative long-term effect is preferable to maximizing short-term individual wealth, even though the negative effect might not happen or might not be so adverse as anticipated. The only way to measure the value of these decisions is in their contribution to the collective welfare.

The principal strengths of the SupraRational Model lie in its application to ill-structured, squishy problems—what Harmon and Mayer (1986, 9) describe as wicked problems—and in its ability to produce comprehensive, superoptimal solutions rather than the piecemeal, suboptimal solutions of the Rational Model.

EVIDENCE OF THE NEED FOR SUPRARATIONALITY

Increasingly, anomalies for the Rational Model are emerging that support the argument for the shift to the SupraRational Model. First, interconnectedness itself is anomalous realtive to the Rational Model because interconnectedness describes the existence of relationships that are not simple. Complex, interdependent relationships incorporate intervening and interacting variables that cannot be separated for the purposes of normal—that is, in Rational Model terms—problemsolving. In an interconnected world, the possibility of separating dependent and independent variables, though essential for the Rational Model, is highly unlikely. Statistical techniques such as multiple regression analysis are designed to deal with complexity and focus on central tendencies; they ignore extreme cases and other than simple interactions.[11]

A second anomaly is the existence of cultural, ethnic, and gender diversity in society, politics, and administration. Such diversity increasingly brings into question the universality of the Rational Model's homogeneous value assumptions. Demographic studies indicate that within the next two decades, European (white) males will be the principal minority in the United States. Organizations, thus, will be increasingly populated and managed by women and minorities of every variation. It is not clear at this point whether such change will result in the identification of a very different set of value assumptions.[12] What does seem to be predictable is that any exclusivity in determining operating values will be increasingly challenged.

A third and critical anomaly is the generally expanded access to information, which has taken several forms, from universal education to global communication networks. Limited access to education has historically been an important means of controlling information. The Medicis, the Communist Party in the Soviet Union, and Southern slaveowners all recognized that education in the wrong hands threatened their ability to maintain the status quo. Thus it was illegal in many Southern states to teach slaves to read, and it is still the practice in some cultures to deny education to women.

In this century, technology informs and educates the masses. Television, satellite communication systems, and computer networks have all transformed access to information to the extent that absolute or even limited control is a deviation from the norm. Evidence of the power of information is all around. Television was a critical factor in developing political resistance in the United States to the Vietnam War. The Chinese, in their desperation to suppress their own youth in the spring of 1989, cut off outside information and created official stories to control their internal affairs. They face a dilemma in the long run, however, since they must depend on outside education to train their people technically. There is no way to control the exposure of these students to the ideas that will ultimately undermine the political regime. In similar fashion, because elites in US politics and administration are increasingly unable to control access to information, their regimes are also threatened.[13]

The expansion and increasing interconnectedness of information presents perhaps the most serious obstacle to the further efficacy of the Rational Model. As interconnections become more apparent through wider availability and use of information technology, it will be less and less possible to pretend that complex relationships can be reduced to unitary dimensions.

Evidence of anomalies can also be found in the increasing inability of policymakers to solve social problems. As Jeff S. Luke notes in Chapter 1, a form of policy paralysis developed in the 1980s as the United States became incapable of devising viable solutions for numerous complex policy issues. The primary stumbling block to the development of comprehensive policies seemed to be the perception that individual welfare (wealth and independence) would be jeopardized by a focus on the welfare of the society as a whole.[14] This is the Rational Model run rampant.

Policy problems, because they are so complex, can no longer be solved through the Rational Model. A shift to SupraRationality is required in order to address the dimensions of interconnected social-policy issues. Once human beings see that all are connected, there will be no return to individualist-centered policy- and decisionmaking.

IMPLICATIONS OF THE SUPRARATIONAL MODEL FOR PUBLIC ADMINISTRATION, POLICY ANALYSIS, AND POLITICS

The Rational Model, used to define and delimit public administration throughout the last two hundred years in the United States, is based on a simple notion: social units, whether individuals, organizations, or nation-states, should make decisions based on narrowly defined self-interests and, in doing so, will not appreciably affect, or be affected by, each other. In other words, problems—whether individual, organizational, or national—can be addressed in isolation from outside events and considerations.

A corollary notion, then, is that events or decisions taken in places other than here have no effect on my organization or nation-state: my success is due to my own efforts and your misfortune is none of my own. Mitigating circumstances, intervening variables, or bad luck are anomalies outside of the parameters of the decision model.

Rational Model organizations are characterized by high levels of control. In order to garner the benefits due them—at least from the perspective of the Rational Model—individuals must be able to guard against the introduction of extraneous influences that unduly complicate the decision problem or threaten to diminish the benefits. It is imperative in such circumstances that if units are to maximize their own welfare, then they must also have the power to minimize any influences that could jeopardize their success. It is no accident of history, then, that public organizations have developed as rigid hierarchies with strict rules and requirements for individual accountability.

A set of assumptions underlies the development of organizations and rules shaped by the Rational Model. One assumption is that relationships are simple; where this is seen not to be the case, as in general systems theory, complex relationships must be broken down into their smallest component parts for problemsolving. The parts are then recombined, or summed, to get the maximum solution for the whole system. Even computer models that purport to represent complexity are constructed on an initial set of simple mathematical relationships. Too many variables in these equations spoil the broth, so to speak, especially where there are complex interactions.

A second assumption is that all situations can be addressed by a uniform set of rules. This relates again to the notion that relationships are simple. Where conditions deviate from the norm, explanations of the situations are made to fit the rules or else the situations are not addressed at all. Thus, individual deviant cases are typically said to fall between the cracks, which implies that although the cases may have merit, the individuals did not have the foresight to define themselves according to the dictates of the rules.[15]

A third underlying assumption is the belief in scientifically derived truth. Through science, so this belief goes, it is possible to identify absolutes that can be used as the basis for the rules and for the training of administrators. Neutral, objective science is also the ideal way to develop control over subjective, value-laden politics and its inefficiencies. For administration, science has been transformed into an assumption that the use of scientific means will necessarily produce the desired ends. Cases that do not fit the norms must *ipso facto* be unscientific and therefore unworthy of further consideration. Scientific administration is a matter of technique and is, by definition, apolitical.[16]

Science is to be desired above all else, even—or perhaps especially—above politics. Allen Schick has observed that public budgeting in the United States, especially the concept of the executive budget, represents the triumph of administration over politics (1980, 6). Ralph Hummel argues further that scientific management (bureaucracy) has transformed politics. Only problems that can be addressed by scientific means make it to the political agenda: "Lawmakers themselves are seduced into accepting the bureaucratic approach viewing politics as technical issues to be decided according to technical (problemsolving) rather than political (problemshaping) standards" (1987, 220).

Although science claims to be objective, the Rational Model, in fact, assumes the existence of a set of universal values, derived from the cultural norms of a homogeneous, middle-class European society. The values determine the acceptability of solutions to problems that have been defined in terms of the values. The principle value for the model is the increase in unit efficiency or welfare. Problems whose solutions would result in no welfare gain, or a gain to a unit other than the deciding unit or even to a universe including the unit, are anomalies for the model and cannot be successfully addressed.

For maximum efficiency, the model also demands an elite model of politics and administration. Only through limiting access to both the political and the administrative arenas is essential control possible. Pluralism, which implies deviation from elitist cultural norms, can be tolerated only to the extent that it can be controlled (Dye 1981, 29). Control through rationality is achieved increasingly by turning to experts, scientific policy analysts trained to design objective solutions. Hummel describes the impact on politics thus:

> When power can be properly exercised only by experts, because these demonstrate their ability to exert control over people and machines, then the claim of the old participants in politics, citizens and politicians, to have a part in controlling such power is rejected. In fact, both the citizen and the politician are disqualified from the new apolitics. They are replaced by functionaries, managers, and professionals. (1987, 230)

Finally, an essential requirement of the Rational Model is that access to information be limited. For elites to have control over the policy and administrative processes, information must be managed in such a way that only the right units have access to the information relevant to them. By assuming that information can be controlled, power elites can legitimate withholding information from the public on the basis that it is for the public's own welfare maximization (e.g., when to do so is "in the national interest").

The SupraRational Model, in contrast, views problems as global and interconnected; they cannot be addressed piecemeal because of the synergism among the parts. Consequently, social units—individuals, organizations, or nation-states—are also interconnected entities.

The problem situation is one of high uncertainty and risk and one that is beyond the capacities of individual decision units to solve. Problemsolving in this context necessitates incorporating ideas from and participating with diverse individuals and sectors; it negates completely the notion of individual accountability or the one best, scientifically correct solution.

Structured hierarchies cannot operate healthily in such an environment. Instead, organizations must be open and fluid, possibly using interlocking small groups with floating memberships. Such groups would be participative and truly democratic (i.e., no superior-subordinate relationships) to exchange information effectively. Accountability would be shared by the entire group.[17] Members of such groups would, of necessity, be interdisciplinary rather than narrowly expert since no problem can be viewed solely through the restrictive lenses of any individual discipline or specialty. This also means that public administrators could not assume that they alone control all relevant information for problemsolving by virtue of their expertise. It would be necessary to incorporate the expertise of agency clients and other publics in a new dynamic in order for the organization to function effectively in the interconnected world.[18]

For public organizations, this means that the classic bureaucratic organization is dysfunctional. Tightly structured hierarchies with their focus on control and individual accountability are fundamentally not equipped to operate effectively in the interconnected world. They are obsolete systems. Public organizations using the SupraRational Model will measure the value of their decisions in terms of social and organizational effectiveness rather than business efficiency.

The SupraRational Model also requires a politics of consensus. This means that protecting and enhancing the common values of the society is the new aim of policy development. A policy is not valid if it creates losers. Once again, the measure of a successful policy is the extent to which it advances the common good and leads toward collective welfare maximization. Since all are winners in this system, individual welfare is also maximized.

To reach collective decisions of this nature requires political systems, public organizations, and international policy bodies to be open and participative democracies, cooperative and noncompetitive. Policy must be developed through a process of consensus building, rather than compromise, so that interests are integrated rather than competitive and the results are synergistic.[19] Such a process is anathema to the Rational Model. Similarly, the bargaining and compromise typical of modern-day US democracy would also become obsolete in the SupraRational Model.

Political bargaining and compromise, whether through formal elite systems of politics or pluralist interest group politics, implies the existence of winners and losers in a zero-sum game. To be successful in these games, one must be willing to trade off some of what is valued in order to obtain the other's cooperation and vice versa. To compromise, then, means that each must lose something, and neither can be fully satisfied with the outcome. Big or powerful losers may become motivated to develop new political forces in order to overcome weaker participants who earlier won a political battle. Policy development is then a continual battle for success among various groups or ideologies, and the focus on common problems and interests is lost.

The rise and fall of regulatory policy beginning in the 1970s illustrates this phenomenon. In the early years of the decade, environmental and consumer-oriented interest groups influenced the passage of a number of laws designed to protect public health and welfare.[20] In each case, these laws were enacted through a political process that involved considerable bargaining and compromise among interest groups representing consumers and environmentalists, industry groups, Chambers of Commerce, state and local governments, and others. Despite the compromises made on all sides, powerful interests, primarily industry groups, perceived themselves to be big losers. Rather than work to implement the laws or to improve them, many of these interests devoted themselves to developing the political strength to overturn the laws or to emasculate the enforcement process.

When Ronald Reagan took office in 1981, deregulation became a major thrust, with environmental regulation a particular focus of this effort. Despite overwhelming evidence that a majority of the public supported stronger policies for environmental protection, the powerful losers in the regulatory battles convinced the political leaders in the administration to reduce the budget for enforcement and to attempt to dismantle many of the laws already in place. Considerable time and money were lost in the continually shifting battle between winners and losers as the environmental interest groups responded to become winners again.

What was lost in this scenario and in other political fights was the realization that all groups are losers when the tradeoffs have negative impacts for all society. In the environmental arena, the battle is usually drawn as a choice between an environmental value (air, water, birds, bunnies, and trees) and economic values (jobs). There is no way to win such a confrontation. A pristine environment without a viable economy will not enable an advanced society to progress. At the same time, an economy in a deteriorating environment will ultimately destroy both the human values that it presumes to promote and the economy itself in the long run. People should not have to endanger their children's health in order to feed their families; nonetheless, that is frequently the choice presented in the Rational Model policy process.[21]

It is often argued that consensual political processes are time consuming and expensive. This is true if one considers only higher short-term costs of consensus building over the more efficient compromise processes. The results of the SupraRational policy process, however, would be policies that are more successful over the long-run, have fewer harmful indirect effects, and are, therefore, cheaper overall. Admittedly, such a process would likely lower the ceiling that winners can achieve in a competitive, winner-take-all process, but it would also raise the floor for the losers and lead to a more hospitable society for all.

SUPRARATIONALITY
AND PUBLIC ADMINISTRATION

The shift from the Rational to the SupraRational Model would change not only how problems and organizations are viewed. The role of the administrator would also be fundamentally different even though many of the tasks and the skills required to perform them would be similar.

The dominant characteristics of public administration and its organizations are presently designed for and dictated by the Rational Model's necessity for control. The policy/administration dichotomy, for example, is the theoretical concept of control by politicians over administrators. Despite the burgeoning literature questioning the reality or desirability of the dichotomy,[22] some theorists and practitioners continue to advance it as fundamental for governance in a democracy.[23] Neutral competence can be seen as the means of control for the bureaucracy over outside influences, principally the citizenry but sometimes also the politicians.

Other characteristics—such as uniformity, equal treatment no matter what the variation of circumstances from the norm, and rules designed to remove the personal element from personnel systems, service delivery, and routines—are essentially means of control by a unit to achieve unit goals. The ultimate goal and the measure of success for the Rational Model is efficiency: profit maximization for private units and cost minimization for public ones or, as Woodrow Wilson (1887) put it, the goal of government organizations should be "business efficiency."

The role of the public administrator would change from neutral expert providing scientifically derived solutions for social problems to facilitator assisting social groups to develop the solutions most appropriate for a given problem in a given situation. The SupraRational Model accommodates complex problems that overlap sectors wherein neither the public administrator nor the private entity alone can possess the knowledge and skills necessary to address the entire problem system.

All sectors intersect with the public administrator, however, and public administration is the only function in the society that interacts with all the others. The public administrator, therefore, is centrally placed. In this unique position, the principal goal of the public administrator must become amelioration, not as the expert imposing a solution on other groups, but as the enabler and the mediator.

RATIONALITY AND THE NEW
PUBLIC ADMINISTRATION

The New Public Administration, as conceived at the original Minnow-brook Conference in 1968, incorporated many of the ideas posited here. For instance, its primary concern was social equity. Proponents also argued that the policy/administration dichotomy was a fiction, that administrators do influence policy, and, therefore, it was the responsibility of public administrators to advocate normative solutions to public problems. As Frederickson put it, *"Administrators are not neutral. They should be committed to both good management and social equity as values, things to be achieved, or rationales"* (1971, 312; emphasis in the original).

The New Public Administration was greeted with acclaim at the time, particularly by younger administrators and scholars influenced by the social upheaval of the 1960s—yet it did not have a lasting effect. Twenty years later, there were few if any examples of advocate administrators in government service. The rediscovery of the policy-administration dichotomy by conservative ideologues in the 1980s indicates that the concepts of the New Public Administration were never sufficiently institutionalized in government so as to demonstrate their superiority for public problem-solving and administration.

Why did the New Public Administration fall so short of its promise? It may have sown the seeds of its own destruction insofar as it was designed to be a threat to the status quo. It was based on the premise that "a Public Administration which fails to work for changes which try to redress the deprivation of minorities will likely be eventually used to repress those minorities" (Frederickson 1971, 311). Public administration was "anxiously engaged in change. *Simply put, New Public Administration seeks to change those policies and structures that systematically inhibit social equity"* (p. 312; emphasis in the original). Although they would work within the system, the New Public Administrationists clearly intended to alter the balance of political power. The vested interests may have been too strong for such changes to occur.

The more fundamental reason for the failure of New Public Administration may be that it did not escape the Rational Model and, therefore, did not escape the bounds of conventional theory. Rather than proposing something entirely new, the New Public Administration simply added a dimension to existing theory. As Frederickson notes,

Conventional or classic Public Administration seeks to answer either of these questions: (1) How can we offer more or better services with available resources (efficiency)? or (2) How can we maintain our level of services while spending less money (economy)? New Public Administration adds this question: Does this service enhance social equity? (1971, 311)

The New Public Administration was nestled in the Rational Model and thus contradicted its own value premises. The primary value of the Rational Model is accountability on the basis of economic efficiency for individual units. Social equity is a fundamentally different goal, and it is an anomaly for the Rational Model unless it can be shown to be cost-benefit efficient. Indeed, Frederickson saw cost-benefit analysis, the principle mechanism for rational decisionmaking, as valuable to the New Public Administration as well as to the old:

Cost-benefit analysis can be an effective means by which inequities can be demonstrated. It is a tool by which legislatures and entrenched bureaucracies can be caused to defend publicly their distributive decisions. The inference is that a public informed of glaring inequities will demand change. (p. 318)

What was not recognized at the time is that cost-benefit analysis is inherently biased against social equity because the benefits of social programs are difficult to translate into market prices, the basic requirement for the calculus. In fact, cost-benefit analysis was used in the late 1970s and 1980s as a force to deregulate government programs and *lessen* social equity.[24]

The role of the public administrator remained the same in the New Public Administration as in the classic model, except that administrators were now supposed to make decisions on the basis of normative values. This supposition presumed that administrators *knew* what those values were. In addition, the administrator was promoted as the expert, the possessor of the knowledge that would be used to advocate the best outcome for suppressed minorities.

This role, which implies continuing control by the administrator, is straight out of classic theory and the Rational Model. In contrast, the administrator's role in the SupraRational Model empowers all parties in the policy situation, enabling them to develop their own solutions rather than designing the best one for them. The critical information needed for policy development is possessed largely by those other than administrators. Administrators, then, cannot be the experts they are presumed to be by the New Public Administration.

While the New Public Administration remained in the Rational Model, it nonetheless held the seeds for theory development toward SupraRationality. Frederickson foresaw the possibility of

> theorists executing a model or paradigm of social equity fully as robust as the economist's market model. . . . If a full-blown equity model were developed it might be possible to assess rather precisely the likely outcomes of alternative policies in terms of whether the alternative does or does not enhance equity. (p. 330)

Social equity is a key measure of decision effectiveness in the SupraRational Model, along with the environmental ethic that Luke describes in Chapter 1 and Etzioni's (1988) deontological theory of social and economic behavior.

CONCLUSIONS

At this point, it is possible to see only the dysfunctions of the dominant model and the outlines of the emerging one. No one can presume to know exactly how public administrators will operate as ameliorators in performing their daily tasks within the multiversalist paradigm. What is clear is that interconnectedness is different from the old ways and requires fundamental changes in the way public administrators and citizens view their worlds and their public organizations.

Classic public administration saw the world as black and white. In such a world, there existed the possibility for right and wrong answers, even revealed truth. The New Public Administration saw many shades of gray and resisted the concept of absolutes. Nonetheless, by presuming that there were normative (or right) solutions to public problems and, further, that administrators knew what they were, the New Public Administration never broke away from the classic view and the rational model of decisionmaking. It still saw a static world.

The world, however, is multicolored, diverse, complex, and constantly changing. To make effective policy decisions in this world, we must adopt a multiversalist paradigm in which we accept the truth that answers are situational and temporal, that risks and uncertainties are par for the course, and finally, that the best that can be achieved is amelioration of today's problems as we await their new permutations tomorrow.

NOTES

1. For a full exploration of the notion of separation and its consequences see both Stivers in Chapter 3 and White in Chapter 7.

2. I am indebted to the literature and educational programs of Beyond War, 222 High Street, Palo Alto, Calif., for the ideas presented here.

3. Those of us who see a different reality and are criticized by our colleagues who do not recognize it can take comfort in knowing that Copernican astronomy was not accepted by the scientific community for two hundred years. Copernicus was threatened with excommunication for heresy and other young scientists were warned away from this radical theory. See Boorstin (1983) for an account of the development of Copernican theory.

4. See any text on microeconomics or policy analysis for a description of the Rational Model. Examples are Apgar and Brown (1987) and Patton and Sawicki (1986).

5. See Matzer (1984) for an explanation of the time value of discounting.

6. See Huber (1980) for a description of rational decisionmaking.

7. The Reagan Administration used this technique to defer developing air-pollution policies to reduce acid deposition.

8. Quotation appearing on a commercial poster, *circa* 1977. This echoes Aaron Wildavsky's Law of Large Solutions; see Luke in Chapter 1 for a discussion of the limitations of such an approach to problemsolving.

9. Supra-rational: not understandable by reason alone; beyond rational comprehension. *The Random House Dictionary of the English Language* (New York: Random House, 1967).

10. Since the Rational Model requires data to establish cause-and-effect relationships, it can only deal rationally with events that have already occurred. Global warming can only be verified by collecting data for several years after it has already happened. This will be too late for the development of effective policies to moderate its effects since it is likely we will not prove that climate change has happened until up to fifty years after the fact.

11. Interdependence probably explains why empirical social science tends to find correlations that are generally modest. Rarely do behavioral studies identify correlations that can be said to verify cause-effect relationships, say in the neighborhood of 90 percent.

12. On this point of whether increasing diversity in the workplace will affect the ways in which the work is carried out, see Guy in Chapter 5.

13. The NIMBY (not in my back yard) phenomenon is an example. Federal agencies, principally the Department of Energy, the Environmental Protection Agency, and the Corps of Engineers, can no longer decide unilaterally on placement of waste-disposal facilities, dams, and so forth. Citizens with better information than in the past demand to be included in the decision process.

14. This concern is most notable in policies for deregulation. For example, the savings and loan industry was deregulated in the early 1980s to encourage entrepreneurship. While individuals profited in the short-term, the policy had extremely negative long-term effects on the national and world economy.

15. An example of falling between the cracks is the following: A woman with twenty years experience as a caseworker in Michigan moved to Ohio in 1986 and became employed by Catholic Social Services. She was then required to apply for a state license and was informed that she was ineligible both for the license and to take the exam to be licensed until she had completed twenty-four undergraduate credits in social work. This

rule was enacted in 1985 and provided an exemption for experienced caseworkers employed by the State of Ohio as of January 1, 1984. Similar experience obtained elsewhere does not count. The rule was designed to ensure that caseworkers are qualified and classroom work was designated as the sole measure of qualifications. The woman is no longer a caseworker.

16. The sociopolitical consequences of this apolitical scientific administration are explored in depth by Mayer in Chapter 6, where he examines an empirical manifestation of the Rational Model in US domestic programs.

17. With open group decisions, it would be impossible to determine who is responsible or accountable, since no one could be identified as being in charge.

18. For an outline of a social theory for the paradigm, see Thayer (1981), especially Chapter 4.

19. The best description of the difference between consensus and compromise can be found in Follett (1965).

20. A selection of these laws includes The Clean Air Act of 1970; The Federal Water Pollution Control Act of 1972; The Occupational Safety and Health Act of 1970; The Resource Conservation and Recovery Act of 1975; and The Toxic Substances Control Act of 1976.

21. Some cynics have suggested that a way to solve this problem would be to pass a law requiring chief executive officers to live next door to their own factories. In like manner, water quality would be improved considerably if municipalities were required to take their drinking water from the river downstream from their sewage-disposal plants.

22. See Denhardt (1981) or Hummel (1987), for example.

23. Then-Attorney General Edwin Meese, speaking to the American Society for Public Administration annual meeting in Boston in 1987, articulated this position for the Reagan administration.

24. The Reagan administration used cost-benefit analysis as a mechanism to achieve its goal of crippling or eliminating social spending programs.

3

"A Wild Patience":
A Feminist View of Ameliorative
Public Administration
Camilla Stivers

Despite marginal fluctuations and fleeting challenges, the intellectual history of public administration reflects continuing emphasis on the professional application of proven techniques to achieve control over events and processes. From the "one best way" of scientific management through Herbert A. Simon's "satisficing" and Charles Lindblom's "muddling through" to the contemporary focus on public management, accountability, and the enlightened exercise of administrative discretion, the individual administrator's determination to bring order out of disorder persists. Theorists have disagreed about how far this enterprise could succeed but rarely about its desirability. The New Public Administration, despite its newness, was no exception. It failed to constitute an effective framework for decisionmaking because—instead of achieving a transformation—it simply added "relevance" (advocacy of social equity) to the Old Public Administration's "rigor" (efficiency, objectivity and neutrality). Although they disagreed about the stance and approach the individual public administrator should adopt, both the New and the Old Public Administrations believed not only that control was possible but that it was necessary. The quest for control, for effectiveness, has been the hallmark of the public administrator; indeed, it has been held to be *his* sacred duty.

This collection of essays is occasioned by—and, in fact, aims to broaden—awareness that a new understanding of the nature of reality has dawned and may be about to supplant the one in which the possibility of control could be safely assumed and reasonably desired. Initial writings about the new interconnected reality portray public administrators as encountering a unique form of complexity, one that evades and renders fruitless their best efforts to bring it under control. Attempts to do so are seen as akin to "wandering in the wilderness" (Gawthrop 1989, 195); the new complexity "bedevils" the public administrator (Ventriss 1989, 173); it is associated with "uncertainty, instability, . . . conflict, and risk" (Radin and Cooper 1989, 168). Administrators are advised that this intractable form of complexity requires them to "constrain visions" to that which is "judged . . . to be realistic, . . . [since] a meaningful long-term vision is neither reasonable nor perhaps even possible" (Guy 1989, 220). Realistic practice from this vantage point entails facilitation and amelioration, which replace problemsolving and the achievement of results as the proper aims for public administration.

The purposes of this contribution to the dialogue are to:

- Suggest that the new complexity is only the latest version of a persistent theme in public administration;
- Examine that theme's origins and the less-than-obvious purposes it may serve;
- Reflect on the ideas of control and effectiveness in public administrative practice;
- Differentiate between expert control and a practice guided by substantive visions of the public good; and
- Argue that, in moving beyond the Old Public Administration's rigor and the New Public Administration's relevance, public administration should resist the temptation to equate realism with accepting the impossibility of positive change.

The proposal to deal realistically with complexity is actually a permutation of the persistent desire to bring order out of disorder that has characterized Western public thinking at least since the decline of feudalism and the advent of the scientific revolution. Reexamining these issues from a feminist perspective suggests that Western common-sense understandings of "complexity" and "realism" can be traced to a perception of the self (the individual knower and actor) as a being necessarily separated and isolated from reality, which is to be known and controlled. This is a view in which the knower is understood as male, and reality—that which is to be subdued, if it is not to overwhelm—is understood as female. The following discussion on the relationship between the nature of reality and the nature of the self suggests a different interpretation of the meaning of both complexity and realistic action.

The search here for a fresh outlook is prompted by some unease over the concept of amelioration as the proper goal of practice in the multiversalist paradigm. This paradigm has been put forward (see, for example, Bailey in Chapter 2) as the orientation necessary to comprehend adequately the interconnected reality facing public administration. To put it plainly, I am concerned that turning to the idea of amelioration as a response to the command "Be realistic," could—by resurrecting the idea of neutrality—further mire public administration (not to mention society at large) in the slough of the status quo. Realism in this context too easily implies chastened acceptance of government's inability to make meaningful improvements in the conditions of people's lives. The mood of resignation reinforcing this tendency germinated in the misguided perception that the United States "lost" (i.e., was incapable of winning) the War on Poverty. This public malaise has been taken advantage of during the Carter and Reagan eras to advance the view that it is inappropriate for society to use government to try to combat social ills. The result is not *lessened* use of government, of course, but a *redirection* of its use—as the widening gulf between rich and poor in the United States attests—along with a general degradation in the quality of the public conversation and in opportunities for ordinary people to participate in public decisionmaking.

If embracing amelioration means moving away from a continuing faith in comprehensive rationality, managerialism, and design science, I am all for it. If, however, the public service is to be a force for good, if it is to be trustworthy, if it is to be legitimate (not just legitimated), then practice must cast amelioration in substantive, proactive terms, so that "taking complexity into account" means more than expert facilitation of so-called market approaches, combined with neutrality with respect to oppressive inequities. An alternative reaction to complexity is not separation of self and world but is, instead, a form of integration. Feminist poet Adrienne Rich writes, "A wild patience has taken me this far." I offer wild patience as an idea that may help integrate substantive visions with clear-sighted facilitative or ameliorative practice.

THE SEPARATED SELF

The view that complexity requires one to be realistic implies that the world out there is what it is. Reality will not bend to the will of public administrators, goes the message; therefore, public administrators had better accept it as it is and do the best they can with what they have. "Being realistic" assumes, first, that the view of the environment of modern public administration as complicated, diverse, interconnected, and rapidly changing is in some sense objectively correct. Second, it assumes that the appropriate response to this finding is to give up a long-term vision, lower one's sights, and proceed cautiously, if not timidly. It is worth taking a closer look at these assumptions rather than accepting them at face value. The argument here, based on feminist ontology and epistemology, is that at least some of the threatening complexity imputed to the world comes out of a particular view of the nature of the self and its relationship to everything else. ("Everything *outside* the self" already buys into the position that self and not-self can be sharply distinguished.) Understanding this perspective of the *separated self*—which is deeply interwoven into the fabric of much of what is done and said in Western society—means recognizing how it contributes to the powerful effect that realism has on us, an effect that is ideological. Public administrators are advised to be "realistic" about the expectation that public administrative practice can be used as a force for good, for increasing social and economic justice. The result, however, is to support the use of government to retard progressive change, as well as to maintain administration itself.

"The Cartesian Masculinization of Thought"[1]

The rationalist project that is a prime mark of the Western world's transformation from medieval to modern is frequently symbolized by Rene Descartes's famous dreams in 1619. The mode of knowledge Descartes formulated was based on detachment of an inwardly felt self from a universe lying outside it. Such a relationship between self and world can be seen as being in distinct contrast to the medieval sense of relatedness:

> The background picture [before the scientific revolution] . . . was of man as a microcosm within the macrocosm. It is clear that he did not feel himself isolated by his skin from the world outside to quite the same extent that we do. He was integrated or mortised into it, each different part of him being united to a different part of it by some invisible thread. In his relation to his environment, the man of the middle ages was rather less like an island, rather more like an embryo. (Owen Barfield, *Saving Appearances: A Study in Idolatry*, quoted in Bordo 1987, 255)

Descartes's well-known *cogito ergo sum* represents an assertion of the only indisputable knowledge, that is, knowledge of the self's existence.

All else—the outside—cannot be known with the same surety. Although in the later *Meditations* Descartes claims to have extricated himself from doubt and celebrated the vigilance of reason, the epistemological gulf opened up by the *cogito* evoked a profound anxiety and sense of alienation from the object world—feelings never quite dispelled by the assertion of triumphant rationalism.

Numerous observers have interpreted Descartes's project as "the masculinization of thought" (see sources quoted by Bordo 1987). On what basis can the postulation of an interior self decisively separated from an external world be seen in these terms? The answer is reflected in the imagery surrounding the world—or Nature—that prevailed in sixteenth- and seventeenth-century Europe. Nature was seen as female: both as the kindly Mother Earth who provided for the needs of mankind, and as a disorderly virago, bringer of tempests, plagues, and famine. Fear that Nature's order might break down into chaos was a common sentiment in Renaissance writing. For example, in 1594 Richard Hooker warned that "if nature ceased to observe her own laws, the celestial frame might dissolve, . . . the wind die out, the clouds dry up, the earth's fruits wither, and then chaos would ensue" (Merchant 1980, 128).

The disintegration of feudalism and the disorder of the Reformation lent impetus to the masculine desire to exert control over the forces and fates dealt by a threatening female Nature. According to Machiavelli,

> fortune is a woman and it is necessary if you wish to master her, to conquer her by force; and it can be seen that she lets herself be overcome by the bold rather than by those who proceed coldly, and therefore like a woman, she is always a friend to the young because they are less cautious, fiercer, and master her with greater audacity. (quoted in Merchant 1980, 130)

Similarly, Francis Bacon portrayed the scientific method as having "the power to conquer and subdue [Nature], to shake her to her foundations" (E. F. Keller 1985, 361) or "to follow and as it were hound nature in her wanderings. . . . Neither ought a man to make scruple of entering and penetrating into those holes and corners, when the inquisition of truth is its whole object" (quoted in Harding 1986, 116).

The rationalist project of the Scientific Revolution, symbolized by Descartes's dreams, aimed both to subdue and to exploit the female earth. In this effort, connection with Nature, such as is reflected in the medieval organic view of the universe, "muddies the clear lake of the mind" (Bordo 1987, 261) and weakens the masculine effort at control. Knowledge requires that Nature be conceived of as wholly other; only if mind and Nature are completely distinct can mind truly grasp and thus be able to subdue Nature, the object. The knowledge from which power will emerge is a matter of "measurement rather than sympathy" (Charles Gillispie, *The Edge of Objectivity*, quoted in Bordo 1987, 258).

Object Relations and Science

The Western conflation of Nature/the Other with the feminine and the self/knower with the masculine has been pointed out in feminist philosophy since Simone de Beauvoir's classic, *The Second Sex* (1957). It appears, for example, in the mythology of the hero, which has shaped Western ideas about what it means "to be a man," that is, to be a full human being—one whose questing ego encounters the world in order to conquer, one for whom excellence is achieved through tests of autonomy. Catherine Keller describes the significance of this heroic image:

> The archetypal [hero's] . . . philosophical descendent is the separate, self-enclosed subject. . . . Its relations do not affect its essence. Indeed, to sustain its sense of independence, such a subject is always liberating itself from its bonds as though from bondage. Intimacy, emotion and the influence of the Other arouse its worst anxieties, for somehow it must keep relation external to its own being, its "self." (1986, 7)

Feminist theory has attempted to account for the masculinity of this separated self and the anxiety surrounding issues of separateness and autonomy by turning to psychoanalytic theory, especially the branch known as object-relations theory (Chodorow 1978; Dinnerstein 1976; Gilligan 1982; Flax 1978). This theory seeks to explain the development of the self in terms of both innate drives and actual relations with others. Feminists working from this perspective argue that in societies where children are cared for primarily by women, both male and female infants must struggle to reach a sense of self in the context of women's care. As a result, male and female children adopt distinctive models of the self. Males develop through a process of separation and individuation from an "other"—a kind of person who they biologically cannot become. Personhood becomes equated with the achievement of autonomy and fairly rigid ego boundaries are formed. In contrast, females' personalities develop in relation to persons like themselves, the kind of person they will in fact one day grow to be. Maturity thus becomes defined in terms of the maintenance of attachment, and ego boundaries remain relatively permeable.

Feminism has found object-relations theory useful because it suggests that gender is at least partly constructed by means of a social and cultural process, allowing feminists to argue that childcare arrangements substantively and fully shared by men and women would lead over time to a reduction in the distinctiveness of the two genders. For present purposes, the most interesting use of the theory is to account for the persistence of cultural stereotypes linking science and ideas of objectivity and detachment with masculinity (reflected, for example, in the distinction commonly made between "hard" and "soft" data). Evelyn Fox Keller argues that "adherence to an outmoded, dichotomous conception of objectivity might be viewed as a defense against anxiety about autonomy" that has its roots in the male struggle to separate himself from the enveloping presence of the mother/other (1985, 85). She suggests that the conflation of science and objectivity with the masculine colors the Western view of science. That is, cultural preference for the masculine leads one to see as scientific only that mode of knowledge that is objective in the sense of being arrived at through processes of detachment.

Keller's argument suggests that, because of male preference for masculine modes of thought, generalized male dominance in society leads to the elevation of masculine interpretations of what constitutes real knowledge. Objectivity becomes equated with detachment, and the resulting knowledge is seen as the only true form instead of a particular conceptualization rooted culturally in the developmental experiences of half the population. Universalization becomes possible because the half in question is disproportionately influential in shaping societal ideas and ideologies. Thus, the entire society comes to see the particular as the essential, and alternative ways of knowing appear comparatively limited, partial, and less trustworthy.

Autonomy and Choice

Ideas of the separated self and objective knowledge will not seem strange to readers of Thomas Hobbes, John Locke, and other classical liberal political philosophers. O'Brien points out that Hobbes aimed to perpetuate the idea of sovereignty because he felt that the "atomism and competitive particularity of autonomous individuals" made it necessary (1981, 160). Both the notion of a prepolitical state of nature inhabited by self-sufficient beings and the case for individual political rights based on property ownership have analogous roots—as does *homo economicus*. The liberal, just society is premised on the idea of agreement among individuals exercising free choice in their entrance into a contract that binds them in limited ways.

The idea of individual rights is a persistent theme in liberal philosophy, which continually stresses the necessity in a legitimate state for the free exercise of the individual will. The emphasis on free will or choice is linked to the idea of the autonomous knower, for whom knowledge consists in the mastery of Nature so that she yields up her secrets to him. The scientific method empowers the knower, enabling him to choose knowledgeably and thereby to best *fortuna*. In contrast, as feminist philosophers point out, women's experience, which includes childbearing and—culturally—childrearing and the care of other vulnerable persons, is steeped in the limits on choice, in the irremediable given-ness of certain aspects of existence, and in the contingencies that must be taken into account, all of which inevitably bound the free exercise of the individual will. As Gilligan puts it, "Since the reality of connection is experienced by women as given rather than as freely contracted, they arrive at an understanding of life that reflects the limits of autonomy and control" (1982, 172).

The Autonomous Public Administrator

The image of the separated self reverberates in familiar concepts and tendencies of public administration. One obvious place to find the separated self is in the figure of the neutral administrator, whose legitimacy lies in detachment from partisan politics. Neutral expertise depends on the possibility of objective (in the sense of detached) knowledge arrived at through study of an "out there" reality. Although the idea of neutrality is now widely regarded as simplistic and outmoded, it still has a hold on those in the field. As Rosenbloom argues, the administrative culture that grew up in the reform period (1877-1920), of which neutral scientific competence was a hallmark, persists today despite the challenges of Herbert Simon, Robert Dahl, Dwight Waldo, and Paul Appleby in the 1940s (1987). Rosenbloom quotes Harold Seidman's diagnosis to the effect that if 1937 marked the "high noon" of the orthodoxy, then someone "apparently stopped the clock" (p. 78). Perhaps the contemporary value of neutrality is most obvious in the frequency with which fairness and impartial judgment are held up as important qualities of the legitimate public administrator, abilities predicated—at least implicitly—on the possibility of detached analysis of situations.

In a recent fresh examination of Woodrow Wilson's famous essay, Daniel Martin (1988) offers further evidence of the central place detachment still holds. He asks why the politics/administration dichotomy persisted, when it appears that Wilson abandoned his original formulation of it—the result of his mistranslation from German sources—within a few short years. Martin answers that the dichotomy became a valuable resource as administrative reformers were transformed from outsiders to bureaucratic insiders intent on professionalizing their pursuit. Although the reformers knew only too well that the dichotomy failed to jibe with their experience, Wilson's idea symbolized "*strength through isolation*," (emphasis added) an enduring ideal in a "changing world" (p. 635). An autonomous public service thus had, and continues to have, prescriptive value in a system widely perceived as fragmented, competitive, and frequently threatening to administrative interests.

Another image of the separated public administrator is that of the entrepreneur. Doig draws on Joseph Schumpeter's portrait for the decisive characteristics (1988). According to Schumpeter, Doig argues, the entrepreneur is "the most rational and the most egotistical of all," one who has "the dream and will to found a private kingdom . . . to fight, to prove oneself superior to others . . ., [who] seeks out difficulties, changes in order to change" (p. 22). Doig's research indicates that this model corresponds closely to the personalities of the public leaders he studied. Significantly, he takes pains in his work to dispel the picture painted in much public-administration literature of the bureaucrat as one who can accomplish little, and more importantly, whose accomplishments cannot be distinguished from the ongoing flow of events. Doig sees Herbert Kaufman's assessment as cautionary:

> In the short run . . . the only perceptible changes are likely to be small compared to the continuities; your contribution to them will be so mingled with the contributions of others that you will have trouble identifying it. (p. 3)

The ideal in Doig's argument is the public administrator about whom one can pinpoint decisive accomplishments, whose impact can be isolated and earmarked.

In this respect, Doig is in a longstanding tradition. Perception of how important it would be that public servants be able to achieve perceptible greatness dates back to the nation's founders. They saw the incentive to attract "the better sort" to public life to be the public fame that such deeds would win. Public virtue, according to the founders, had to be visible; that meant that individual deeds must be separable from the course of events. Green's (1988) portrait of the Hamiltonian administrator conceptualizes the virtuous administrator as one who acts before an audience of the wise and the good and who by his performance wins public respect, if not acclaim.

The image of the public administrator as professional also reflects important elements of detachment. The hallmarks of the professional include the exercise of autonomous judgment and the right of members to police themselves. The claim to autonomy is based on the profession's access to a scientific, objective knowledge base—professional knowledge and its application are so specialized that no outsider is considered qualified to say whether a member is competent. Bledstein's discussion of the development of the idea of professionalism in the nineteenth century makes clear this grounding in the image of the separated self:

> The culture of professionalism emancipated the active ego of the sovereign person as he performed organized activities within comprehensive spaces. The culture of professionalism incarnated the radical idea of the independent democrat, a liberated person seeking to free the power of nature within every worldly sphere, a self-governing individual exercising his trained judgment in an open society. (1976, 87)

Thus the public administrator as neutral bureaucrat, as entrepreneur, or as professional, implicitly (if not self-consciously) trusts in the ongoing existence of the separated self as able to hold itself apart from the hurly-burly of the world in order to make sense of that world, be effective, and feel legitimate. Because the separated self is culturally and historically masculine, the self-identity of the public administrator of either sex—partaking as it does of these central and persistent images—is also significantly masculine.[2]

THE GENDER OF COMPLEXITY

The multiversalist paradigm sees the environment of late-twentieth-century public administration as irremediably—and even threateningly—complex. While the nature of present-day complexity may be unique in some ways, the perception of complexity has been a long-standing tendency in Western culture, which raises the question of why this is so.

The Search for Order

There is little need to attempt an exhaustive analysis of the theme of complexity: remembering its importance for those late-nineteenth-century reform efforts from which modern public administration sprang may be enough to convey the sense that perceiving the threat of complexity is nothing new. Woodrow Wilson's 1887 essay begins with the argument that the study of administration is necessary because of complexity: Once, "the functions of government were simple, because life itself was simple." But now, "present complexities of trade and perplexities of commercial speculation . . . perennial discords between master and workmen . . . assume . . . ominous proportions." Similarly, "the functions of government are every day becoming more complex and difficult, [and] multiplying in number." The answer to this dilemma, of course, is the science of administration and the development of sound principles that will make it possible to "run a Constitution."

Wilson's essay is only the most familiar expression of a characteristic stance taken by reformers of that period in response to what they perceived to be the threat not only of complexity but of complete societal disintegration. As Wiebe paints the picture, by the early 1880s nationalization, industrialization, mechanization, and urbanization were producing bewilderment and spiritual dislocation in the United States. Swift change and an increasingly entangled network of social relations evoked the widespread sense of an alien social environment. Specific phenomena such as successive waves of immigrants, labor unrest, and the demands of agrarian Populists were particular sources of anxiety for those in positions of authority. While people from all walks of life were shaken as they confronted what seemed to be an incomprehensible world, members of corporate and governmental elites in particular "reached out for . . . mastery" in an effort to "quash all disorder" (1967, 76-77).

Wiebe argues that bureaucracy was the perfect response to this sense of complexity and chaos, not because it attempted to wipe out these threats, but because it acknowledged their inevitability and sought to meet them *on their own terms*:

> The ideas that filtered through and eventually took the fort were bureaucratic ones, peculiarly suited to the fluidity and impersonality of an urban-industrial world. They pictured a society of ceaselessly interacting members and concentrated upon adjustment within it. Although they included rules and principles of human behavior, these necessarily had an indeterminate quality because perpetual interaction was itself indeterminate. . . . Thus the rules, resembling orientations much more than laws, stressed techniques of constant watchfulness and mechanisms of continuous management. (p. 145)

Wiebe suggests that proponents of bureaucracy were "resilient" precisely because they "presuppos[ed] the unexpected" (p. 154). Bureaucratic thought envisioned the creation of unity from diversity through procedures and processes that would mesh all parts of society together. Complexity would be dealt with not by ignoring or trying to suppress it, but by meeting it head on. The principle weapon in this effort would be science. By becoming experts, bureaucrats would rise above narrow partisanship and personal ambition:

> The product was the perfect bureaucrat, whose flawlessly wired inner box guaranteed precisely accurate responses within his specialty. The latitude he enjoyed in administration existed only because no one could predict the course of a fluid society and the expert *would require a freedom sufficient to follow it.* (p. 161; emphasis added)

Wiebe's argument suggests that, although the fear of disorder was real enough both in society-at-large and among the elite, administrative reformers—self-consciously or not—made ideological use of the threat of disintegration, taking advantage of pervasive anxiety to advance an approach that prevailed precisely because it did not depend upon eliminating the menace to which it was a response. Wilson's essay exemplifies the argument: scientific administration is vital because the world is complex and disorderly; we cannot make the world simple once again, but we will make it run efficiently.

Present-day arguments in support of administrative discretion argue in similar terms: because government is fragmented and the course of events is unpredictable, the administrative expert requires the freedom to devise flexible strategies. This means that the administrative interpretation of situations is to be the determinative one. For example, Gary Wamsley (1990) calls for "agential leadership" on the part of public administrators through the exercise of strategic discretion, which acts as a guidance mechanism for steering the otherwise chaotic course of the ship of state. Norton Long (1981) has argued that it is a good thing public administrators are asserting their role in governance, because other branches of government are not exerting the necessary control. Such arguments reflect not only mere acceptance of the inevitability of complexity but also advocacy, in Wiebe's terms, of those "mechanisms of continuous management" that maximize *administrative freedom*, a permutation of the boldness Machiavelli felt was necessary in order to master *fortuna*. "Realistic" administrative practice uses the diagnosis of complexity to *perpetuate*—rather than to temper or transform—administrative autonomy, which represents the public administrator's masculine separated self. Let us examine more closely the gendered character of the complexity that this masculine figure confronts.

Disorder Is a Woman[3]

As argued in examining the separated self, since the beginning of the early modern period Nature/matter/the other have been associated with the feminine, while culture/mind or spirit/the self with the masculine. The new science of the sixteenth century, by displacing age-old hierarchies with the discoveries of Copernicus and Vesalius, contributed to a generalized sense of impending disorder in the universe. Because of their childbearing and childrearing responsibilities, women were seen as closer and more attuned to Nature than were men; therefore, the unease over a changing cosmos fixed itself more readily on women. Works of art and literature of the period depicted them as disorderly, lustful, insolent, and dissolute. The clearest manifestation of this perception of woman's nature was the phenomenon of witchcraft, inflamed by the fifteenth-century antiwoman tract, the *Malleus Maleficarum*. Witches were represented as wild and lustful creatures engaged in frenzied activity, wreaking revenge on those unfortunate enough to earn their enmity and manipulating the natural world with their magic spells (Merchant 1980).

While witchcraft was perhaps the most vivid emblem of the cultural meaning of femininity at the beginning of the modern period, the general distinction between nature and culture, each with its attached gender associations, took many other forms. For example, John Knox identified women with passive, base matter and men with spirit. He argued that the body politic, corresponding to the "natural body of man," required that the head rule the body. In society, the ruler—the head—must be a man, for woman's rule would be a monstrosity (Merchant 1980, 145). The "monstrous regiment of women" feared by Knox was still being evoked in the late nineteenth-century United States Congress by a legislator in dread of female suffrage (Gay 1984).

This image of the masculine head of state controlling the archetypically feminine masses is a persistent one in Western political philosophy. Landes demonstrates that the absolutist monarch of pre-Revolutionary France "unman[ned]" (the word used at the time) all other members of the kingdom because of his unlimited power (1988, 21). Brown (1988) has pointed out the gender dimensions of key philosophical terms: political action, or virtue, from *vir* (man), consists in giving form to matter (*mater*, or mother—woman). Machiavelli's body politic is a woman's body, its head a male head. The true prince renders the people "submissive, grateful, loyal" (pp. 87-88, 109-110). By taking political action, men outwit *fortuna*—they rise above contingency. Controlling the body politic, they can move into the realm where freedom means not being confined by bodily necessities—by sheer subsistence. Political men can become pure mind, that is, the ultimate separated self.

What emerges, then, from feminist reflection on the Western common-sense view of self and the Other is a unitary, rational, clearly bounded, masculine self separated from and confronting a complex, threatening, feminine world. Despite the widespread acceptance in modern times of Freud's theory of the human psyche as tripartite and only partly conscious, most Westerners appear to continue to lead their lives assuming that the thinking selves of which they have immediate conscious knowledge are their whole selves. Feminist philosophy suggests that this failure to take into practical account otherwise commonplace knowledge persists because the heroic, masculine ego (an image that ideologically governs the self-understanding of both sexes) is unable to deal with its own inner complexity and so has projected that complexity onto the world. The universe must be complex so that human beings can assure themselves of being unitary unto themselves; the threat must come from the world—hence from each other—and not from inside themselves. Thus Westerners postulate a world made up of individual human atoms, in competition and conflict, able to cooperate only to combat commonly perceived threats (Whitbeck 1983).

This line of argument does not aim to "prove" that the world is not complex but to point out that the question of the world's complexity cannot be answered "objectively," because complexity is an evaluative term. In practice, we in the West tend to define complexity in relation to that which we see as not complex—our thinking egos. Complexity in the universe thus serves as the stalking horse for the inner fragmentation and mystery we seem unable to accept—and, if Wiebe is correct, complexity also functions ideologically to underscore the necessity for the free exercise of administrative discretion. The latter is an idea that depends heavily on seeing public administrators as autonomous decisionmakers whose free choices are a balance wheel in the fragmented complexity of modern government and politics. Public administration so construed needs the threat of complexity so that the world will need public administration to handle the threat. Status quo politics uses complexity to perpetuate the perception that government is incapable of meaningful action in pursuit of substantive justice.

BEYOND RIGOR AND RELEVANCE

The beginning of this essay suggests that, in the context of the call to be realistic so as to exert maximum control over events, the notion of amelioration runs the risk of bowing to the dictates of things as they are, thus reinforcing the link between public-administrative practice and maintenance of the status quo. Although the New Public Administration failed to achieve a paradigm shift, it undercut the Old Public Administration's apparent neutrality and objectivity by defending the proper place of substantive political values in public-administration thinking. A key question for the multiversalist paradigm is how to conceive of amelioration so as to preserve the New Public Administration's substantive commitment without reasserting the Old Public Administration's neutral expertise—that is, how to move beyond the rigor-versus-relevance debate to something truly transformative. To do this requires dealing with feminist ideas about the self, its relation to knowledge and to political life, and the implications for ideas about complexity.

The Art of Personhood

The New Public Administration's call for relevance was a reaction to conceiving of public administration as a science, that is, in the masculine, objectified sense. In the ensuing years, relevance fairly quickly acquired a bad name. It came to be equated with inappropriate partiality and the lowering of standards of excellence in knowledge production—grounds, it should be noted, that depended for their force on the very mode of thought that the proponents of relevance sought to supplant. Clearly, however, whatever permutation of relevance is sought in the multiversalist paradigm must also deal with questions of the relationship between self and the Other.

As suggested above, feminist theorists working from an object-relations perspective have argued for replacing the separated, autonomous self, which they trace to the process of male personality development, with the *different*, more relational and altruistic self linked to the development of the female psyche (see, e.g., the title of Carol Gilligan's 1982 near-classic, *In a Different Voice*)—or, if not replacing the masculine with the feminine, at least making room for a worthy alternative. But, it has been observed, such moves do not deal directly with the opposition between a unitary self and a complex world, for the different self is still seen as atomistic and fixed (Ferguson 1987). Feminists attempting to move beyond the different self have adopted a developmental perspective that suggests viewing the self as arising out of social practices and in relationships with others, therefore varying within different cultures and constantly changing. The idea is not to get rid of the notion of the self (the anxiety that inevitably arises when the masculine self is challenged), but to see personhood as an art learned gradually in childhood and practiced throughout life (Code 1987). From this perspective, the self has many aspects developed in different practices (Ferguson 1987), some of which might even conflict with each other—for example, female public administrators struggling to balance career aspirations with family responsibilities might feel these two aspects of their selves are at odds from time to time.

This developmental view emphasizes the social nature of the self: human beings develop in relationships that are not merely oppositional but frequently enabling. We gradually acquire both our sense of our own uniqueness *and* our sense of being like other human beings through listening and speaking with—and influencing and being influenced by— others (Code 1987; Whitbeck 1983). Thus, these theorists argue, the authentic self is able to deal with the fact of its own dependence on others and its origins in social interaction, as well as with its own autonomy and freedom.

Politics and Knowledge

Replacing the separated self with a developing, multi-aspected self has clear political implications. Because of the separated, unitary ego's interest in controlling the world, which includes other human beings, the prevalence of that ego's ideology in classical liberalism and its philosophical descendants reinforced the dominance of male-identified political systems.

The developmental self, on the other hand, can be the grounds for an authentic political philosophy, one which aims at facilitating both freedom and reciprocity. In addition, the politics of the developing self address the human characteristics needed for a full, substantive democracy. The necessity and benefit of educating people for democratic citizenship is an age-old idea, but one that has had difficulty prevailing against the separated, unitary ego's view of human nature as fixed. The influence of social relationships on the development of the self points to factors that help form the democratic character, especially the dynamics of family life. Gould suggests that the attainment of full democracy in the public sphere requires freedom and reciprocity in personal relationships in the private sphere, including inside the family: "Someone accustomed to dominate or to be subordinated in personal life is unlikely to be able to treat others as equals in the context of democratic decisionmaking" (1983, 8). In a democratic society, there can be no "head of household."

Reciprocity in personal—as well as public—relationships requires giving up the idea of the separated self, not only because of the issue of control, but also because the objectifying ego and its politics aim to wipe out differences among people in the interests both of knowledge and liberty. In detaching himself, the Cartesian strives to eliminate the contaminating influences of his unique being in order to have true knowledge of the world. The implication is that all knowers are—or should be conceptualized as—alike, for only if the identity of the particular knower *makes no difference* on the outcome of the search for knowledge will the results be valid. The objective knowledge that comes from detached observation transcends the experiences and characteristics of the observer, who in his role as knower is only a standardized instrument. Denying his own inner complexity and changeability—thus objectifying himself as a object of his own knowledge—the Cartesian knower then performs the same operation on other selves. They become manipulable objects of knowledge, the epistemological analogues of the liberal state's atomized, competitive members, because

> the patriarchal subjectivity of control cannot distinguish connection from conformity. It creates what it fears: a collective sameness, a proscription of difference, a prohibition against wandering. It projects this fear onto women. . . . The separative cadence of other-opposition and self-preservation creates not difference but sameness: the project of self-identity through time preserves a fantasy of solid subjective unity amidst the Others out there. (Keller 1986, 204)

Alternatively, a state composed of developing multi-aspected selves will predicate itself on the acknowledgement rather than suppression of difference and on the inherent connectedness of self and world in the knowledge process. Such a perspective has its prototype in the culturally feminine experience of the care and nurturance of developing persons that is carried into—in order to transform—the culturally masculine public space. Whitbeck (1983) describes the requisite ontology as nondualistic: differentiation—that is, distinguishing self from other—does not depend on opposition, but on relationships among analogous beings. The Other is not considered opposite to the self, therefore others can be like, as well as different from, the self. Relations among these analogous beings are mutually created, developing through both identification and differentiation. From this perspective, one cannot become a person without relating with others.

For such selves, knowledge is a matter of interconnection with that which is to be known. The development of communal standards for knowledge is not only accepted but emphasized. As Code (1987) points out, objectified knowledge systems mislead in their emphasis on detached observation, for in practice very little of what counts as knowledge comes through direct observation. Instead, most of the time one must count on the testimony of others. Therefore, the development of adequate bases for trusting in testimony is paramount. Trust, of course, develops out of authentic interaction and the tangible demonstration of good faith, rather than as a result of adherence to specified procedures analogous to the scientific method.

This view of knowledge is predicated on respect for difference and complexity in the world rather than on the desire to reduce difference and to control, if not eliminate, complexity. Evelyn Fox Keller's (1983) portrait of Nobel Prize-winning botanist Barbara McClintock provides an interesting example of such an approach to knowledge in a natural science. McClintock's work on the genetics of corn was successful because of her painstaking process of "listening to the material" and her "respect" for the minute differences among various specimens:

> McClintock's feeling for the organism is not simply a longing to behold the "reason revealed in the world." It is a longing to embrace the world in its very being, through reason and beyond.

> For McClintock, reason . . . is not by itself adequate to describe the vast complexity—even mystery of living forms. Organisms have a life and order of their own that scientists can only partially fathom. (p. 199)

From such a perspective, the complexity of the field is both inherent and interesting, not threatening. The scientist is motivated to *embrace* the world, not to control it. By practicing the patience to "hear what the material has to tell you," one reaches "a completely new realization of the relationship of things to each other" (pp. 198, 207).

A Realistic Relevance

Drawing from feminist theory the ingredients of a possible relevance for the multiversalist paradigm, one can say first that connectedness between person and world is the *new* realism and recognition of it the new rigor. If the self develops in relationship with others, beginning in infancy and continuing throughout life, then "being realistic" involves recognizing how artificial and *un*-realistic it is to argue that one must bow to things as they are. Relevance—that is, relatedness—is not only valuable, it is required. It involves McClintock's listening to the material, which is more a dialogue than a passive waiting for what comes from the field; it involves abandoning the idea of control over the environment in favor of developing processes and skills for working with the environment, that is, for interaction, social learning, and collaborative creativity. And it involves an ongoing *inner* dialogue among the multiple aspects of the self. Somewhat analogous is Hannah Arendt's view of thinking as a "soundless dialogue between me and myself" (quoted in Young-Bruehl 1989, 25), but in this case it is a dialogue expanded to encompass relationships with the emotional and nonconscious aspects of the self. Finally, relevance requires an attention to the quality of politics, to the quality of families, and to the material conditions necessary to enable the formation of the democratic character, both in early childhood in nonhierarchical nurturing relationships and in adulthood in nonhierarchical relationships in the public sphere. With these ingredients, public administration can integrate the positive features of both rigor/realism and relevance/relatedness to evolve a substantive ameliorative practice.

A WILD PATIENCE

The feminist perspective aims to transcend dichotomies like self versus Other, nature versus culture, rigor versus relevance, because feminists believe that such oppositions are all grounded in the historically masculine struggle to define once and for all the heroic ego—to say what the ego is by pointing to and by denigrating what it is not, namely, the feminine Other. Thus, to move toward an ameliorative practice from the feminist point of view is to move beyond rigor versus relevance to something that integrates the positive qualities of rigor *and* relevance, transforming each into something truly new.

In other words, let the difference between rigor and relevance stand,[4] because it is no longer necessary to define either term as *not* the other. Adrienne Rich's "wild patience" may be an appropriate analogue for the multiversalist administrator's standpoint, because it suggests a realism both clearsighted and committed. The idea of patience captures the sense of taking the time to develop and practice awareness of the world—in order to sense (but not obliterate nor subdue) its diversity—a world in which those who are engaged in practice are inherently and intimately involved. Patience involves the development of ways of knowing that take advantage of the social nature of reality, especially those that involve direct interaction with people in the field—McClintock's "listening to the material" becomes listening to and working with people. Patience is the facilitative administrator's praxis.

A *wild* patience, however, is an awareness that refuses to settle for whatever comes—realizing the interweaving of our own human selves into the fabric of the field, wild patience grounds us in purpose—not so that we lose touch with process in obsessive concern with outcome, but so that process is not vacuous. Wildness might be thought of as a rigor that depends on attachment rather than detachment—on affiliation with people in the world, on anchoring in personal and communal values. Wildness, in fact, draws strength from awareness that all that human beings know of the world comes as a result of attachment to it; otherwise, without this awareness, we are, as interpretive philosopher Wilhelm Dilthey once said, trying to see without an eye. Or, as Mary Parker Follett put it, interpretation is part of vision, not something you do afterwards (1951, 27).

From the stance of wild patience, the complexity of the environment is not a threat. Nor is it a basis for legitimating either the political-economic status quo nor the unilateral authority of bureaucratic experts engaged in the management of a fragmented and disorderly system. Because we, as human beings, *share in* this complexity, it is neither alien nor remote. Such a realization should help us to become aware of the extent to which the perception of complexity disarms and disables us and makes possible the persistence of want and injustice. Our interconnectedness with everything—and everyone—around us does not mean, however, that the world can be whatever we think it is. Thus wild patience preserves both the Old Public Administration's courageous rejection of wishful thinking as the basis for decisionmaking and the New Public Administration's bold assertion of concern for justice. We need not transcend the world, as the masculine separated self does by being not-Other, in order to make sense of what we do and to believe that it is meaningful. We can, instead, find meaning in immanence—that is, in the substance and conditions of people's lives—and in what we can do to ameliorate those conditions.

If we do not trust in process—in discussion, in facilitation, in communal activities, in the "interweaving of willings" (Follett 1965, 69)—we risk continually giving in to the lures of mastery, domination, and control. But if our prime concern is the neutrality of process, then we have set about separation and transcendence again, leaving the necessaries of this life to others—metaphorically, to the women.

The world as it is must make us patient—but it should also make us wild. In a stance of wild patience, we must join with those from whom we are never truly separated. Together with people in the complex and ultimately uncontrollable environment of public administration, we have an opportunity to make wildness and patience, as Adrienne Rich says, blend and "breathe" in *all* of us "as angels, not polarities."

NOTES

1. Much of the material in this section is based on Susan Bordo's (1987) essay, the title of which I have used as the title of the section.

2. I can only note here, without being able to discuss it, the problem this creates for women in public service in terms of achieving a sense of authenticity in practice. Given how differently females and males are socialized in our culture, for women taking on the identity of public administrator almost inevitably involves conflicts with widely shared social expectations of appropriate female behavior, or with their own deeply felt values and self-expectations.

3. Much of the material in this section is drawn from Merchant (1980).

4. I owe the idea of "letting difference stand" to Cynthia McSwain.

4

Humanizing the Workplace: Incorporating Feminine Leadership
Carol J. Edlund

This essay argues for incorporating a feminine leadership style into public administration theory. Since traditional theory favors control—as clearly argued in several of the essays in this volume—rather than humanistic organizational structures, a new leadership style is necessary in order to take into account the interconnectedness and interdependency that is the hallmark of today's public administration world.

A feminine leadership style is a necessary element in the developing multiversalist paradigm. The concept refers not to leadership by women but rather to a leadership style that contrasts with the dominant masculine leadership style. The qualities of either style can be possessed by both men and women; in addition, in individual instances the styles are likely to be mixed. The basic assumption here, however, is that men *and* women, in order to be successful in bureaucratic organizations, have had to adopt the masculine style almost exclusively, one that is dysfunctional in the inter-connected world of today.[1] A feminine leadership style incorporating traits usually attributed to women offers more potential for management and problemsolving in the present environment than does the masculine style alone.

The concept of a feminine leadership style incorporates Jeff S. Luke's notion of catalytic leadership in Chapter 1 and is compatible with the SupraRational Model of decisionmaking outlined by Mary Timney Bailey, described in Chapter 2. It is my hope that as more women achieve leadership positions in public organizations, feminine leadership styles will gain legitimacy as a means of managing complex, interconnected, and interdependent organizations. The evidence that Mary Ellen Guy provides in Chapter 5 suggests that gaining this legitimacy will not be easy, particularly if changes in leadership style are not supported and enhanced by changes in organizational structure. The purpose here, however, is limited to conceptually clarifying the feminine leadership style.

A TIME FOR CHANGE

Data from public-opinion polls reveal that people have lost confidence in public leadership (Denhardt 1981; Lipset and Schneider 1987). This loss of faith in the leadership of government and other public organizations is critical because, among other things, these institutions play significant roles in the lives of the workers they employ. The traditional, bureaucratic model of leadership by itself is not adequate because it fails to meet the needs of an enlightened workforce and to take into account the totality of the human psyche. A masculine leadership style with its emphasis on rational (head) thinking gives little value to the relevance of feminine (heart) thinking.

A new reality is emerging in the public workplace in which there seems to be an awakening to the human needs of workers (Cohen 1989). Employees yearn for a more caring, livable work environment. They believe that love, family, and labor can be integrated. It is not that people dislike work per se, but rather that they find it uncaring (Cohen 1989). They have feelings of meaninglessness and alienation, believing their work is monotonous and routine, and many are just marking time until retirement (Lenz and Myerhoff 1985). Neither men nor women are especially enthusiastic about their jobs, nor do the majority of public employees, especially in the federal service, believe they are treated fairly (Lewis 1990).

In addition, workers perceive a work-home schism in which life itself has a wholeness and sense of community but work is a separation (Hummel 1987). Attitudes that work is no longer challenging are played out in a number of ways. Employees resist paternal authority, distrust power, and are ambivalent toward rationality (Maccoby 1981). They resent both the lack of recognition from management and a work environment that devalues individual contributions and personal needs. The result, according to the Volcker Commission, is serious morale problems in the public service (Lewis 1990).

Public organizations are not always satisfying places in which to work (Hummel 1987). Most male and female managers lack effective interpersonal and communication skills, instead relying on the traditional, masculine leadership style that perpetuates values more suitable to a mechanistic model of domination and control. The preferred style is a task-oriented rather than a process-oriented approach, with scarcity and efficiency the dominant concerns. The measure of success is too often equated with quantity of production, position in the hierarchy, and the size of one's paycheck.[2]

The rationalism of "head work" is valued over the vagaries of the judgmental heart (Hummel 1987). Head thinking recognizes those aspects corresponding to a previously defined reality, rather than those exploring the possibilities of new ideas and discovering creative ways to solve problems. Because bureaucracy is structured according to rational principles in order to serve instrumental values, bureaucrats are designed to be instruments. Their beliefs about human norms are rendered insignificant and replaced with technical skills. Psychologically, bureaucrats are required to be techno-rational experts incapable of emotion, with a language that is not reciprocal but consists instead of one-way commands. Hummel (1987) likens bureaucracy to a "bomb that threatens humanity" and a "heartless" structure in which only the "dehumanized" survive. Consequently, bureaucracies impose enormous human costs by degrading labor and people (K. Ferguson 1984).

The changing nature of the American worker, combined with the interconnectedness and interdependency of the organizational environment, calls for a new leadership style. Contemporary public employees are influenced less by the Puritan work ethic and more by quality of work life and job satisfaction. Promises of promotion and status are not the major driving forces they once were. Employees are less attracted to power and instead seek interesting work and satisfying personal relationships (Maccoby 1981). Not only are workers better educated, but they are influenced by an ethos that prefers self-fulfillment, participation, and autonomy.

Envisioned in this scenario is a worker who relies on an ethic of self-development. These "self-oriented" or "New Age" employees desire flexible schedules, meaningful work experiences, and the opportunities to give their best (Maccoby 1981). They desire the freedom to question and challenge, to be recognized as individuals rather than machines, and to be treated with justice, fairness, and dignity.

Even those successful in their jobs are often dissatisfied with how organizations are managed. In his seven-year study of "new breed" careerists, LaBier (1986) found many successful bureaucrats who were troubled or emotionally damaged by their work. He describes the situation as "modern madness," wherein career professionals are in conflict between work demands and personal lives. In a survey of working women, Ciabattari (1986) found that 55 percent of the respondents believed that managers do not make employees feel important as individuals; 53 percent believed that managers demand unreasonable work loads; and 48 percent reported a lack of performance feedback.

From the evidence, it appears that while employees perceive respect from management as an important indicator of job satisfaction, they are not receiving it. For these respondents, incentives of big salaries, benefits, or bonuses do not make the real difference. Rather, it is how managers lead, the work environment they create, and the standards of personal performance they practice that make people feel good about themselves and their work. For the contemporary worker, the human component is as critical as technical skills.

With the supply of qualified male managers dropping 50 percent in the last decade (Johnson 1987), competition for talent has become intense. The search for talented managerial candidates must expand so that leaders in public organizations are the best and brightest. One obvious talent pool is women. Continuing to move women into middle and upper management makes good sense because it diversifies the workforce and opens career opportunities for talented employees. It may also enable the organization to operate more humanely and, thus, more effectively. Women are in the managerial pipeline, but only 2 percent have moved into executive positions in the private sector (Kagan 1986). This low percentage rate indicates that women have not been successful in developing managerial careers in most private-sector organizations (Fitzgerald and Shullman 1984). In the federal workforce in 1987, over one-quarter (28%) of the managerial segment (general schedule grade 9 and above) were women; only 12 percent of the middle-management positions (General Schedule 13-15) were occupied by women.

Merely integrating women into existing organizations will not, however, change the situation (K. Ferguson 1984). Women have not done very well as male clones because they still do not fit in the male system; consequently, they should stop acting like men and start "standing out" (Cohen 1989). There is evidence that female managers are judged negatively when they exhibit such masculine traits as domination and aggression. When women changed their behavior so that it was perceived as cooperative, they did not receive negative evaluations. As Fitzgerald and Shullman point out, "behavior that is consistent with accepted sex-role behavior is evaluated more positively than where it is out of role" (1984, 66). In other words, women are considered to be more successful when they use their culturally natural style.

TRADITIONAL LEADERSHIP MODEL

In general, a masculine bias still permeates most organizations (Loden 1985), because existing management theories have developed primarily with the orientation of male managers in mind (G. Powell 1988). The traditional bureaucratic organization is structured on a military/game model characterized by masculine traits. A masculine leadership style, for example, relies on competition and aggression. The goal is to dominate and subdue the opposition; the more aggressive the behavior, the greater the chances of winning.

Gamesmanship stresses a reward system based solely on individual performance and internal competition (Maccoby 1981). Such an emphasis requires that those at the top struggle to win, while those at the bottom strive to beat the system. Gamesmen retain their power as long as subordinates prefer this reward system and do not seek success from other satisfactions. Because this model suggests that everyone cannot win, competition rather than trust and cooperation are emphasized. The work atmosphere is unfriendly and individuals feel anxious and alienated. However, people can no longer be controlled by promises of more, especially where one worker's gain is another's loss.

A primary characteristic of the traditional masculine model is top-down control. Because obedience to authority is paramount, a boss-subordinate structure prevails. The primary goal is to accomplish the task as efficiently and rationally as possible; thus, decisionmaking tends to be analytical, strategic, and objective. Americans place a high value on objectivity, so logical, rational thinkers are given high regard (French 1986). There is little room in this model for nonrational thinking; concrete ideas have preference over abstract concepts and feelings are discounted. Ours is a masculine culture with a hardened heart (Castillejo 1990).

For most female employees, the traditional workplace is an alien culture. "Women do not follow male-constructed or sex-typed managerial standards and therefore must learn the rules of the game in order to succeed in a man's world" (Rizzo and Mendez 1988, 10). Since women are neither socialized through team sports nor share a common history of military experiences, these models of gamesmanship fail to incorporate women's life experiences.

Bureaucracies, which are designed to promote and reward male behavior, equate success according to masculine values. Factors promoting successful leadership for men, however, often operate as barriers for women. For example, to be effective, leadership requires access to knowledge. This factor is built into both the formal and informal structure. While there is usually equal access in the formal structure, "insider" information is frequently unavailable to women, because they have limited access to the male informal network (Lipman-Blumen 1982). They are excluded from the executive washroom and all-male private clubs. Since credibility comes from knowledge acquisition, a manager who does not transmit information loses credibility and trust. Failure to give women critical information creates a spirit of distrust and erodes self-confidence (Peterson 1984).

Communication, as practiced in the traditional masculine model, further alienates women from leadership roles. Bureaucratic language is semi-secret and one-dimensional, and seeks to control rather than facilitate communication (K. Ferguson 1984). Women are less likely to feel they have effective two-way communication with male managers, nor do they believe they are kept informed of how well they are performing (Lewis 1990). In mixed-sex groups, their talk is interrupted more frequently; they are heard, but not listened to (Peterson 1984). Not only do men talk more than women, they initiate and follow through on more verbal acts (Lipman-Blumen 1982). Men are also more likely to influence others' responses. They also offer more task-related suggestions, whereas women provide support and encouragement. Since organizations most often seek task accomplishment, male activity is the more highly valued behavior (see Stivers in Chapter 3).

Another barrier operating against women as leaders in the traditional sense is access to resource allocation. Political, financial, and legal help are distributed by the male executive informal system (Lipman-Blumen 1982). Because it is harder for women to tap into this structure, they lack the necessary resources to power. Consequently, information frequently must come from mentors, and then only when they are willing to share knowledge and advice.

In addition, the masculine model alone is inadequate because it perpetuates communication distortion, discourages employee participation and creativity, offers limited incentives, and represses feelings and emotions. Bureaucracy's need to control is incompatible with people's need to care for each other (Hummel 1987). Public organizations can no longer prefer managers who control people and resources; rather they should seek leaders who are capable of creating an environment where power is shared, and individual differences are appreciated (see Luke in Chapter 1). To meet the demands of interconnectedness requires an expanded definition of leadership, one that acknowledges the full potentiality of the human psyche. The place to develop this ethic of self-development is the workplace (Maccoby 1981) and, more especially, public organizations.

TOWARD A FEMININE LEADERSHIP STYLE

The traditional model defines leadership as

a pattern of philosophy, beliefs, attitudes, feelings, and assumptions
. . . that affect the individual's behavior of managing people. More
specifically, style refers to the individual expectations about how to
use a leadership position both to participate and involve other people
in the achievement of results. (Lau and Shani 1988, 49)

A new leadership style requires a definition more congruent with the
present, interdependent reality, one that includes the capacity to energize
workers, create new meanings, and restructure the organization. With this
purpose in mind, leadership can better be defined as

the character of the relationship between the individual and a group
or organization that simulates or releases some latent energy within
the group so that those involved more clearly understand their needs,
desires, interests, and potentialities and begin to work toward their
fulfillment. (Denhardt 1981, x)

"Feminine leadership" refers to a managerial style that reflects characteristics normally associated with women. In this context, I rely on the
Jungian concept of dividing the human psyche into the anima—feminine
("diffuse awareness")—and the animus—masculine ("focused consciousness") (Castillejo 1990). Feminine traits include empathy, intuition, relatedness, nurturing, and cooperation (Cohen 1989), while masculine traits
are more commonly associated with analytical thinking, competition,
rationality, hierarchy, and quantity (Loden 1985). These qualities belong
to both men and women in varying degrees, but the feminine more often
pertains to women (Castillejo 1990).

The theory of feminine leadership finds an intellectual home in several
schools of thought. For instance, human-relations theory developed in
reaction to Scientific Management, with its emphasis on division of work
into tasks and a one-best-way leadership style. This humanistic perspective, by focusing on individuals as human beings, stresses the importance
of developing meaningful work and participatory problemsolving (Kaplan
and Tausky 1977). From this perspective, leaders energize the group,
encourage initiative, and draw out of people what they have to give (Follett
1973). They influence coworkers while they are influenced by the group,
a circular response. The concept of power changes from domination

(power over) to group or shared power (power with). In this way, power assumes a relational effect that emphasizes integration and cooperation. The common end, rather than the leader's definition of the goal, is sought, and leaders seek opportunities to create situations that develop individuals. Thus people are neither followers nor subordinates but "workers with."

Theory Y, a motivational concept, emerged later in human-relations theory. It assumes that workers have the potential to develop their capacities and share a willingness to accept responsibility (McGregor 1960). Accordingly, people want to be productive both for themselves as well as for the organization. Management's responsibility, then, is to provide opportunities for employees to achieve personal needs such as skill development, acceptance, and respect. Consequently, managerial behavior presumably has a major effect on worker performance and satisfaction.

Behavioral science also informs feminine leadership. This school of thought concerns small group interaction, shared responsibility for fulfilling mutual goals, and specific managerial role behaviors (Lau and Shani 1988). It acknowledges the importance of feelings and emotions and asserts their presence in human interactions. The professional-manager style of leadership is an outgrowth of behavioral theories. It is appropriate for contemporary organizations because it suggests an eclectic approach to managing a diverse and complex workforce. It combines a task- and people-oriented style and includes several aspects relevant to feminine leadership: (a) high performance standards, (b) meaningful involvement of employees and managers, (c) group problem solving and decisionmaking, and (d) self-direction and actualization (Lau and Shani 1988). Within this framework, the manager's role is facilitator, coach, educator, and change agent.

A fourth theoretical base is trait theory, the oldest literature on leadership theory (Rizzo and Mendez 1988). Trait theory assumes that leaders possess certain personal features or qualities that are appropriate to leadership. Some of these characteristics include emotional balance, an expectation of high performance standards, fairness, integrity, inner direction, and sociability (Stewart and Garson 1983). These traits are commonly associated with women; thus, by inference, an assumption could be made that certain feminine qualities are appropriate leadership traits. The limitation of this theory is that in stressing universal traits of leadership, research results have not yielded consistent findings (G.N. Powell 1988). Nonetheless, until it is known to what extent feminine traits contribute to managerial effectiveness, trait theory can be considered a useful intellectual framework.

Finally, feminine leadership is normatively grounded in the liberal notion of equality: people are equal in their humanity and, therefore, deserve equal treatment and opportunity. That *all* human beings experience similar feelings and have the same basic needs of survival, recognition, and affiliation demands true equality and not just equal treatment in the usual liberal sense. Thus, a more expansive theory of equality is needed.

Emphasizing social equity is a more helpful approach; in addition to being treated equally, human beings are also individuals and thus deserve differential treatment. Their differing abilities make important contributions to the workplace. For example, when dissimilar jobs have equal value to the employer, they are paid equal wages. Comparable worth is a pay strategy that is designed to address the undervaluation of women's work. Hence, true equality occurs when people are treated equally as human beings and differentially as individuals. In this respect, the goal is equality of results.

THE PRACTICE OF FEMININE LEADERSHIP

Feminine leadership addresses the limitations of the one-sided masculine model. It is offered as a complement, not as a replacement, to the traditional approach. The feminine leadership model allows women to be successful in their own right without having to repress their feminine traits or take on masculine qualities that do not seem natural. A feminine leadership style also offers men the opportunity to tap into their feminine side while at the same time retaining those masculine traits that are useful to the organization. The feminine approach introduces a balance into the workplace by allowing men and women to develop their full potential.

A feminine leadership style is rooted, generally, in women's life experiences. The concern of the female principle is for process, life forces, and values (Janeway 1987). Culturally, women are conditioned to value the social relationship, and through the mothering role model, women are more likely to develop a language of empathy, sensitivity to emotional needs, and higher tolerance for conflict and ambiguity. They learn the importance of sharing information and personal feelings. Thus, from their collective history, women can bring a different perspective into the workplace.

Women in organizations place a higher value on respect from peers, satisfaction from clients, and meaningful interpersonal relations (Wajahn 1986). They redefine success as a balance between work and family or personal life, control over their own destinies, and "knowing in your gut" that what you are doing is right for you (Lenz and Meyerhoff 1985). Feminine leadership uses different measurements of success. Unlike the traditional male role model of wheeler-dealer, feminine leaders seek different objectives, such as consensus building and team development. Consequently, this model offers alternative values that can result in a redefinition of work and a different leadership style.

Feminine leadership can be applied in four managerial functions: (a) using power, (b) coordinating work relations, (c) resolving conflict, and (d) solving problems. An important aspect of managerial behavior is the use of power. The traditional definition of power is domination (power over) or position power. From this perspective, power belongs to the position and is not transferable; hence, it is external to the individual (Loden 1985). Because this type of power is considered to be scarce, it is sought relentlessly. Feminine leaders, on the other hand, prefer personal power (power to) or empowerment (power with). In this concept, power resides in the person and relates to management in the following ways. Empowerment negotiates rather than rules; examines rather than threatens; cooperates, listens, and seeks connectedness rather than separation (Cohen 1989). Employees are considered individuals not subordinates, and they are encouraged to participate in decisionmaking. While deference to rank and authority characterize position power, personal power relies on shared goals and mutual respect.

A second function of managerial behavior is coordinating work relations. This responsibility includes performance standards, group participation, and interpersonal effectiveness. Women often set unusually high performance standards for themselves because they believe they have to be twice as good as men (Loden 1985). Since women usually do not have equal access to power brokers and the informal male network, they associate success and recognition with hard work and competence. Consequently, female managers place greater emphasis on productivity and prefer leading by example. Not only do they set high performance standards for themselves, they also expect the same from others. They have little patience for a declining work ethic, office politics, or mediocrity.

Feminine leaders have a different perception of teamwork. Because they believe employees should have access to the entire process, they encourage input from everyone. A person's position in the organization does not matter; that is, you do not have to be "someone" to be respected and have your opinions validated (Janeway 1987). Rather than the win-lose concept of the masculine style, theirs is more a win-win attitude. Where men were socialized as boys to win, women—as girls—were told to do "the best they can." Bringing this attitude into the workplace encourages people to feel they are capable of doing the best work possible (Gilligan 1982). The focus is on self-sufficiency, winning as personal achievement, and connectedness. This reframes the game metaphor from competition to cooperation and network. For the feminine leader, the issue is centeredness rather than the top-down authority inherent in the masculine-model hierarchy. Where the masculine model sees teamwork as individual competition and stardom, team emphasis in the feminine leadership model is personal best and shared success. Where the traditional manager sees participative management as a threat to authority and influence, a feminine leadership style considers participative management as opportunity, trust, energy, and freedom (Loden 1985).

Interpersonal effectiveness is another contribution feminine leadership offers to the management of work relations. Feminine leaders regard quality in relationships as an end in itself and seek to rethink human values with regard to sexual relations, social intimacy, and love (Lenz and Meyerhoff 1985). Rather than discouraging these relationships, they are more open and accepting of them.

Feminine leaders have the capacity to bring into the organization finely developed interpersonal skills such as sensing, listening, caring, and feeling. Feminine leaders emphasize tact, empathy, and understanding. Empathy gives leaders the ability to understand how others feel (to "walk in their shoes"). For instance, because the feminine principle knows there are times when family responsibilities take precedence over work responsibilities, the feminine leader understands employees' needs to attend their children's school activities and to be home when they are ill. The feminine does not separate work and family. In order to integrate the two, workers are calling for policies that recognize personal needs: childcare, parental leave, flextime, job sharing, and elder care (Cohen 1989).

Female leaders are often concerned with fair treatment because of their own experiences with inequity and discrimination. They know how it feels to be outsiders, to earn less money, and to have their career paths short-circuited. Since they are familiar with difference, women may be more aware of workers' varying needs and preferences. They believe that diversity is best dealt with by giving employees more flexibility and autonomy. For this reason, they promote personnel practices that transform the workplace into a more feminine culture: innovative work patterns, self-management, open space, individualized office decor, networking, and social activities (Lenz and Myerhoff 1985). Instead of treating everyone the same, women believe that individual needs should be acknowledged and managed accordingly.

A third managerial function is conflict resolution. Conflict is the tension that occurs when values are in opposition. It is an inevitable condition in today's complex, dynamic organizations. The key is not whether conflict is present, but how it is managed. Here, as with the other functions, the two leadership models have different ways of resolving conflict. In general, the masculine seeks to win, escalating tension through anger and physical force. The feminine, on the other hand, is the peacemaker and seeks to relieve tension through conciliation (Loden 1985). Where the masculine seeks resolution through action and short-term solutions, the feminine prefers accommodation, less action, and more time. For the latter, the intent is to preserve relationships because, in the long run, these are more important than outcome.

The ability to vent stress is an important quality in the feminine model's favor. Where men, through the masculine model, are trained to ignore emotional signals, women are socialized through the feminine model to release their emotions and talk about their feelings. This creates a dilemma in the workplace, however: when women express themselves, they are considered weak and ineffectual. Yet women provide a good role model in this respect. Not only do they often acknowledge their feelings, but they do not hesitate to seek help when the going gets tough.

Problemsolving is a fourth managerial function. The feminine model relies more on intuition to resolve problems than does the masculine model. Intuition is an internal way of knowing, an ability to judge a situation on the basis of limited conscious data. It also provides the capability to handle uncertainty and complexity in decisionmaking. Davis argues that "women have certain cultural advantages when it comes to expressing their inner lives . . . And . . . certain biological opportunities for developing intuition through childbearing and child rearing" (1989, 3). Intuition is generally considered a female trait and, as such, a nonrational approach; not perceived as an applied skill, intuition is often not taken seriously in traditional management settings. Because nonrational thinking is not quantifiable, it is regarded negatively in those settings as neither scientific nor valid. However, as Jeff S. Luke and Mary Timney Bailey argue in Chapter 1 and 2, respectively, today's social problems do not easily lend themselves only to logical, deductive rationality. Complex problems cannot be resolved with one-dimensional thinking; instead, they require alternative solutions and strategies. Qualitative and inductive skills offer an appropriate complement to traditional rational thinking. This cognitive approach allows hunches, speculation, and gut feelings to be explored. As a feminine way of knowing, intuitive thinking is an additional way to process information, solve problems, and make sense of the world.

CONCLUSION

This model of feminine leadership seeks to arouse awareness of and appreciation for the contributions feminine leadership can make in public administration theory. The concepts suggest that when the workplace is humanized, organizations are more effective and satisfying. A feminine leadership style would soften the work environment and strengthen personal power, which would be to everyone's advantage. The impact of this approach is freedom: allowing people to be themselves. Women and men do not have to repress the feminine to be successful, nor do men and women have to rely solely on masculine traits to be successful.

When people are free to be fully human, gender issues will no longer be relevant. Until that happens, however, it is important to differentiate the two styles. Unless these concepts are understood separately, they cannot be integrated. Both leadership styles have their strengths, but a holistic approach is preferred because it uses the full range of human capabilities. We cannot know if women manage differently from men until they are free to use their feminine traits. If they take on the masculine model and perpetuate the status quo, then it makes little difference how many women move into leadership positions. Women must enter the bureaucratic world not to equalize it but to alter it. They cannot coopt the existing leadership style because cooptation prevents change. Feminine leadership is a new style that does not replace the traditional model but coexists with it. This new model advances our understanding of reality because it questions, rather than merely describes, traditional public administration theory.

Knowledge of feminine traits is hardly recent, but knowing those traits is one thing; integrating them into the workplace is another. As more women move into positions of leadership, feminine qualities should, and will, be legitimated. They need to be integrated into managerial behavior because those qualities recognize human differences while retaining similarities. Everyone benefits when humanistic values are incorporated into organizational structures. A workplace that welcomes their inclusion will in the end be a more human, healthy, and satisfying environment. And a theory that acknowledges and incorporates interconnectedness should do no less than unite the human psyche.

NOTES

1. This dysfunctionality is thoroughly documented elsewhere in this volume; see, for instance, Mayer's discussion in Chapter 6 of the sociopolitical consequences of the technological modes of thinking-and-acting inherent in the recent American administra-

tive state. Also see Guy in Chapter 5 and Stivers in Chapter 3 on the issues surrounding feminine leadership styles.

2. On this commodization process, see Mayer in Chapter 6.

PART 2

Reality and Other Challenges to the Emergence of New Public Administration Practice

The authors in Part 1 paint a bold picture of a changed and changing public administration practice forced by the demands of an emerging paradigm. To achieve these changes, however, public administrators must meet the challenges and overcome the barriers posed by contemporary realities.

In this set, Mary Ellen Guy and Richard T. Mayer find little evidence of the projected changes in the findings of their studies of contemporary American bureaucracy. Guy looks closely at the issues of feminization of public administration raised by Camilla Stivers and Carol J. Edlund. Examining the literature of women in management, she is unable to find evidence that women managers at higher levels are very different from their male counterparts. It appears, rather, that managers adopt androgynous characteristics that may be appropriate to the nature of the job. Guy specifies ten hypotheses that need to be investigated to test whether women can indeed transform management.

Mayer outlines an operant theory of social control, a pattern that emerged in his study of the laws and regulations between 1960 and 1980 governing three federal agencies. Although his findings confirm the rational, instrumental described by Jeff S. Luke, Mary Timney Bailey, and Stivers, he is not as sanguine about the ease with which public administrators are likely to overcome these present conditions.

Mayer finds that the administrative state has become dependent on rationalistic methods because, in part, they ensure the stability of the state. The rules and processes have become more important than the outcomes; abandoning these conditions would expose the state to the chaos and turmoil of uncertainty.

5

The Feminization of Public Administration: Today's Reality and Tomorrow's Promise
Mary E. Guy

The greatest waste of human resources in the United States today is the underutilization of intelligent women.

Daniel H. Kruger (1964)

It is incumbent upon public administration to respond to the interrelated complexities that, woven together, comprise the fabric of contemporary society. To borrow from Paul Appleby's (1949) argument, public administration is the enterprise of making a mesh of things. In today's world, "to make a mesh of things" means integrating the strengths that diverse interests and forces bring to governing.

This essay focuses on one aspect of this charge: the integration of women into the fabric of American governance. The central question raised here is whether women are changed in the process of gaining leadership and power in the field of public administration, or whether they themselves will transform public administration in the ways envisioned by feminist theory. The question cannot yet be fully answered for two reasons. First, women—while making up a significantly large portion of government's laborforce—constitute a significantly small proportion of governmental decisionmakers in the United States. Therefore, the jury is still out; until women form a substantial part of the decisionmaking apparatus, it will be difficult, at best, to determine whether they bring something special to management in public administration.

Second, in order to assess whether feminist theory is a useful predictor of the effects of integrating women into the workplace, it is essential to develop a set of reality-based hypotheses to be tested. This chapter traces the history of women's integration into the public service in order to develop such hypotheses. The ten hypotheses offered here place changes in the status of women in public administration in the context of changes in the role and status of women in society and organizations generally.

WOMEN'S INTEGRATION
INTO THE PUBLIC WORKFORCE

Up to this point in time, the direct effect that women have had on government in the United States has been slight; fortunately, their indirect impact has been far greater. Today, as in the past, women must convince men and other women that their demands for governmental action are legitimate before their desires can be transformed into policies, programs, and services. This is because men—not women—hold the vast majority of decisionmaking positions in government. In legislative chambers and top-level executive posts, women's voices are most often still heard only through the mouths of their husbands, fathers, brothers and sons. When Abigail Adams reminded her husband to "remember the ladies" as the U.S. Constitution was being drafted, he responded to her in jest. The thought of incorporating the rights of women into the Constitution was considered frivolous. Two hundred years later women's political status has improved, but women remain dependent on the goodwill of the men around them, rather than on a constitutional mandate that directly legitimates rights equal to those of men.

In 1923 the Woman's Party persuaded a Congressman to propose, for the first time, an equal rights amendment to the Constitution. Every year for forty years, from 1923 until 1963, members of Congress debated a resolution demanding such an amendment; inclusion has yet to be agreed upon by the American people. It is possible that the United States will march into the twenty-first century still unwilling to ensure equal rights for women. This ambivalence is mirrored in the difficulties that confront women as they attempt to ascend into decisionmaking posts in government.

Women's integration into the public service has been gradual. By the mid-1800s, it had become acceptable for women to fill clerical positions. Federal legislation concerning female clerks was passed in 1864, setting women's pay at half that paid to men (Van Riper 1976). As more women filled clerical positions, popular images promoted the "feminization" of the clerical laborforce. Female stenographers were described as especially capable because of their ability to radiate sympathetic interest, agreeableness, and courtesy in the office (Kanter 1977). In fact, women in the workforce have always been characterized as having those traits most conducive to performing tasks that offer lower prestige and lower pay. For example, in 1897 the U.S. Bureau of Labor reported that women were favored over men for unskilled factory jobs because they were better adapted, cheaper, and more reliable than men. A century later, although female clerks are no longer restricted to earning only half that of their male peers, clerical jobs have become a pink-collar ghetto where earnings are far lower than earnings in traditionally male-dominated jobs requiring less training and lower skill levels. Over the course of the century, the proportions of women and men in clerical jobs completely reversed themselves:

    1880   4% women, 96% men
    1890 21% women, 79% men
    1910 83% women, 17% men
    1920 92% women, 8% men
    1981 99% women, 1% men

The expansion of administration over the years clearly brought women into numerical dominance in the office but almost exclusively in clerical rather than managerial positions. The number of women appointed to high-ranking decisionmaking positions has increased at a snail's pace. For well over one hundred years following the formation of the federal government, no woman was named to a cabinet-level post or even to head a bureau. The first female bureau chief was finally appointed in 1912 when President Taft named Julia Lathrop to head the Children's Bureau. The first female cabinet member was named in 1933 when President Franklin D. Roosevelt appointed Frances Perkins as Secretary of Labor (Sealander 1983).

As women entered factories and offices, they slowly began to gain acceptance in managerial ranks. Similar to the literature of the 1800s touting the attributes that women presumably brought to clerical and unskilled factory work, a 1963 article describing women in management editorialized that they were good listeners and sympathetic in nature and thereby brought a humanizing influence to managerial ranks (*Wall Street Journal* 1963). Just as they were so credited a century earlier, women supposedly humanize organizations while men rule them. Convincing male employers that women are capable of effective performance in powerful positions has proven more difficult. Even as the same 1963 *Wall Street Journal* article announced that the number of women in managerial positions had doubled in the preceding twenty years, it boasted that

> Finance isn't especially hospitable to women, but a number of them have triumphed over firmly held male convictions that the female brain can't cope with money matters more complex than a household budget. (p. 16)

Not until 1963 did the Harvard Business School admit women to their masters in business administration program. Nine years later, another *Wall Street Journal* article, touting that employers were coming to grips with demands for women's equality on the job, closed with "You might as well face it—women aren't going to go away" (Morgenthaler 1972, 17). The words are equally true for both public- and private-sector employment. In both, women are finally penetrating midlevel ranks and knocking on the doors of high-level posts.

The Struggle for Equal Opportunity

The mid-1900s saw economic and social pressures combine in such a way that women began entering the workforce upon completion of their formal education and remaining in it, with only sporadic absences to accommodate childrearing responsibilities. The years between the end of World War II and the mid-1960s were thus a watershed in which the laborforce participation of women changed dramatically. Prior to the postwar years, middle- and upper-class women left the workforce once and for all when they became pregnant; only working-class women remained in the workforce throughout their adult life. Today the laborforce participation rate for new mothers continues to climb steadily. The year 1987 marked the first time that a majority of women reported they were working or actively seeking employment within a year of giving birth. The increases in the percent of working-age women in the workforce are displayed in Exhibit 5.1.

After years of lobbying, the 1960s brought some degree of legislative relief for women who suffered from discriminatory employment practices. By the beginning of that decade, it had become socially acceptable to question inequities in employment opportunities and wage disparities. The Civil Rights Act of 1964 provided a milestone for women's employment in the federal government by requiring that all employees be treated

Exhibit 5.1   Working-Age Women in the Workforce

Year	% of Working-Age Women in the Workforce	% of Working-Age Women in the Workforce with Children
1950	34	22
1978	51	53
1987	56	65
2000	61 (projected)	

Exhibit 5.2   Women as a Percent of the Federal Workforce

Year	Percent		General Schedule	
1910	10		**8 or below**	**9 or above**
1939	19	1960	99% female	1% female
1945	37	1987	72%	28%
1947	24			
1960	25			
1968	34			
1978	37			
1987	48			

without regard to sex in every phase of employment. The Equal Employment Opportunity Act of 1972 amended the 1964 Act to bring state and local governments, governmental agencies, political subdivisions, and any governmental industry, business, or activity within its coverage (Grossman 1973). Rapid spurts soon increased the proportion of women in the public service, especially in the higher grades. The federal Acts caused a significant change in the dispersion of women in the federal workforce; see Exhibit 5.2.

Women generally fare better in public-sector jobs than they do in private-sector jobs in terms of salary equity but continue to occupy the lower ranks in both sectors (Ahn and Saint-Germain 1988; Welch *et al.* 1983). However, projections show that women continue their climb into decisionmaking posts. For example, between 1976 and 1986 the number of women in federal general schedule (GS) grades 13 through 15 jobs— middle-management positions—more than doubled from 5 to 12 percent of the total (Barnes 1988). In that same decade, the number of women working for the federal government grew by 20 percent, while the number of men dropped by 6 percent (Hudson Institute 1988). Among entrants under the age of 35, the female share tripled to 27 percent. While women made up only 1.4 percent of all federal employees in grades 16 to 18 in 1970, they comprised 6.1 percent by 1985 (Fox 1987). This gradual integration of women into managerial levels is mirrored at the state and local levels. For example, in only two years, from 1986 to 1988, the number of women hired by the Virginia state government grew by 4 percent, and the number of women hired in the upper managerial grades increased 60 percent (Moss 1988).

Windows of opportunity open in ironic ways. Between 1976 and 1986, the share of federal general-schedule jobs held by women increased 6.5 percent, while the white-male share of these jobs decreased from 50.2 to 41.8 percent (Lewis 1988). These were the years in which presidential candidates campaigned for office by railing against the inadequacies of the federal bureaucracy. They were years of low morale and declines in real pay. Thus, it appears that societal biases against government provided an opportunity for women to make greater than usual inroads into the public service. As of 1986 women were two-thirds of the employees in the U.S. Department of Health and Human Services; women held about 10 percent of the air-traffic controller jobs, a traditionally male-dominated occupation; more than one-quarter of the women in general-schedule and equivalent pay plans were in grades 9 and above; and the average female worker was about thirty-nine years old, while the average male worker was about forty-two (P.A. Kaplan 1987).

The statistics reporting the proportion of women working in public agencies suggest that women are only slightly underrepresented in public service as a whole. A closer look, however, shows that women are concentrated in low-level positions, with only a disproportionate few in managerial and administrative positions. For those who do make it further up the hierarchy, many are locked into low-to-middle management positions, where their exercise of authority is limited (Bocher 1982; Franklin and Sweeney 1988; Kanter 1977; Smith 1980). Women who aspire to rise to the top of the nation's public agencies seem to collide against a "glass ceiling," an invisible barrier that stands between them and further advancement. In 1977, the Carter White House earned bragging rights when 12 percent of its major administration appointments had been filled by women. The women holding those positions agreed that they found little or no problem at the executive level, but they expressed acute awareness that women in key public-service jobs, as in most other fields, still had a long way to go before approaching the numbers and influence of males (*U.S. News & World Report* 1977). Over a decade later, the same situation exists.

In a nation in which 51.4 percent of the population is female, only a small minority hold top-level positions in local, state, or federal government. Yet representation of women in all public-sector jobs is more nearly balanced with the number of women in the population than is representation of women in private-sector jobs (Barnes 1988). But inside this silver lining to public employment is a cloud: Although the absence of women in top administrative posts is noticeable in any agency, it is particularly perplexing in the human-service agencies. Women are grossly under-represented in top management of these agencies even though they comprise well over half the users of most major social programs. Women make up 65 percent of all Medicare recipients. Female-headed households or women living alone receive 70 percent of all housing subsidies, while over 81 percent of the adults in homes receiving Aid to Families with Dependent Children are women (Nelson 1984). Among Americans age 65 and over, there are one hundred women for every sixty-seven men. In state agencies across the nation, low-ranking female employees deliver services in healthcare centers, hospitals, public welfare agencies, and employment-security offices. But men are at the top, directing the agencies (Dometrius 1984).

It is very clear that women will not have influence commensurate with their proportion in the population until the number of women in decision-making positions increases dramatically. It will be many years before the number of women in management is proportionate to the number of women in the workplace. Even for the years immediately following equal-employment legislation and affirmative-action initiatives, there is no evidence that women who make it to the top are given preferential treatment, put on managerial fast tracks, or leapfrogged over more-quali-fied men into management positions. In fact, the credentials of women who arrive in such positions are equivalent to those of men (DiPrete 1987; Dometrius 1984). If progress toward integrating women into top manage-ment continues at the pace set by the first six years following passage of the Equal Employment Opportunity Act of 1972, *it will take at least sixty more years* for women to gain perfect representation among career agency leaders (Dometrius 1984).

The Struggle for Equal Pay

It was in 1963 that Congress passed the Equal Pay Act requiring that women receive equal pay for equal work. Despite this legislation, sexual inequality in earnings remains a major problem (Cooney *et al.* 1980; National Committee on Pay Equity 1989; Smith and Ward 1984). Fully employed women who were high-school graduates with no college edu-cation had less income in 1979 on the average than did fully employed men who had not completed elementary school. And in that same year, women with four years of college had less income than did men with only eighth-grade educations. By the latter 1980s, the inequity had changed little. In 1987 the annual female-male earnings ratio for full-time work-ers—known as the wage gap—was 65 percent; that is, on average, women earned sixty-five cents for every dollar men earned.

Because of women's lower status in the workplace, pay scales decrease as the number of women in a job category increases. Since 1955 the wage gap for fulltime, year-round workers has hovered around 60 percent. It has been as low as 57 percent in 1973 and 1974 and as high as 65 percent in 1987 (Smith and Ward 1984). In spite of recent progress, there is ample evidence that women are more likely to be in occupations that pay relatively low wages in local, state, and federal civil service as well as in private-sector jobs (Lewis 1985). The irony is that when the annual wage gap increased five percentage points, from 60 to 65 percent between 1979 and 1987, only 70 percent of this improvement represented growth in women's earnings, while the remaining 30 percent represented a decline in men's earnings due to declining employment in high-wage industries.

Women's integration into the public workforce has been a bumpy ride. More women are currently positioned to move into high-level decision-making posts than ever before; yet if history provides any guidance, further upward movement will be anything but smooth. Women who have shown management potential at lower-level jobs are being promoted when op-portunities arise. For example, the proportion of women promoted into federal administrative positions between 1973 and 1977 was twice the proportion of women hired from outside the federal system into those administrative ranks (DiPrete 1987). After more than twenty years of affirmative action efforts, however, the percentage of higher-level jobs held by women is still far beneath the proportion of women in the population. There is no empirical data to support an overwhelming enthu-siasm that change is imminent and that women are going to break through into power positions (Huerta and Lane 1981). Despite clear advances in the workforce and more access to education, women throughout the 1990s will remain under-represented in upper echelons and over-represented in the lower ranks. Pink-collar ghettos may even increase (J. Bailey 1988), and comparable-worth battles will continue to be played out in the courts as well as around family dinner tables.

Lessons from the struggle for career advancement and pay equity give rise to two closely related hypotheses:

Hypothesis 1: Women are more likely to gain entrance into tradition-ally male positions when the status of those positions is in decline.

Hypothesis 2: As a position becomes predominantly female, it diminishes in status and salary.

CURRENT ISSUES REGARDING WOMEN IN THE WORKFORCE

Currently there are several unresolved debates regarding women in the workforce, one of which is the "mommy track" versus the "career track." Felice Schwartz (1989) points out that with the changing workforce of the future, employers will have to select more women for managerial positions if they intend to place the best and the brightest in those positions, simply because there will be proportionately fewer men and proportionately more women from whom to select. Hiring more women requires that employers take the need for pregnancy and family leave into consideration. Schwartz argues that employers lose talented personnel when they fail to design jobs that accommodate women when they need to take leave to care for family members. To remedy this, she suggests employers develop "mommy track" positions to accommodate mothers' needs. The tradeoff in job flexibility would be accomplished by offering lower job benefits. On the other hand, women who do not have family responsibilities could be slotted into "career track" positions, which would be similar to career opportunities afforded to men.

Those who oppose Schwartz's proposal argue that the mommy-track positions with lower pay and more flexibility are those positions women have always been offered. Opponents contend that it is career-track positions that women have been struggling to achieve for decades; the proposal simply institutionalizes what has always been the case. Although proponents and opponents of the proposal often shed more heat than light on the subject, the time has come for alternative job designs for employees with family responsibilities. Schwartz's proposal highlights how differences in men's and women's family obligations typecast employees and affect employment issues and opportunities.

From the time women began achieving managerial rank, male employers have been concerned about their need to take prolonged leaves of absence. In 1963 the *Wall Street Journal* made reference to the liability all women have because of their potential to get pregnant: "Many firms hesitate to promote women to key posts because of well-founded fears they will depart to raise a family just as they learn the job" (p. 1). Even today, those who advocate not promoting women into high-level decision-making posts argue that it is not worth the agency's costs to train a woman because she is likely to quit if she becomes pregnant. Those who agree with this argument subscribe to the myth that women have higher turnover rates than do men, and that the turnover is due to their putting family obligations ahead of career interests.

Gregory Lewis and Kyungho Park (1989) debunked this myth of female turnover with an investigation of the turnover rates for women and men employed in the federal civil service. Although women's turnover rates were overall about one-third higher than men's in the federal civil service from 1976 through 1986, Lewis and Park found these aggregate statistics to be misleading. Female-male differences appeared to be almost entirely due to differences in average age, salary, and length of service. Women and men in similar circumstances had very similar turnover probabilities. Age, experience, and salary were more important predictors of exit probability than was sex. This makes the mommy-track-versus-career-track argument moot: When women who want a responsible position gain it, they are as loyal to it as men are in comparable positions. Similarly, women who have reached top managerial levels in state governments report that the most important factors for career success are the same for women and men: continuous fulltime employment and continuous employment in one agency or lateral moves within state agencies (Hale and Kelly 1989).

Working a Second Shift

Another debate surrounding women in the workforce is the degree to which they must work a second shift in the home. This is primarily true of women with children or elderly parents for whom they are responsible. Women are still expected to be the primary caretakers in a family. As with other social changes, people's personal lives have changed more quickly than their institutions or social customs. Suzanne Bianchi and Daphne Spain (1984) report that studies of time spent doing housework and taking care of children continue to show that working women do the major share of household tasks at the expense of leisure. In 1987, 56 percent of married women worked outside the home (USDOL 1987a). In families where both spouses work, the wife is still expected to do most of the household chores in addition to her employment.

One recent study indicates that men are less satisfied with their jobs when their wives work. Perhaps a reason for this lowered satisfaction is that husbands of working wives must also bear at least partial responsibility for household chores, and this takes time, energy, and rewards away from concentrating on their jobs (Parasuraman *et al.* 1989). If this speculation is correct, then perhaps the converse is also correct: that married women in the laborforce experience lower job satisfaction than men do because the women must share their commitment to their jobs with their commitment to maintaining their homes. This interpretation leads to speculation that women who have time- and energy-consuming household responsibilities will experience lower job satisfaction than will those who are free to devote a much greater proportion of their time and energy to their careers.

While 90 percent of top-ranking men are married, only 60 percent of top-ranking women are (Bayes 1987). Women in high-level positions who have children generally compete with men who also have children but whose wives either do not work or work part-time and, in either case, assume responsibility for childcare (Vertz 1985). These two facts present obstacles to women's advancement. For instance, when they are responsible for childcare, the women are not as free to work late in the evenings and travel overnight at short notice because they must also pick up children from schools or daycare centers and see that the children receive the attention they need.

Another aspect of the second shift for women who work stems from the fact that they do not have wives. When a married man has a responsible leadership post, both he and his wife, for all practical purposes, are employed. Women who work do not have the added advantage of a supportive wife waiting at home, eager to serve as a charming escort at work-related social gatherings. A fact of life in organizations is that the closer one gets to the top, the more traditional and nonmodern the system looks. Thus, men in top management positions in both the public and private sectors are much more likely than other men to be married and to have wives that do not work outside the home (C.L. Cooper 1987). These differences in lifestyle combine to diminish the amount of satisfaction that a woman will experience from achieving a position usually held by a man.

On the job, the effects of these various hurdles combine to diminish the likelihood that a woman will be (a) motivated to seek promotion, (b) able to demonstrate competence and confidence in informal settings, (c) visible to decisionmakers, and (d) judged to be as productive as a man in her position would be (Kanter 1976; Lewis 1986).

Additionally, because many achieving women are not married, they are excluded from social gatherings where attendance by the guest and the guest's spouse is the norm. In traditional gatherings, a single woman presents an awkward problem because customs are designed to accommodate couples, not singles. When she is accompanied by a husband, he often presents an even-more awkward problem because accommodations for spouses typically consist of accommodations for wives. These lifestyle contrasts lead to the following hypotheses:

Hypothesis 3: The greater a woman's family responsibilities, the lower her job satisfaction will be.

Hypothesis 4: The greater a woman's family responsibilities, the lower the rank she will attain on the job.

FORCES AFFECTING FULL INTEGRATION

A number of forces affect the integration of women into public administration. Most of these derive from the confluence of economic and demographic changes that is creating a changing workforce, increasing the educational achievement of women, extending life expectancy, seeing more women win election to office, and introducing more flexible working hours and conditions.

The Changing Workforce

In 1950, 34 percent of all adult women in the U.S. were in the workforce; by 1979, this increased to 51 percent (Newland 1980). According to the Hudson Institute (1987), 61 percent of all women of working age are expected to have jobs by the year 2000. The demographics of the workforce are changing because of decreased fertility among whites, increasing education, and increasing divorce rates. From 1970 to 1985, the U.S. laborforce grew each year by 2.2 percent; it is now growing by only 1 percent each year (Bloom and Steen 1988). These factors suggest continuing high laborforce participation rates for women (Lichter and Costanzo 1987; N. Stone 1989). The U.S. Department of Labor estimates that 60 percent of the increase in the civilian laborforce between 1975 and 1985 was attributable to more women joining the ranks of the employed (USDOL 1986b). Women are expected to account for another 60 percent of the growth in the laborforce between 1984 and 1995 (Fullerton 1985). The Department of Labor estimated women's participation rates in the workforce in 1985 in the following work categories and percentages:

Part-time workers 66
Administrative support workers 80
Retail and personal services sales workers 69
Executives, administrators, and managers 36

Between 1972 and 1980, the number of female managers and administrators more than doubled, while the number of male managers and administrators increased by only 22 percent (Forbes and Piercy 1983). While this trend is expected to continue into the coming years, women's advancement will be tempered if the following projections hold: Although the nation's economy is projected to generate more than twenty-one million new jobs between 1986 and 2000, this 19 percent increase would be only about half the average annual rate of increase that occurred between 1972 and 1986 (Silvestri and Lukasiewicz 1987). This projection would mean that competition for the best jobs will remain stiff. The glass ceiling for women may rise some, and there will be crevices and cracks, but by and large, it is likely to remain lower than the ceiling above men's heads (Morrison 1987; Morrison *et al.* 1987).

Educational Achievement

By 1979 the average female worker was as well educated as the average male worker: both had completed a median of 12.6 years of schooling. Education is significantly related to the development of managerial skills and personality traits that contribute to securing managerial jobs (Brenner 1982). In fact, education seems to be the most important variable, far more important than sex or prior work experience. Recently, the lengthening of the years of women's schooling and their increased acquisition of specialized training have enhanced their potential earnings, thereby encouraging them to maximize their time in the laborforce. The lengthening of the time spent in education has reduced the participation of young females in the laborforce, thus expanding the demand for older women.

Forty percent of the growth in jobs is projected to be in those jobs requiring educational attainment: executive, administrative, managerial, and professional workers and technicians. It is impossible to overstate the importance of education as a positive influence on the promotion of women into decisionmaking posts. While the number of employed female workers age 25 and older increased by 89 percent between 1950 and 1970, the number of college graduates among them increased by 147 percent. In contrast, the percentage increase among men college graduates of the same age in the same two decades was only 134 percent (Johnston 1973).

A fact often hidden by the rising number of college-educated women is that they continue to major in education, the humanities, and the health sciences to a far greater degree than do men. In 1986, women accounted for slightly more than 49 percent of the nation's 13.9 million professional specialty workers, but female professionals remained concentrated in relatively few job categories. Sixty percent are in just two categories: noncollege teachers and registered nurses (USDOL 1986a). Men are not nearly as concentrated. Their two largest fields—engineering and noncollege teaching—together accounted for only 37 percent of their professional employment. In 1981, women were 42 percent of the employed workforce, but they were 99 percent of the secretaries and only 1.6 percent of the electrical engineers (Crocker 1984).

Elected Female Officeholders

Even though their numbers are still minuscule, women have made great strides in winning elective office around the nation in the past decade. As of June 1989, according to the U.S. Conference of Mayors, 115 (13.1%) of the 880 mayors of cities with populations greater than 30,000 were women. Thirty-one of these female mayors served in cities with populations over 100,000. The advances have come only recently, however. Of the seventeen female mayors of cities among the nation's hundred largest, thirteen took office for the first time since 1985 (*PA Times* 1989). But most female mayors operate in council-manager settings where the real power is often located in city managers' offices, which are still dominated by men.

The number of female officeholders has also increased in state government. State legislatures are slowly but surely being penetrated by more female legislators. In state legislative races, female candidates raise the same kinds of money as do male candidates in comparable situations, tend to run in the same kind of races, and are treated similarly by the voters at the polls (Burrell 1989). Furthermore, female legislative officeholders are just as effective as their male counterparts in comparable situations (Blair and Stanley 1989). Exhibit 5.3 shows that although women are represented at all levels of elected government, they have a long way to go before the number of women in elected office is proportional to their numbers in the population (Center for the American Woman and Politics 1989).

Although feminist theory asserts that women clearly have an effect on the policy process different from that of men, the point has yet to be proven. The evidence has yet to be presented that women practice policymaking in a way that produces policies different from those created by men. Men and women differ in the importance they ascribe to military-spending and social-welfare issues, but these differences are obscured by their vast common agreement. By the time a final decision is made, so many alternatives have been winnowed away that the remaining small number of alternatives are those over which there is substantial agreement among both men and women. There has been hopeful speculation that an enduring difference will prevail between men and women in decisionmaking posi-

Exhibit 5.3   Percentage of Elective Offices Held by Women in 1989

U.S. Congressional Seats	5.0 (28 out of 535)
Statewide elective executive positions	13.6
State Legislative seats	6.9
Seats on county elective governing boards	8.9
Mayors of cities with populations over 30,000	13.1

tions, whether they hold elected, appointed, or career positions. This difference is thought to be in the arena of moral reasoning (Gilligan 1982; Stewart 1985), but the evidence has yet to show that the differences are so great that they are made manifest in public policy or agency procedures.

Public administration is in the midst of a reorientation to a globally based environment and economy, sophisticated technology, increased demands for scarce resources, and increased demands for social equity. This interactive mix of economic, political, technical and social issues will inevitably have an effect on the society in which tomorrow's children grow up. But the truth is, American society is patriarchal and there are no indications this tradition is changing. The general public expects men to take the lead when men and women share authority positions, regardless of the quality of the man's or the woman's actual performance (Geis *et al.* 1985).

A fundamental challenge confronting women's integration into public administration is the political economy of "lip-service equality." The Equal Employment Opportunity Act is in place and functions well for entry-level positions. Before equal-employment opportunity can become a reality at all levels of the public agencies, the values and attitudes of those who control the top positions must favor promoting women. This is where the political economy of the status quo becomes apparent, namely, that equality for women in management is a zero-sum game. As more women move up the ladder, fewer opportunities exist for men. As far back as 1965, researchers were reporting the resentment of many younger men who considered the growing presence in management positions of married women who "do not need to work" as a block to their own advancement (Bowman *et al.* 1965). In other words, as women get close to parity, the doors slam shut. Competition increases, and only one person can be promoted into a single position that several people want. Male resistance therefore occurs once women are represented in anything more than token numbers.

These forces combine to influence and temper the integration of women into managerial positions. The following hypotheses balance today's reality with tomorrow's promise:

Hypothesis 5: As educational levels increase, women will express more distinctly feminist policy preferences.

Hypothesis 6: As women are needed in the workforce, childcare and parental leave will become standard benefits.

MANAGERIAL STYLE OF WOMEN VERSUS MEN

Scores of empirical studies have investigated the differences and similarities between women and men in federal, state, or local administrative positions (Ezell *et al.* 1982; Freedman and Phillips 1988). Some report that while female managers perceived themselves to be as competent as male managers, they view female managers in general as being less competent than male managers (Ezell *et al.* 1980). Others report that there are no significant differences between male and female executives either on any decision tasks (Muldrow and Bayton 1979) or in their desire for responsibility and their ability to wield power (Lynn and Vaden 1979).

Of men and women in similar positions, men report that the most important personal attributes for their own success are skills and abilities, attitudes, self-concept, motivation, and education. Women note for themselves the same traits but rank them differently: Attitudes, self-concept, and motivation are ranked first, followed by skills, abilities, and education. Women give more credit than do men to mentors and to those who provide them with emotional support (Agassi 1979; Hale and Kelly 1989). It is virtually impossible to determine empirically whether the differences in basic work values that are found in surveys of employed women and men are due to sex differences, positional differences, differences in perceived career opportunities, or merely differences in the way men and women express similar concerns.

Rosabeth Moss Kanter has been grappling with this question for years. A decade after she had published *Men and Women of the Corporation* (1977), she revisited the subject and concluded that her original conclusions were still correct: productivity, motivation, and career success are determined largely by organizational structure and the nature of the social circumstances in which people find themselves. This means that differences in the behavior, and success, of women and men have more to do with what they are handed by the organization than with inherent differences in ability or drive (Kanter 1989b). When men and women are dealt similar cards in the organizational game, they behave in similar ways. The problem, of course, is that men and women rarely are dealt similar cards.

Contrasting women in management to men in management polarizes issues and exaggerates differences. Assumptions that women are less competitive, afraid of power, unskilled in interpersonal relations, or unwilling to take risks are not supported. After studying high-ranking federal and California state administrators, Jane Bayes (1987) found no significant differences between women's and men's management styles. Both men and women expressed deep concern for people, advocated participatory styles of management, and criticized other managers for micromanaging. A study of Texas public administrators reports similar conclusions. Management style appears to be dictated more by the department and the position than by the person occupying the position, regardless of sex (J.R. Stanley 1987).

When differences are found in the effectiveness of female managers compared to male managers, they tend to result from factors other than gender. Differences disappear when the contexts of the jobs are the same. Age, education, experience, and training of leaders and subordinates, in conjunction with type of occupation and rank within the organization, are more salient than the gender of the manager (Riger and Galligan 1980). Top-ranking officials in the same agency have similar work-related attitudes and habits, whether they are male or female. The organization's culture guarantees this because people who are subject to the same occupational experiences tend to converge in their work-related attitudes over time. Occupational socialization reduces any attitudinal or behavioral gap between the sexes: There is more difference between women at the top and bottom than there is between women and men at the top.

Routinely promoting men and disregarding women restricts choices unnecessarily because most managerial skills are gender neutral. In fact, the most effective manager uses an androgynous leadership style, whether the leader is a man or a woman (Fitzgerald and Shullman 1984; Schein 1973; Steinberg and Shapiro 1982). "Androgyny" means a blend of the best that is both masculine and feminine, with the extremes of neither. It means combining the sensitivity of the feminine side with the assertiveness of the masculine side. Since women have the capacity to encourage nurturing, expressive behaviors, building upon these qualities as strengths rather than denying their worth is constructive (Grant 1988; Steinberg and Shapiro 1982).

Women as Low-Level Peacemakers

Although women are expected to provide a humanizing influence on organizations, and are rewarded for doing so, the downside is that they become invisible in the process. Women who exhibit effective and "appropriately feminine" interpersonal skills succeed at being peacemakers, mediators, or compromisers. The price of their success is that they become invisible, because the reward for being a successful mediator is that the negotiating sides develop an amicable settlement and the mediator is able to phase out of the situation. Peacemakers and compromisers are heralded for their ability to bring others together—but it is the others on whom the limelight shines. When women restrict their performance to that for which they have always been praised, then they function as support staff to men who receive the limelight.

Power and Powerlessness

More female managers are found in government agencies than in private business, but they are concentrated in those agencies with the least policy discretion. This includes health and human-service agencies that provide rulebound entitlement services in which the executive is afforded little discretion. It is possible that the reason women are promoted in rulebound, rigid organizations is that women may have greater opportunities for promotion when the rules are followed in hiring and promotion. Perhaps in more flexible organizations, women get left out in the guise of promoting men who characterize traditional leadership qualities. This reasoning is less plausible than the explanation that the position in a rigid organization is more likely to be filled by a woman because it has lower status than does one with more discretion.

Powerlessness tends to produce those very characteristics attributed to female bosses: rulebound, rigid adherence to policies and procedures and centralization of control (South *et al.* 1982). Female bosses are more likely to be found in tightly supervised and rule-conscious hierarchies. Restrictive organizational environments reward strict adherence to rules and inflexible interpretation of policies. People respond to the restrictiveness of their own situation by behaving restrictively toward others. Powerless authority figures who use coercive tactics provoke resistance and aggression, which prompts the authority figures to become even more coercive, controlling, and behaviorally restrictive. For those who have little power, but who must lead or influence others, their control of the rules can represent one of the few areas of personal discretion. When differences in organizational power between male and female supervisors are controlled for statistically, *only* the supervisor's power accounts for the differences in all the variables studied. Closeness of supervision, showing favoritism among subordinates, emphasis upon the value of workgroup membership, and job satisfaction: all of these variables disappear as reasonable explanations for the difference between male and female supervisors (South *et al.* 1982). This leads to the conclusion that as women move up the managerial ranks, their supervisory styles will more closely resemble those of their male counterparts, because the demands of the position shape the person.

Women as Tokens

As women make more inroads into jobs previously inaccessible to them, they pay a price. Being the only member of their sex in that position, they are likely to be a "solo" (Crocker and McGraw 1984; Kanter 1977), which carries the burden of tokenism. When women represent only a small minority of decisionmakers in an agency, their general behavior is different from that of someone wholly integrated into the decisionmaking process. There are predictable characteristics of tokens:

- They feel "on display" and so must be conscious of their appearance, words, and deeds;
- They feel more pressure to conform and to make few mistakes;
- They are more likely to be excluded from informal peer networks;
- They are stereotyped and placed in role traps that limit effectiveness; and
- They have fewer opportunities to be mentored because of the rarity of people like them at higher levels in the agency.

Because women do not fit in traditional male-dominated management groups, they tend to be clustered in those parts of management with the least uncertainty. They are in jobs where processes are routinized and discretion is limited, such as lower-level managerial positions and staff positions without line authority.

While tokens feel they have to do better than anyone else in order to be seen as competent and allowed to continue, they also must walk a fine line of doing just well enough but not too well; being visible enough but not showcasing one's performance. As tokens, their performances are always in the limelight. If they fail at tasks, they bear the burden of responsibility for all other women. Each woman's performance is a test not only for herself but for all women who follow. Because tokens are different from others, they are noticed as much for their being different as for their skills. They must work not only at doing their job but also at trying to increase the level of comfort that others have with them.

When Frances Perkins was named Secretary of Labor in 1933, she was wary of being identified as a special champion of women. She felt everyone was watching her to see if she appointed too many women. Consequently, she went to great lengths to quell such fears by not catering to concerns of women in the department's Women's Bureau (Sealander 1983). Such is the dilemma of tokens. If they respond too directly to the expectations of the group of which they are a token, they lose credibility in the eyes of the dominant group. If they ignore the expectations of their own group, they are accused of being *mere* tokens.

The characteristics of female tokens are inversely related to the proportion of women in high-level positions. As the proportion of women in management increases, each individual becomes less surprising, less unique, less noteworthy, and less blameworthy. There is some question whether achieving a critical mass of women in management will help or hinder the promotion of more women. Despite the assumption that as women reach parity with men in managerial ranks they will be more accepted, the opposite threatens to be the case. Studies show that while men are most likely to encourage women when there are very few, as more women enter a rank, they are segregated by their male peers and receive less support. There appears to be an inverse relationship between the encouragement for promotion women receive from their male supervisors and the number of women in any one rank (South *et al.* 1982). The "tipping point" is where women in management are no longer so few that they are treated as tokens.

A countervailing view, however, is that when tipping occurs, men resist further advances of women (Markham and Corder 1982). When the tipping point is reached, those in the majority no longer feel it is necessary to assist the minority's integration and, instead, slam the door shut in the face of the newcomers. As resources become scarcer, former friends become foes as they compete for plum positions. (For example, this is an explanation for what happened, relative to minorities, in the reverse-discrimination cases decided by the U.S. Supreme Court in the latter 1980s.) The possibility of this reaction anticipates a fend-for-yourself attitude by men toward women. This includes men who formerly were supporters of women in their efforts to integrate into the workforce. Some fear that this backlash will result in an attempt to return to rigid gender roles of the past, just as the Reagan presidency attempted to harken back to the Norman

Rockwell image of the traditional family. (In fact, by 1986 this traditional family accounted for only 3.7 percent of all the nation's families [USDOL 1987b; Kosterlitz 1988]). The challenge becomes one of increasing the number of women in management, not just to the tipping point, but far enough beyond it that women become equal players in all situations. Before women are fairly represented among public personnel, they will have to move up the ladder to create a critical mass for mentoring others. The message of the tipping point is that to stop pushing is to lose the momentum that has been slowly built up.

Feminist Theory

Feminist theory asserts that women's influence in the workforce will result in significant changes in the workplace:

- Organizational hierarchies will become less rigid;
- Organizational climates will become more cooperative, less competitive and less aggressive; and
- Values of trust, openness, and acceptance will replace the quest for individual power.

When employed men and women are interviewed to test these assertions, the results show that women and men are more alike than they are different (Colwill and Erhart 1985). Respondents do tend to agree that changes have occurred in the workplace: women are no longer afraid to stand up and be counted, they are more likely to be accepted and respected in the workplace, and they are less likely to be merely tolerated. Women are also seen as being more qualified, more responsible, and more career oriented than they were twenty years ago. Women manifest a stronger desire for responsibility, authority, and financial independence on the job. The workplace has become increasingly flexible with men and women feeling freer to quit, take leaves, work part-time, and make career changes. Respondents, however, are unwilling to attribute these gradual changes to the integration of women into the workforce. Respondents do not report a decline in the rigidity of organizational hierarchies, and many report that the workplace has become more competitive and aggressive and less cooperative. Women have a greater scope of responsibility and opportunity, increased confidence and competence, and a greater sense of independence.

Feminist theory argues that women's biological and historical role as the bearer and nurturer of children teaches them not about the autonomy of individuals but their essential connectedness. Women have learned how people must depend upon each other to survive. For girls, knowledge is contextual and social. For boys, knowledge comes from the struggle to separate themselves from one another, and they interpret maturation as becoming independent and learning to achieve autonomously. Feminist theory puts forth the expectation that women in management positions will be change agents, and both advocate and practice management styles that place a high priority on participatory, nonhierarchical interactions between managers and employees (Belenky *et al.* 1986; Ferguson 1984; Gilligan 1982; J.R. Stanley 1987; also see Edlund in Chapter 4). The assumption is that the advantage to having female administrators is that they contribute caretaking, nurturing, compassion, and empathic qualities. Female administrators are assumed, in feminist theory, to speak with a different voice, that is, to base their actions on principles that highlight relatedness rather than dominance. Various productivity techniques, such as quality circles, are designed to elicit what feminist theory claims as women's unique contribution to organizations: worker participation in a manner that emphasizes communication, cooperation, and pragmatic problemsolving.

While feminist theory argues that women, regardless of their rank in an organization, will hold attitudes and promote behaviors different from those of men, empirical evidence has yet to support this. The differences manifested between women and men in the workplace occur as a function of where they stand in that workplace. The exigencies of job demands and the perspective provided by rank and role seem to be the determining factors. Men and women at GS-11 levels and higher do not differ from each other on important personality dimensions, such as self-esteem, aggressiveness, and other personality traits that contribute to the ability to work effectively with people and to excel within a work environment (Gomez-Mejia 1983; Guy 1984 and 1985; Holsti and Rosenau 1981; Rehfuss 1986). There are significant differences between upper-level and lower-level women, however, just as there are differences between upper-level and lower-level men (Vertz 1985). The one exception to this rule is that women in advanced positions have more nontraditional attitudes toward the role of women than men in similar positions. Women in high-level positions have no preference as to the sex of their supervisor, while men in similar positions are more likely to prefer male supervisors. In fact, men, regardless of their organizational location, have more traditional attitudes toward the role of women than do women (Vertz 1985).

James A. Lee (1988) became interested in the question of how much change actually occurs in managerial values over time. After hearing the optimistic forecasts hailed in the latter 1960s for the 1970s, in the latter 1970s for the 1980s, and in the latter 1980s for the 1990s, he reported on an empirical test for the presence of such changes. Between 1965 through 1986, he found very little change taking place in the rankings of common managerial values. What was most important to respondents in 1965 remained most important in 1986. What was least important in 1965 remained least important twenty-one years later. These values included preferences on decisionmaking style, the worth of planning and being innovative, believing in subordinates, being loyal and sensitive, and maximizing ethical values and personal friendships. He interprets this continuity by explaining that managers cannot change values or attitudes in a vacuum. All other elements in the social system will change very slowly and in a generally synchronized manner. In other words, marked discontinuities occur only rarely. In terms of the full integration of women into decisionmaking posts in government, Lee is probably correct as well. A drastic discontinuity will not occur. As long as women are the primary caregivers to family members, they will have to keep one foot grounded in the homefront with the other grounded in the workplace. They will not be as fully integrated into the workplace as men are because caretaking affects productivity, absenteeism, morale, and turnover (Magnus 1988).

The debate about women's advancement into administrative positions, the unique qualities women bring to the workplace, and the presence or absence of differences in administrative styles are reflected in the following hypotheses:

Hypothesis 7: Acceptance of women in managerial ranks increases up to a point, then the opposite happens and either further advancement of women is opposed, or men leave the field.

In terms of women being invisible when they play the peacemaker role, the "warrior" hypothesis applies:

Hypothesis 8: Making peace among protagonists has lower prestige than being a winner in a competitive situation.

Societal biases will continue to favor men in decisionmaking posts. Only through actual exposure to competent women will people's attitudes change. Women's skill as managers must gain acceptance by example.

Hypothesis 9: Positive attitudes about women's administrative skills are created by exposure to female managers.

The ultimate test of feminist theory is whether the following hypothesis is supported or refuted. It tests whether the position shapes the person or the person shapes the position.

Hypothesis 10: Women in management positions use feminist qualities and skills that men do not.

CURRENT REALITY AND TOMORROW'S PROMISE

So the question remains: Are women changed in the process of gaining leadership and power in the field of public administration, or will they, themselves, transform public administration in the way envisioned by feminist theory? The ten hypotheses posed in this chapter lay the groundwork for substantiating or refuting a feminist impact on public administration. Settling the questions raised by the hypotheses will resolve the contradictions about differences between men and women and the implications of those differences for public administration. Not until these questions are answered will the field know whether feminist theory provides a useful source for developing a theory for managing interconnected organizations. If differences between men and women make a difference in the workplace, then the feminine strengths of mediation, facilitation, and consensus building are too valuable to ignore. As has always been the case, competing demands on government require negotiation and consensus-building strategies. Yet women are still on the outside looking in when it comes to managing important public purposes.

That women tend to pay attention to the human dimension is not sufficient reason to insist that they be sequestered in powerless positions. In fact, because they tend to pay attention to the human dimension is exactly the reason they should step out of the shadows and take center stage as this nation grapples with the economic implications of a unified European market, the end of the Cold War, a changing workforce, the transition from an industrial economy to a service economy, a troubled educational system, an inadequate healthcare system, and a world in which environmental hazards threaten not just the nation but the planet. If ever there were a need for building bridges, it is now.

If this chapter presents a mixed message of whether men and women are different or the same, it is because the debate is still open. Testing these hypotheses will perhaps provide answers because they invite serious examination as public administrators grapple with the complex web of purposes and problems. When supported, these hypotheses can become manipulable levers useful for fostering constructive change.

Integrating women into public administration requires reweaving the fabric of societal expectations about the rightful place of women. These trends will move forward only with constant pushing. The two-hundred-year history of the women's movement for equal rights and opportunities in the United States tells us that initiatives that seem eminently reasonable to women have only been secured by persistent, patient pushing. No societal climacteric has occurred that has catapulted women into prominent policymaking positions in government or business. Only very slowly will women be found in important positions. Not until women are so commonplace in high positions that no one bothers to count them, and debates such as those raised in this chapter are laid to rest, will it be obvious that women have fully integrated public administration.

6

The Tug of History: The Operant Theory of Social Control and the American Administrative State
Richard T. Mayer

The argument in this chapter is grounded in an earlier empirical study that isolated the logic of instrumental rationality inherent in administrative action and captured changes between 1960 and 1980 in federal law and regulation in three domestic, intergovernmental programs: highways, community-development programs, and welfare.[1] Those changes were analyzed in terms of the patterns that emerged both within and across the programs over the twenty-year period in order to assess the extent to which there were collectively exhibited structural characteristics of an operant social theory, specifically one of social control. (An operant social theory is a theory of how the world works—a world view—that is operating within society and that produces effects.) A key assumption in that study was that the range of programs provided a sufficient array of activities so as to enable a plausible discussion of the administrative state as a whole.

This essay takes off from that point and describes the cumulative interaction of the characteristics of the operant theory of social control. This theory, insofar as it represents an active orientation of administrative actors, circumscribes the arena within which *any* efforts at reform or amelioration can operate.

The operant theory of social control is therefore quite relevant to the themes of this volume—interconnectedness and interdependency—which are not only descriptive of today's public administration environment, but also point toward a normative vision of the future of U.S. public administration, one that emphasizes horizontal rather than vertical relationships, consensus rather than coercion, and information sharing rather than resource utilization. These themes represent a set of value orientations that directly counter those of the operant social theory.

This chapter focuses on two recent decades of the American administrative state, the 1960s and 1970s. By the end of that period, the administrative state had reached a particular fullness that can be seen most clearly in the federally funded intergovernmental programs providing domestic assistance; it is this fullness that is encompassed here by the concept of the operant theory of social control, the focus of this essay.

Simply put, when a significant portion of administrative activity was scrutinized, a number of patterns over time emerged that cut across program areas and across laws and regulations. Taken together, these patterns constitute an operant social theory, specifically, a theory of social control.

The operant theory of social control, if it accurately represents the social reality facing U.S. administrators, is the empirical reflection of Mary Timney Bailey's Rational Model in Chapter 2, Camilla Stivers's separation of self in Chapter 3, Carol J. Edlund's traditional masculine model, and Jay D. White's modernism in Chapter 7. Similarly, insofar as the operant social theory meaningfully represents a structuring of the field for discourse, it also represents a significant barrier to Robert C. Zinke's rhetorical republic in Chapter 8 and Jeff S. Luke's environmental ethic in Chapter 1.

This theory of social control is ascribed to the administrative actors only insofar as it represents a way to talk about the patterns that emerged from the investigation and the way those patterns appear to interact with one another. The operant theory of social control, however, is ultimately a construct of the researcher used to describe patterns that appeared across the studied program areas and were generalized to the administrative state. One must be cautious not to reify this construct and transfer to it the responsibility for decisions that people have made in their own historical contexts. At the same time, even though individuals are deciding and acting, there are still patterns that go beyond individuals' specific motives in specific cases; it is the combined array of these patterns that is posited here as the operant theory of social control.

All of this is important to the idea of developing a multiversalist paradigm in sync with the interconnected and interdependent reality that is today's environment. If what is described in the pages that follow is accurate in magnitude and direction, then the task ahead is not an easy one.

The remainder of this chapter is divided into two sections: The first describes the technological orientation of the operant theory of social control and lists the patterns that emerged from a detailed examination of federal laws and regulations during the 1960-80 period. The second section details those patterns with the objective of illustrating the manner in which they interlock and reinforce one another.

THE OPERANT THEORY OF SOCIAL CONTROL

The operant theory of social control reflects structural patterns in administrative activity that emerged from an empirical examination of federal laws and regulations covering the twenty years of intergovernmental domestic-assistance programs. As arrayed in Exhibit 6.1 in relatively abbreviated form, these patterns are listed alphabetically to underscore that the order of presentation suggests no priority or weight.

Tinkering with the Process

Individually, the patterns in Exhibit 6.1 are generally self-explanatory and relatively mundane. Some are more pervasive than others, just as some appear to have more significance. Each pattern is relatively benign, and each, insofar as it is consciously pursued, is usually considered as a good in its own right. Who, after all, would not want better management of resources or clearer accountability? And is not the centralizing and specializing of authority an effective and efficient means of attaining desired ends? The issue, however, is one of cumulative consequence and reinforcement.

The common element in these patterns is a technological orientation toward administrative work.[2] This is not surprising, given the cultural dominance of technology and technique, particularly in the form of labor-saving devices and enhanced productive capacities, that has been a hallmark of twentieth-century progress in the West.[3]

The intent of this technological orientation is to rationalize administrative processes.[4] This rationalization of processes both broadly encompasses bureaucracy in all of its variations and narrowly includes the routinization of interactions between client and worker, employee and manager, citizen and representative. Technological orientation speaks first to the nature of the relationship in each instance, rather than to its substance. The technological orientation is at play in any relationship to the extent there is routinization for specific instrumental purposes. For example, reading a Miranda card at the point of arrest can have several different substantive purposes. In addition, this action also helps routinize the relationship between law officer and suspect. No single instance of

**Exhibit 6.1   The Operant Social Theory: Patterns Across the American
Administrative State, 1960-80**

Accountability:
of the federal agency to the public
of state and local agencies to the public
structures within programs
Bounding the process with rules to direct outcomes
Centralizing:
authority into the executive
within the executive
federal authority
state authority
Commodization:
of benefits
of equity
of politics
Controlling:
the administrative process with documents
administrative discretion
Explicit emphasizing and orienting:
around quantification
managerial control
planning
Fiscal incentives as a means of control
Hierarchical task specification
Manipulating rules
Quantifying:
outcomes
purposes
Specializing:
authority
work
Substituting values:
of accountability for responsibility
of horizontal equity for fair treatment
of rule-ordered relationships for interaction between individuals
of mandatory coordination for discussion and sharing
of surrogate realities for administrative realities

such regularizing of behavior is likely to affect the overall relationship
between law officers and suspects; cumulatively, however, as an increasing number of relationships are routinized in a number of ways, the sphere
of potential human interaction in each subsequent relationship is qualita-
tively reduced.

Similarly, each pattern by itself does not necessarily enable more control
of the process of administration. For example, requiring more openness in

the administrative process suggests less direct control by administrative actors as more players come onto the field. The effect over time, however, is just the opposite as those players (a) are brought into the rulemaking process, the legitimate means of playing the game, (b) which makes the process more routinized and ritualized, and (c) therefore, turns interactions into commodity trading rather than social interaction. This is not to suggest that aspects of these patterns may not have been initiated with different intents, carried out with different purposes, or even later serve different motives while also reinforcing the operant social theory.

Essentially, the operant theory of social control shapes the sociopolitical relationships of administrative actors, both with each other and with the citizenry with whom they interact and on whose behalf they act.

THE OPERANT SOCIAL THEORY: PATTERNS ACROSS THE ADMINISTRATIVE STATE

The discussion in this section is guided by the patterns listed in Exhibit 6.1 and is essentially a Weberian analysis focusing on the role of instrumental rationality and the process of bureaucratization.

Accountability

Over the period 1960-80, as the legislative and the judicial arenas expanded as arenas of administrative control (with the intention, for example, of holding federal agencies more accountable), more publicly justified administrative decisionmaking was mandated. To the extent that the accountability trends described below were successful in prying loose the cover from the administrative black box, the normal closed-system workings of the operant social theory were less regular and often more politicized.

One mechanism for increased accountability of the federal agencies to the public during the period was the requirement for explicit responses to public comments on draft rules and regulations. Working in a similar manner was the transference of documents, such as quality control manuals and policy-and-procedure memoranda, into the public record (either through reference or publication). Internal working documents often become public documents; because they were made public, greater care was taken to ensure their specificity and clarity. What once were working handbooks became policy documents.[5]

Another aspect of the public accountability of federal agencies was in the congressional arena. Over the period, an increasing number of oversight reports were required of federal and state agencies. A review of General Accounting Office (GAO) reports by year shows an increase in the number of GAO studies and suggests that their primary focus shifted from a straight accounting orientation early in the period to very specific management assessments of programs by the end of the period.

The Congress increased its specification of the law over the period. While these specifications were intended to limit administrative discretion, they had the effect of reinforcing the quantifying and task specifying that are central to operant-theory logic.

Finally, the sheer volume of litigation involving federal agencies increased over the period, as did the number and types of administrative reviews. Both litigation and administrative reviews were mechanisms of accountability that emphasized assessing recorded administrative behavior against previously specified rules.

In this situation, there are three ironies of increased accountability to the public. The first is that the emphases on public justification and public accountability reinforced (and were reinforced by) other trends in the administrative state, such as increased quantification. Thus, the various mechanisms that evolved became highly task and procedure oriented. The net result was that those mechanisms—by their legalistic nature—supported exactly the kinds of activity they were intended to limit, namely, aggrandizement by the administrative state.

The second irony is that this general increase in "sunshine" became itself more routinized and procedurally oriented over time. (Litigation and the adversarial process, after all, are strongly procedurally based.) Most of the rules surrounding administrative reviews, for example, emphasize the importance of determining exactly what category of activity is subject to which category of review and in what manner.

The third irony is that the increased use of adversarial proceedings (either in courts or before administrative law judges) also emphasized a clearer and stronger demarcation between "we" and "they"—a characteristic of the operant social theory—with those "working for" the administrative state on one side of the line and those "treated by" or "working against" on the other. The particular irony here lies in the fact that those who chose to take on the administrative state had to do so on *its* terms. For instance, one has to have standing as an applicant or recipient in order to contest treatment as an applicant or recipient. Similarly, one has to follow the administrative rules of appeal in order to get information or documents.

Meanwhile, state and local agencies were being hit from two directions during this period. The same "sunshine" sentiments were also at work, though not necessarily with equal success, in the halls of state and local government. Meanwhile, the federal government demanded increased accountability as well.

In all instances, these external accountability structures regularized the relation between citizen and government, with two consequences: First, organization begot organization. The most effective comment, the most effective oversight, the most effective means for being heard all came from being organized. As the channels for citizen input became more special-ized, more specialized knowledge—best pooled through organization—was needed; one result was the professionalizing of advocacy.[6] In the second consequence, overt accountability was ultimately a political proc-ess. As the processes became regularized, participation in them became a commodity for barter, which ultimately meant commodization of that part of the political process.

In addition to the above, there were also attenuated accountability structures within programs themselves. In the Community Development Block Grant (CDBG) program, for instance, grantees eventually had to account for how non-CDBG and nonfederal funds were to be used in community development.

This centralizing of accountability was accomplished through ever more-intricate reporting rules and forms and an increased number of oversight points. The intricacy was in large part a function of the defining and redefining of concepts and categories within each program. As a result, compliance with the rules rather than achievement of purposes became the operating measure in the programs. There were, by the end of the period, more points in the process at which the federal (and the state, in the case of many local projects) agency had to concur than there had been at the beginning.

The language of the regulations in particular became one of financial incentive and disincentive, that is, of granting and withholding financial favor. On the one hand, this is not surprising: One rationale of the categorical grant is that acceptance of the federal funds requires acceptance of the federal rules, and, therefore, it is logical to turn to those funds as a means of enforcing the rules. On the other hand, however, to the extent that this happened, those concerned with the accountability of funds (rather than those concerned with the exercise of programmatic responsibility) tended to take precedence. This was particularly clear in the Aid to Families with Dependent Children (AFDC) program, for instance, with its construction of an entire bureaucratic system around fiscal allowances and disallowances.[7]

As a means of enforcing within-program accountability downward, federal agencies organized themselves in ways that were intended to ease their oversight function; that is, to make that function more efficient from their point of view. This included, among other things, extensive reliance on self-reported data collected from state and local agencies. The meaningful link between, on the one hand, the appropriated federal dollar and, on the other, the sewer, the daycare center, and the food stamp that the dollar ultimately reached became highly attenuated, as did meaningful discourse about carrying out societal purposes.

In addition to these considerable accountability activities, there was also extensive activity in relation to citizen participation as a form of accountability. All of this appears to run counter to the thrust of the operant social theory, as indeed was their intended purpose. What is striking, however, is that over the period all of the efforts in these areas appear to have come under the spell of the operant-theory orientation. As the proceduralism of these activities increased, the number of specified rules for participation doubled and trebled, and the objectives shifted from participation and substantive accountability to compliance with those rules and procedures. In other words, while these activities may have achieved their stated purposes, it is also true that those purposes often came to be redefined in terms more conducive to the operant social theory.

Bounding the Process with Rules To Direct Outcomes

Written rules constitute abstractions from present and past reality that are used to shape the future. A useful distinction can be made between "soft" and "hard" rules. Soft rules suggest a general orientation, a framing of potential action. Early in the period, much of the highway, CDBG, and welfare law and regulation was of this nature. The rules provided a direction, a general bearing, a purpose; they set boundaries on what were acceptable activities and what were not.

Hard rules, however, are much more precise and exact, a directing and specifying of future action. They define the outcomes expected from the rule-directed activity. For instance, by the end of the period, the general purposes of programs were no longer general; instead, they were quite specific and included such things as highway-safety ratios, percentages of low- and moderate-income families to be included in funded projects, and error rates in the payment of AFDC grants. This specification of objectives was also accomplished by specifying *how* the objective was to be accomplished; the process, in other words, became increasingly managerial, with coercive power (in the form of the threat of fiscal sanctions and disallowances) transmitted through hard rules to be applied in concrete situations.

Bounding the process with hard rules that were (by definition) abstractions made the process itself abstract, just as happened with the public-accountability processes. Delimiting the administrative process also meant that communication between human beings was then mediated by a set of abstract, rule-bounded structures, thus creating a series of surrogate realities for all the players. Such surrogate realities not only disable authentic communication; they also enhance the domination of one administrative player over another.

Centralizing Authority

The law became more specific during this period; in doing so, it also centralized more authority into the hands of the executive at all levels. Thus, each additional area of legislative interest in the highway program—safety, beautification, materials usage, and so forth—generated additional legislative language; in each case, this language specified executive action: the National Traffic and Motor Vehicle Safety Act of 1966 required the Secretary to establish highway-safety standards and mandated that each state have a highway-safety program designed to reduce traffic accidents.

This pattern of centralizing authority into the executive was not limited to the federal government but occurred at all levels. For example, federal law and regulation often required that a single state agency be assigned as the accountable agency and designated the governor as the accountable official in the state. The federal agency in many programs dealt directly with parallel (i.e., executive) local entities. Though procedures varied somewhat by state and over time, the net effect in any case was to give pre-eminence to the state executive agency over the state legislative body in determining the use of available state resources.

Naturally, this centralization meant an increase in the amount of authority, relative to the legislative and judiciary branches, that came to reside in executive branches. Throughout this period, there was also an explicit strengthening and increased use of executive authority, *as a type of authority*, at all levels in programs and in all branches of government. In other words, the use of executive (i.e., administrative) power became the dominant mode for organizing programmatic power.

The overall result was centripetal, whereby legislative authority became increasingly unable to cope with the multitude of administrative actions engaged in at any one time. Legislative activity—by definition inefficient, requiring as it does discussion and consensus—necessarily focuses on only a portion of the administrative world. As the logic of the operant social theory came more into play, legislators were increasingly called to task for not better managing even those small portions; in response, legislators tended to choose areas they assumed to be most manageable. Legislatively, for instance, it was easier to manage the amount of error in federal financial payments in the AFDC program than it was to manage reducing or preventing dependency, the ostensible purpose of the AFDC program.

A second centripetal effect of the centralizing pattern resulted from the specialization of executive authority across the administrative state. In welfare, for example, even as there was a specialization resulting in an increased number of programmatic authorities (Child Support Enforcement, Title XX, etc.)—in essence, a centrifugal effect—there was simultaneously within each new federal agency a centralizing of authority, which was then required to be mimicked at the state and local level as well. This centralizing within specialization, done in the name of more efficient and accountable management, necessitated an increased use of management systems as a means to control information and internal rulemaking. Management-information systems, reporting systems, accounting systems, concurrence-and-approval systems, supply systems, planning systems: each of these subsystems repeated in microcosm the centripetal and centrifugal tendencies of the larger system. Each subsystem required its own data, its own hard rules, and, ultimately, its own language, filling out the larger system in a way that was systematic in name only.

A third centripetal effect was the centralizing of federal authority relative to state and local authority. With each passing year, the controlling force became more clearly the federal agency (though most often out of its area offices, rather than out of Washington). This was bolstered by the legislative purpose of ensuring that funds were spent appropriately; more and more, this meant on projects affecting low- and moderate-income individuals, which in turn meant more stringent specifications and reporting requirements.

The early days of this period saw a tremendous amount of latitude, particularly at the local level, in terms of how and where federal resources were to be allocated and used. By the end of the period, the area of nonfederally directed choice in using federal funds was severely constrained.

Federalizing programmatic purposes was the explicit intent of numerous political agendas. In many cases, the argument was that local or state problems, such as economic or environmental problems, were often intractable because their locus was not in fact local or state but national or regional. This view was supported by the management-planning orientation in the administrative state. In systems terms, an important component of that orientation, demarcations such as "city" and "state" represented arbitrary and political (and therefore illegitimate) truncations of natural systems that therefore needed to be bypassed. This attitude was very prevalent, for instance, in the health and mental-health fields, both of which moved strongly toward regionalizing their provision of services during this period. It was also the logic behind planning, water, and highway districts, all of which were either created or given greater impetus during this period. In this fashion, yet another political agenda fitted snugly within the orientation of the operant social theory.

Centralizing federal authority resulted in a relative strengthening of that authority. By the end of the period, in a growing number of programmatic arenas the federal authority was *the* authority by which most related activity in that arena was defined. At a minimum, this reinforced the hierarchical command-and-control vision that permeated domestic policymaking. At a maximum, it enabled the uniform application of national norms of behavior, most notably in the areas of civil rights and the treatment of individuals and groups. What evaded U.S. society during this period, however, was how to avoid the costs of the minimum and yet obtain the benefits of the maximum.

A final centripetal effect of the centralizing pattern was that within each state authority was centralized in state rather than in local hands. Particularly early in the period, the federal government increasingly dealt directly with local agencies in the case of many categorical grants. Most of these grant programs, however, involved small amounts of money; in the big-ticket items, such as welfare and highways, the movement was steadily toward holding a state agency or regional authority accountable.

Commodization

Commodities are movables, articles of trade, useful things. In a money economy, the ultimate commodity is money itself. The beauty of commodities is that they are easily quantifiable; comparisons of commodities are simplified by using dollar values as surrogates for the commodities themselves.[8] With the growing insistence over the period on the use of quantified measures and on the primacy of financial relations, benefits (not only for individuals, as in AFDC, but also for states and localities in terms of grants) came increasingly to be treated as commodities, that is, as things measured by their utility. Utility, in turn, was itself increasingly specified in terms of surrogates (such as ratios and percentages), ultimately begging the question of useful to whom?

Commodities have use values and exchange values. They have a utility in themselves, as well as a utility in being exchanged for other things (or for money). In the setting here, there was a double shift. The first shift was to turn values, relationships, and other intangibles into utility-bearing objects; that is, to assess their use values. The second was to rearrange the human interaction (i.e., the social relation) into an exchange relationship between the resulting commodities.

For example, in the case of CDBG grants, there was an expanding requirement of purpose, which was to be detailed in each grantee's Housing Assistance Plan. Simultaneously, this purpose was translated into dollars, with those dollar amounts coming to represent (i.e., stand in for) the specified purposes. Insofar as this happens, oversight focused on *how* the dollars were spent—primarily in terms of whether proper accounting categories were used—and only tangentially on the *outcomes* produced by the program (i.e., by the organized activities themselves).

The same phenomenon of commodization occurred in both equity and politics. One of the clearest ways this happened was through the increased use of funding formulas. Once definitions and formulas were in place, they became surrogates for the equitable treatment of units of local government in relation to one another, regardless of which state they were part of or how intractable their particular problems were. The effect was to turn the issue of equity into commodities to be bargained for in the political arena.

The introduction of the flat grant into the AFDC program had a similar effect in the commodization of benefits, equity, and, ultimately, politics. Until the mid-1960s, the individual welfare grant in each state was determined by a complex calculation regarding estimated needs for food, shelter, clothing, and utilities. The circumstances of the individual applicant were used to determine that individual's need relative to state need standards; for instance, varying shelter and utility costs were taken into account. The resulting benefit, based on the principle of reducing or preventing dependency, was thus intended to correlate with that individual's circumstances. The rationale of the needs-based grant, in other words, is that there should be a rough equity amongst individuals in similar circumstances.

With the flat grant, some or all of applicants' expenses are generalized and applied to all applicants. For instance, in the early 1970s Illinois was divided into six regions, of which Chicago was one, the upper northwest another, and the Peoria area a third. The grant amount (for the same number of individuals in a case) varied between these regions primarily on the basis of the state's calculation of shelter and utility costs. The flat grant, in other words, treats individuals as members of group similar in geography, family size, and income; it therefore pays all similarly situated group members the same amount. The benefit is no longer connected to an individual's unique circumstances, but rather becomes a commodity to be determined by external criteria. (The intense pressure during this period on states to reduce errors in the AFDC Program provided an incentive by the late 1970s to many states to use flat grants. This mechanism is less prone to error exactly because it does not take into account individual circumstances.)

Membership, consisting solely of having the same externally defined characteristics as others, becomes prevalent during the period. Thus, membership was stripped of any affective or intentional meaning and was a designation of the observer, not of the observed. Equity in benefit amounts thereby no longer meant equity of circumstances but instead equity of membership in an abstract class. The politics surrounding the changes in benefit amounts during the period went from a politics of dealing with specific and unique conditions into a politics of commodities, trading off an increase or decrease here with a decrease or increase there.

The commodization of benefits, equity, and politics represents the operant social theory's logic at play in the political arena, as each of the three was broken down into mass-produced objects manipulated by applying hard rules and other abstractions in order to regularize interactions. The political arena became a marketplace in which values such as equity lost their fundamental meanings, representing as they did merely bargained equations for the treatment of collectivities. Even at the level of individual and agency, equity became merely treatment according to reality-abstracted, predetermined hard rules.

Controlling the Process and Administrative Discretion

As the centripetal effects increased, so did the use of documents as a means of controlling the administrative process, and the key document was the ubiquitous form. As federal agencies become more involved in more activities, their inhabitants discovered a parallel need for more overall control, as well as clearer control of each activity. (The need for control was a not-unreasonable response to the demands of public accountability that were being made.) This need provided the basis for requiring evermore information, primarily as data, to enable judgments about those activities.[9]

Early in the period, there was a generally clear distinction between forms (which had preassigned categories that were to be filled out by supplying data) and reports (which were responses to requests for information). By the end of the period, the two were virtually indistinguishable in most instances and were treated here as meaningfully identical. In its most simplistic form, data represents the facts about a situation, while information represents an interpretation of that situation. The increasing emphasis on information needs was actually an escalating call for data. Thus, at the national level, the increased federalizing of purposes required (from the federal perspective) ever-larger quantities of data in order to be able to assess the state and local situations independently.

Early in the period, the required forms were relatively fewer in number, shorter, and more oriented toward narrative explanation. (One can see this at all levels, from application forms for individual benefits to the required state plans for highway funds.) By the end of the period, the form was extremely category dependent; seldom was there room for narrative explanation, except as a response to specific questions focusing on a category of needed data.

Another use of the form reinforced the emphasis on planning: a standardized format was required for reporting the future as well as the past. The plan became the controlling document: control and authority, while still residing in individual officials as human beings in a titular sense, become embodied in the planning documents. The form, in other words, became the currency of the administrative state. As a currency and a commodity, the form leveled meanings as part of ritualizing them.

The increased use of the form to communicate both planned and actual activities also had the effect of controlling agency discretion because the form created a public justification for those activities. ("Public" is used here in the sense that, for instance, forms became part of the public record, even when they might be kept from public view for reasons of privacy or security.)

Over the period, there emerged a pattern of limiting agency discretion by carefully defining the areas in which the agency—federal, state, or local—in fact had discretion. This was particularly the case as legislative bodies attempted to increase control over administrative agents by demarcating appropriate agency territory. Central to this process was the form as a means of both specifying the areas and bringing any boundary questions into public discussion. In this regard, the legislative bodies used the form to control the activities of the administrative agencies by requiring regular reporting about their activities.

Agency discretion was also controlled through hierarchical specification of tasks. The definition of tasks requires categorization of work into recognizable subunits. A review, for instance, of state-plan requirements in AFDC illustrates this progression toward more clearly articulated categories that, ultimately, bound the discretion available to the recipient agency.

Finally, the opening up of the administrative process (both through litigation and through sunshine requirements) was also intended to control agency discretion. Parallel with this were increasing requirements that agencies justify actions by pointing to an existing record. The issue over time was less whether a specific agency action was in itself justifiable; rather, it was instead whether the action can be justified in terms of the appropriate requirements and previous pronouncements.

These activities, all of which center on controlling administrative discretion, also reinforce the commodization of benefits, equity, and politics by turning matters of political debate into matters of documentation, formulas, and regularized reporting.

There were also a number of ways in which the discretionary actions of individual administrative actors were controlled. The most obvious was in the AFDC arena, where the discretionary actions of individual caseworkers were, by the end of the period, severely controlled by hard rule and by form. In the same way, discretionary actions of individual applicants and recipients also were controlled with augmented requirements for providing information about individual circumstances and for participating in parallel programs (such as Child Support Enforcement and work programs).

The discretion of individual administrators was also controlled, in the highway and the CDBG programs for instance, through funding allocations and predefined statements about priorities. The county road commissioner and the county executive were limited, respectively, in those two programs because of limits on exactly how and when funds might be used for specific purposes.

Ironically, discretion—viewed negatively in a command-and-control model such as that engendered by the system of hard rules surrounding the use of funds—was at the same time seen positively during this period in terms of carrying out one's public charge or responsibility. This put administrative actors in the position of needing to manipulate the existing rules to fit a unique situation. While considered fraud when done for personal gain, such actions—when done for public purposes—were considered essential in order to execute one's job as an administrator properly. This, of course, was the dilemma of the New Public Administration's concern for social equity: how does one provide it and still maintain the integrity of the larger system?[10]

Discretion is simply the freedom to act on one's own; administrative discretion, however, also carries with it both a limit to that freedom (the legal bounds of action) and a responsibility to the public good in enacting that freedom. From within the framework of the operant social theory, however, discretion came to be narrowly viewed as a potential negative, namely, license to act willfully. From this view, those with discretion in an administrative setting were thus, by definition, unpredictable because the premise of the operant social theory was that stability was of paramount importance (i.e., efficient operations must first be stable operations) and unpredictability was the antithesis of stability. Projection into the future (i.e., planning), for instance, requires reasonable expectations of future actions—in other words, stability. This represents a significantly different interest in controlling administrative discretion than does the public-accountability argument behind, for instance, the actions of legal-rights organizations. The latter saw discretion as potentially allowing uncontrolled private interests, which have a bias relative to the public interest, to hold sway. The two motives—maintaining stability and controlling bias—were mutually supportive, however, within the framework of the operant social theory. As a result, the sense of responsibility within the notion of administrative discretion became a requirement of accountability and was dampened to the point of inarticulateness.[11]

Explicit Emphasizing and Orienting

One of the clearest orientations that developed during the period was the explicit use of and preference for quantitative measures. Such measures were required for the initial justification of funding, for the justification of how funds ultimately were used, for describing how various populations would be or were in fact affected by administrative action, for determining whether treatment had been equitable, and so on. Over the period, quantified measures also came to be the accepted form of public justification for nearly all proposed or completed administrative action.

The emphasis was not only on using abstract numbers to represent social reality; it was also on using derivative quantitative symbols, such as ratios and percentages, to describe that reality. Manipulation of the symbols (e.g., reducing the ratio of accidents to miles traveled) was then assumed to represent—indeed, to be—the reality. This manipulation strengthened the commodization of benefits, equity, and politics insofar as the processes and outcomes relative to each were represented and then manipulated through such derivative realities.

Hierarchical (top-down) directing was a second explicit orientation during the period. This orientation supported a third explicit emphasis, namely, management. Within the setting of the administrative state, management came to mean specialization, task specification, and control of the process through promulgation of hard rules to cover future unique circumstances. By the end of the period, the administrative generalist was gone, or at best seriously devalued. Programs in the administrative state tended to shift from an explicit orientation of carrying out a national purpose to one of managing resources efficiently.

Management, no matter how one dresses it up, is control by coercive, authoritative means. Within the framework of the administrative state, management came to mean relying explicitly on coercive hierarchical control, particularly between levels of government and between government and citizen. This stress on management made it difficult to maintain the important U.S. precept of government for the people and by the people.[12] The latter is an important legitimating myth particularly because of the U.S. culture's general distrust for bureaucratic government. It is as though the very task of stabilizing—always the first managerial act—has the potential to undercut the legitimacy of the administrative state, which then begins the vicious circle of increased managerial control (and more rules, more sanctions, less discretion), which in turn further cuts away at the legitimacy.

An element of the explicit managerial orientation was the increasing belief in the efficacy of planning. Like management, planning was no longer merely a tool; it became a normative stance toward the administrative world. Quantitative measures, codified hard rules, and the extended use of forms: all reinforced the planning mode. Planning, like management, attempts to stabilize the surrounding environment with the objective, at least initially, of forecasting future action. To the extent that the plan is interactive with that environment (that is, one is able to readily and quickly adapt it to changing circumstances), it indeed stabilizes those interactions. To the extent, however, the plan becomes solidified, it defines that environment in a surrogate fashion; that is, it interposes itself between the administrative actor and the social reality and even, in the extreme, becomes that reality.

The net result is that required plans become less future oriented and more past driven. The plan, in other words, often became a self-inflicted set of rules that must followed. In required plans, specific elements were generally left to the grantee, who was then held to those elements despite the ways in which the environment may have changed in the meantime.

The next question is the extent to which the existence of the plan is taken to certify the existence of the reality to be acted on. For instance, in the CDBG program, the federal agency had to certify that each grantee had a written plan; only later in the period, by requiring that copies of the public comments on the plan accompany the program evaluation sent to the federal government, was there any extensive attempt to match plan to reality. In a similar fashion, the required highway-safety plan and the corrective-action plan (to correct errors discovered through the quality-control process in AFDC) came to be considered surrogates for the activities themselves.

Fiscal Incentives as a Means of Control

Programs in the American administrative state, with more frequency toward the end than in the beginning of the period, used fiscal incentives as a means for controlling agency and individual behavior. Most often, these incentives were negative—threatening to withhold grant funds in the absence of certain behavior—but, especially toward the end of the period, positive incentives appeared as well.

Fiscal sanctions (i.e., withholding grant funds) had particularly notable effects in at least two programs. In one instance, states were required to pass speed limits of fifty-five miles per hour or lose a percentage of highway funds. Most states quickly, if reluctantly, responded; the requirement, however, then became a cause celebre in the fight for local determination and against alleged excessive federal regulation.

In the other instance, the threat of sanctions against states for allegedly excessive errors in the AFDC program brought no such furor or public outcry. Ultimately, congressional action in the form of the so-called Michel Amendment gave legitimacy to the notion of using the club of fiscal sanctions in the fight against perceived inefficiency, even though removing money from the program would most likely hurt the beneficiaries—poor families. One consequence in the AFDC program during the latter part of the period was that the administrative objective shifted almost completely from "reducing or preventing dependency" (in the words of the enabling legislation) to making error-free transactions.

Hierarchical Task Specification

The pattern of hierarchical task specification necessarily follows from and supports emphasis on management and planning, the use of hard rules, the increasing use of negative incentives, and so on. Task specification was the means by which the work of government came to be articulated and structured. It occurred across all three programs.

The emphasis on the hierarchical ordering altered the relationship between units of government in the federal system. Intergovernmental relations, a primary subject of the Constitution itself, have always been relatively complex. Hierarchical task specification introduced an element of presumed line authority, as a means of increasing managerial control and accountability, that only further complicated those relations.

Manipulating Hard Rules

The methods for controlling the administrative process rely almost exclusively on rule manipulation. Just as the plan became a substitute for the reality, the hard rule became a substitute for intended action. Looked at from the other end, behavior was measured by compliance with the rule; presumably, behavior could be altered by changing the rule. Hard rules, by their nature, focus on overt behavior; a strong emphasis on following the hard rules means a corresponding de-emphasis on anything outside of the rule framework, such as attitudes, treatment (except in a procedural sense), and quality of life. Thus, highway construction moved rapidly ahead without concerns about the more-complicated issues of the relationship of transportation to the environment, just as public participation in planning efforts for community-development projects and state welfare plans each became merely a pro forma meeting of the requirements.

Given the programs' planning orientation, and therefore orientation toward the future as the past, hard rules required increasing levels of abstraction in order to specify increasingly broader areas of activity. The rule written today was based on yesterday's and today's prediction about tomorrow's environment in which that rule would be applied. In a hierarchical system, rules are also written by those who are not experiencing the condition the rule is intended to cover. (This, it should be noted, was considered a positive from within the framework of the operant social theory because the rulemakers could be objective about the situation needing to be bounded.) Further, hard rules once written and promulgated became real; that is, they had a legitimacy and a coercive force that remained until they were changed.

The combination of all these factors made rulemakers and rulebook holders very powerful relative to the rule followers. It is the former rather than the latter who ultimately determine the meaning of social reality in particular settings. Likewise, compliance with the rules became an overt motive, irrespective of the purpose of the rules, with consequent goal displacement.

Quantifying

The pattern by which outcomes were more regularly quantified should be obvious from the preceding discussion. With increased reporting requirements, emphasis on measurement, and use of quantified standards, the original legislative purposes of the programs themselves became quantified. Thus, safe highways were the aggregated roads in a state (but only Classes A and B, not C) that saw better than a specified ratio of deaths (or accidents) per million road miles. A good community-development program, according to reported percentages, assisted the proper proportion of low- and moderate-income individuals. A good welfare program had an error rate below a certain tolerance level.

Quantifying outcomes and purposes did two things: First, the only legitimate outcomes and purposes became those amenable to quantification. This severely short-circuited the political discussion insofar as it made illegitimate those public purposes and outcomes that could not be readily captured and quantified. (In the absence of direct quantification, proxies were often used instead, but this only exacerbated this difficulty.) Second, the quantified and proxied purpose comes to be viewed as the actual purpose itself, a substitution of surrogate realities for administrative realities that is explored below.

Specializing Authority and Work

By the early nineteenth century, the specialization or division of work was a defining characteristic of both bureaucracy and industrial production in the United States. In the administrative state, as in industrial production, specialization was justified on the grounds of both efficiency of output and effective control of that output. Specialization occurred in many guises during the period. At the programmatic level, there were the multiple segments of the highway program and the variegated welfare programs. At the administrative level, there were specialized planners and caseworkers.

Program authorities (i.e., the legal justifications for program operation) became specialized over the period. This specialization of authority reinforced task specialization and definition. Even if agencies had been prone to pool resources in order to address mandates such as reduce or prevent dependency, even if the many other factors examined here were not at play, it still would be extremely difficult for both federal and state administrators, in the face of these specialized authorities, to pool their resources and jointly orient their actions toward any generalized purpose. Such coordination, when attempted, was necessarily frustrated by the increased specialization of authority.

Specialized authorities carved up the social reality by which highways tied together communities, community-development efforts changed conditions in cities and towns, and welfare provided a community's temporary and permanent safety net. Accountability, efficiency, management, planning, and fiscal control all provided support for (and were supported by) this specialization. By the end of the period, the result from the community's perspective was a welter of conflicting definitions, inappropriate categories, and unsuitable and often seemingly irrelevant hard rules.

This latter product, the mass of rules, was an unintentional result of a system of rational action focused on improving and manipulating the social world. This unintended product, known variously as red tape and bureaucratic intransigence or indifference, was hardly unrecognized during this period; it generated further calls for rational action. In response, authority was further specialized in order to focus more clearly on different, increasingly problematic aspects of that world; this specialized authority then issued specified rules to solve the problem.

Specialization of authority justifies the specialization of work, yet the extensiveness of the latter cannot alone be explained by the presence of the former. Again, there was an interplay between centralizing, which means more work to be done in one place; management and planning, which require discrete modules of activity to enable efficient use, especially as a means to control discretion; and hierarchical task specification, which forces work to be divided up. Specialization of work, in other words, is a natural byproduct of the other patterns at play.

Part of the rationale for specialization of work and task is that there are techniques appropriate to particular tasks, and specialization enables their utilization. In the American administrative state in this period, not only did specialization divide up the administrative world as a means of better managing it, but it severed the meaningful connections between information and data, on the one hand, and social reality on the other. Information and data are by definition incomplete descriptions of whatever they represent; specialization of work, resulting in specialized purposes for that information and data, produced an even-greater disconnection between the representation and the reality.

Substituting One Value or Stance for Another

Administrative responsibility has always been a slippery concept; it became a nearly unworkable concept in this time of rule specification, quantified measures, and delineated tasks. Administrative responsibility carries a sense of having the authority to act alone without superior guidance; it is, in other words, the justification for administrative discretion. Yet, such discretion is potentially destabilizing (from a managerial point of view) and might well be harmful to individual interests (from a civil-rights point of view).

The result, over the period, was that accountability, particularly rule-bound accountability, replaced more ambiguous if profound notions of responsibility. Legislative language, for example, shifted from talk of general purposes and responsibilities to specific responsibilities, reporting mechanisms, and closely bounded areas of interest. The term "responsibility" was used continually throughout the period in legislative language; its use in particular contexts changed, however, such that it became indistinguishable from the linear sense of accountability.

Holding administrators accountable, particularly through objectified mechanisms such as the production of percentages and ratios, delegitimates ideas of professional and personal responsibility. The latter notions came to be viewed as synonymous with discretion and, therefore, with arbitrary action. (The irony was that, at the same time, there was considerable public discontent with public administrators who merely followed the rules. This discontent was one justification for the social-equity emphasis of the New Public Administration.)

Holding administrators accountable for abstract events (e.g., obtaining ratios and percentages) diffused the responsibility for outcomes. The administrators were held accountable for drafting and following abstract rules instead of for acting as professionals and responsible human beings. All told, administrative responsibility was squeezed like an orange and emptied of its juice. With its moral underpinnings and professional standards removed, there remained but the outer skin of accountability.

A similar goal displacement occurred with equity. Early in the period, there was a clear sense that equity generally means fair treatment in the sense of being treated approximately according to one's circumstances. In the highway programs, for instance, grants early in the program were by and large apportioned according to some general sense of need as determined with the grantee in the political process. By the end of the period, these grants were determined almost solely by formulas. Fairness was numerically determined: the per-capita income of the state multiplied by the percentage of unemployed provided a measure by which to disburse funds across jurisdictions.

Similarly, at the beginning of the CDBG program, care was taken to maintain at the same level the funds going to the various jurisdictions; by the end, funds were distributed strictly according to intricate formulas. In the AFDC program, because of its entitlement nature, there was from its beginning a link between need and funds provided; by the end of the period, the formulas were merely more extensive. In the other welfare programs, such as social services, however, there was no such link; as a result, those programs followed the general path of the highway programs and, by the end of the period, all of the welfare programs were also formula driven.

In all these instances, fair treatment, which had included a broad sense of political worth combined with some articulation of a sense of need by the party in need, was replaced with a mathematical (or at least mathematically oriented) determination of horizontal equity by which all cases within externally defined categories received the same treatment. Such equity is, of course, more amenable to being public defended, less open to favoritism, and more accurately determined; it is also more abstract and removed from individual circumstances, one consequence being that those who appropriate the money feel less responsibility for the ultimate outcomes resulting from the use of the funds.

There are two consequences to horizontal equity necessarily ignoring individual circumstance, except insofar as that circumstance is encompassed by abstract categories applied from the outside. The first is the proverbial falling through the cracks, the plight of the community or individual whose circumstances span several categories but are, in toto, adequately addressed by none. They are treated, in other words, equitably but inappropriately. The second consequence is perceived as a justified necessity in which circumstances are redefined to fit the available categories or else the situation will not come within the purview of an equity claim.

Finally, horizontal equity emphasizes process and procedure over output and result. In a world of fixed resources, ensuring that all who qualify receive their portion entails that the portions be small enough to spread the available resources across the needed recipients. An emphasis on process over result begs the question of whether the results were adequate.

In similar fashion, rule-ordered relationships become substitutes for interactions between individuals. In a sense, this is just another way of pointing out how administrative discretion is controlled. More than discretion, however, was being controlled in the administrative state during this period: interactions of all kinds were more limited, except as they fell within the purview of rule-ordered relationships. The most obvious example is the way in which the application form drives the caseworker-recipient interaction in the AFDC program.

Potentially, rule-ordered relationships can be affectively empty relationships, particularly as hard rules come to bound social interactions. Heavily rule-guided interactions are necessarily interactions between actors in roles rather than between human beings as human beings. The hard rule is written, promulgated, and applied as a means of applying the general to the specific. It therefore always defines the specific as a special case of the general. As the hard rules define the purpose of the relationship in instrumental terms, those in the relationship find it difficult at best to act other than instrumentally.

For example, true assistance of one person by another requires empathy. Empathy, however, like reflection, is not an instrumental act. It requires seeing the other person not only as a client or a case, an applicant or a grantee, but also as a person. Worker burnout is thus the effect in part of the stress resulting from the severe discontinuity and tension between enacting the empathetic role, which is reinforced by professional norms, and the instrumental role, which is demanded by the rule-structured environment.

In a similar fashion, mandatory coordination between entities becomes a substitute for discussion and sharing amongst individuals concerned about a common destiny. As each program element had an ever-narrower administrative focus, even intraprogram communication in the form of discussion and sharing was more and more difficult. Increasingly, there were calls and mandates for coordination. Increasingly, it was the local agency that perforce had to coordinate the services and benefits being provided.

Given the hierarchical, task-ordered structure of the programs, attempts at coordination were always faced with two dilemmas: (a) determining who was in charge (since the managerial ethic and accountability structures require that *somebody* be in charge) and (b) using resources that did not fit into allowable categories (which, if this were not the case, would obviate the mandate for coordination, at least in many instances).

Discussion and sharing, however, are essential elements of human learning. Disabling discussion and sharing disables learning; substituting mandated coordination, especially with the attendant prerequisites of specialized power and authority, make it difficult at best for the individuals in the coordinated setting to be able to learn from each other.

Finally, surrogate realities were substituted for administrative realities. Abstractions of administrative reality—or, at times, even abstractions of estimates of that reality—stabilize the "blooming, buzzing confusion" that is the social world.

At some point, however, these surrogates for *aspects* of the administrative reality become surrogate *realities* themselves. By the end of the period, this was evident in the regulatory discussion of the state plans in AFDC and the Housing Assistance Plans in the CDBG program. It was also clearly the case with error rates in AFDC and safety standards in the highway program. In each instance, the regulatory focus shifted almost imperceptibly from the intended activity (represented by the surrogate) to the surrogate itself. Replacing the often-confusing administrative reality with a surrogate enables executive, legislative, and judicial administrators to manipulate the administrative reality, or seemingly so. Measures of success, such as number of homes built, number of children in school, and the like do tell something about the administrative reality they purport to describe, and as such, they represent useful tools for the administrator. The reification of such measures, however, constitutes the substitution of a surrogate reality, and manipulation of the surrogate is mistaken for manipulation of the reality the surrogate only stands in for. Ideologically, the consequence is that when the surrogate moves in the desired direction (irrespective of the movement within the reality), manipulation itself becomes justified as a legitimate form of interaction.

Tinkering with the Process

The most evident pattern emerging from the legislative and regulatory promulgation over this entire period is that change in the rules is endemic. While goodly portions of that change reflect altered intent, much of change constitutes tinkering with the process. Again and again, as one follows particular sections of laws or regulations through the period, one sees only the substitution of a word here or the alteration of a phrase there. It was as though the Enlightenment belief in the perfectibility of man had evolved into a belief in the perfectibility of the rules. Insofar as one forgets that the rules have human consequences—that is, as the rules become surrogate realities—there is a tendency to want to clean up those rules, which, after all, is so easy to do. The result in this case was turbulence; the result may also have been an ignoring of the changes by those lower down in the administrative system because what was being tinkered with was on the margin of the important work, namely, their everyday activities.

NOTES

1. For the details surrounding the results of the investigations reported here, see Mayer (1988 and 1989).

2. The focus of discussion here is governmental activity; however, the orientation encompassed in the operant social theory clearly describes corporate activity generally, both public and private.

3. On the encompassing aspects of technicism, see Ellul (1964), Barrett (1979), Mumford (1967 and 1970), and Stanley (1978). Although Ellul and Barrett use the term "technique," while Mumford speaks of "technics" and Stanley of "technicism," all are

speaking of the same general, encompassing phenomenon in which instrumental rationality, as embodied in the machine, is used to organize societal activities.

4. "The essence of administration is the ability of the administrator to get things done well and economically without doing them himself," argues Pfiffner (1946, 9) in "The New Public Administration," the opening chapter of his text.

5. A most notable instance of bringing working documents to public view was the publication, and later the litigation surrounding, the Pentagon Papers in the early 1970s.

6. This point is drawn carefully by both Daniel Moynihan (1969) in Chapter 2, "The Professionalization of Reform," and Hugh Heclo (1983). Relative to the political process, this is also the point of Theodore J. Lowi's (1979) attack on interest-group liberalism.

7. This substitution of accountability for responsibility was historically foreshadowed by the rise of the modern corporation. As the capital requirements outstripped the capacities of single owners and partnerships, bankers and financiers took over with the sale of stocks and bonds. The result was often a diminution of interest in technical (i.e., substantive) matters and a corresponding increase of interest in tangible outcomes (i.e., profits). See Chandler (1977).

8. The argument here parallels Karl Marx's argument regarding human labor as a commodity. See Marx (1978, 321).

9. At first blush, a request of information hardly appears to imply control. One must remember, however, that the basic intergovernmental relationship between federal and state agencies was (despite protestations to the contrary) primarily superior-subordinate in many of these programs, a hierarchical attitude reinforced by the proliferation of hard rules. In its simplest form, the provision of public money carries the requirement to report on its use as defined by the provider of the funds. Requests for information were ultimately coercion-backed demands, no matter how politely cloaked.

10. See Frederickson (1971 and 1976) This same theme is echoed in Harmon (1971).

11. Put another way, it should be no surprise that, as several authors in this volume suggest, the New Public Administration's social-equity concerns appear to have made but little headway in the administrative world since Minnowbrook I.

12. On this point, see Karl (1987).

PART 3

Interconnectedness, Democracy, and Epistemology

The argument here has generally been that public administration lacks theory sufficient to address adequately the conditions of interconnectedness. Assuming this is the case, are current research models for public administration also no longer appropriate? More fundamentally, is the U.S. Constitution obsolete? In the interconnected, multiversalist world of the twenty-first century, can this eighteenth-century document still provide a valid political structure? Robert C. Zinke and Jay D. White, in addressing these questions, find that older approaches may work surprisingly well.

Zinke examines the critical question of how can a changing role for the public administrator—from technocrat to ameliorator—be reconciled with constitutional concepts of independent powers balanced against each other? He finds that the Constitution, far from outlining a fixed structure of government, in fact establishes a "rhetorical republic." Because of the possibilities for dialogue and practical discourse, the Constitution and the institutions it prescribes can adapt to new conditions such as interconnectedness.

The necessary role of the public administrator in the rhetorical republic is to maintain the constitutional dialogue. White carries this notion further by arguing for the use of a rhetorical device—storytelling—as a principal research method for the field.

Forged in the Modern Era of the 1920s and 1930s, public administration theory derived its research models from positivist social science. The latter was compatible with public administration theory, which assumed rationality and independence, particularly between facts and values. In the interconnected world, these distinctions are no longer as clearly valid.

White argues for further development of postpositivist modes of inquiry, emphasizing storytelling as a research model that can improve interpretation of facts and values. Its critical role is the development of narratives to aid in the understanding and amelioration of complex problems.

For both authors, the public administrator and public administration play an essential role in the process of narrative construction and interpretation.

7

American Constitutionalism in the Interconnected World: Administrative Responsibilities in a Rhetorical Republic
Robert C. Zinke

Administrative scholars have taken a renewed interest in the way constitutional norms and values have shaped American public administration. The general thrust of this renewed interest has centered on the need to establish the constitutional legitimacy of American administrative institutions and processes. Indeed, thanks to scholars such as Rohr (1986), many in the field now appreciate the important role that constitutionalism must play in the legitimation of the administrative state. At the same time, however, there exists an uneasiness about the relevance of the U.S. Constitution to the concerns of a complex, interconnected world. In a high-tech age of hyperpluralism, interconnectedness, and the multiversalist paradigm, what is the constitutional role of public administrators?

This chapter suggests that one way of understanding the constitutional role of American administrators is to look at what the Constitution does. The argument is that the Constitution establishes a rhetorical republic, where primary governmental activities consist of speaking, listening, and acting expressively and where national unity depends upon the commitment of citizens to learn about moral realities and to participate actively in conversations, debates, and expressive actions that make those realities manifest. This republic embraces a diversity of political and socioeconomic interests but allows no single voice or interest to dominate public discussion. Moral reason and prudence may be potentially expressed by anyone or by any group of discussants or actors. The exclusion of even one voice or expressive action risks the loss of what the rhetorical republic values most: free and open dialogue.

In the American rhetorical republic, the constitutional role of public administration rests with the facilitation of free, open dialogue and debate about the political norms and values that should guide public life. Ultimately, this chapter argues, the relevance of American constitutionalism relies on the recognition that the exploration of common areas of agreement and understanding requires that diverse groups and interests establish and maintain permanent, ongoing institutions and processes that facilitate open dialogue and debate.

IS THE U.S. CONSTITUTION STILL RELEVANT?

Questions regarding the relevance of the Constitution stem from recent criticisms about the American constitutional system (Robinson 1985; Chubb and Peterson 1989). These criticisms focus on two interrelated sets of concerns: that the Constitution no longer fits with the complex realities of the late twentieth century, and that it impedes the ability of the federal government to act in a unified manner in the domestic and international political arenas.

According to critics, the Constitution represents the product of a simpler, less complex era in American political life. At the time of the founding, American politics reflected the social and economic characteristics of a generally homogeneous, agricultural society. Human relationships were formed through personal interaction, while cultural and ethnic similarities in the population provided the basis for a common understanding of reality—socially, politically and economically—and for basic agreement regarding how government should operate. Political communication occurred through verbal exchange or through the transport of written materials (Westin 1987).

Life in the late twentieth century, critics argue, has become more complex, and the Constitution no longer addresses basic contemporary realities. American society has become pluralistic, both socially and ethnically. This makes it harder to truly communicate—and, thus, to sustain—common understandings and agreements. Moreover, modern telecommunication technologies have made the world more politically and economically interdependent. No single nation can act unilaterally without facing immediate reactions and responses. As Marshall McCluhan noted nearly three decades ago:

In the electric age, when our central nervous system is technologically extended to involve us in the whole of mankind and to incorporate the whole of mankind in us, we necessarily participate, in depth, in the consequences of our every action. It is no longer possible to adopt the aloof and dissociated role of the literate Westerner. (1964, 20)

The inability to undertake unilateral action relates to a second major set of concerns regarding the Constitution. According to critics, the Constitution no longer provides for unified action on the part of government. The Constitution fails to provide the Federal Government with the means to speak with a single voice in either the domestic or the larger, international communities. In a collection of papers published by the Committee on the Constitutional System, for example, one study argues that "in an increasingly interdependent world, facing increasingly complex problems, it is essential for a nation with the economic, military and political power of the United States to be able to speak with one, clear voice" (Dillon 1985, 27).

In addition, according to critics, the constitutional separation of powers encourages fragmented political structures that come under the domination of single-issue interest groups and special interests. A recent Brookings Institution study suggests that new institutions and arrangements must be established that "can pursue policies of sufficient coherence, consistency, foresight, and stability that the national welfare is not sacrificed for narrow or temporary gains" (Chubb and Peterson 1989, 4).

Because it neither addresses current realities nor provides for unified, purposeful action, the critics suggest, the Constitution of the United States is largely irrelevant to the concerns and needs of the contemporary world.

WHAT DOES THE CONSTITUTION DO?

In retrospect, the question of the Constitution's relevance has always presented an issue. Since the beginning of the Republic, each generation has faced the problem of applying the Constitution to its own specific needs and issues, and each has had to determine for itself how the Constitution structures American government. Powell suggests that even for the founders, "the Constitution was something unto itself." "Their superior knowledge of its creation," he notes, "did not render its meaning and import wholly clear to them; indeed, at times they suggested that knowledge of the Constitution's origins was a hindrance, a source of bias rather than of enlightenment" (1987, 16). As the result of these interpretive ambiguities, three distinct approaches—theoretical, nationalist, and textualist—have guided the interpretation and implementation of the Constitution throughout American history. Contemporary concerns noted above regarding the relevance of the Constitution represent the latest manifestation of these older interpretive currents.

The theoretical approach sees an example in the way the founders used prevailing political theories to interpret the Constitution and to inform their actions; for the framers, such theories as checks and balances, separation of powers, and federalism provided insights into how the Constitution should be implemented. However, each period in American history has had its own prevailing theories, which have supplanted the theories of the founders (Kammen 1986). The theoretical approach thus emphasizes that every generation uses contemporaneous thought to guide the implementation of the Constitution. The political theory and philosophies of each age are brought to bear to meet the demands of that age's social and political realities (Powell 1987, 20-34). The arguments above concerning the complexity of contemporary life in the late twentieth century reflect the theoretical approach to constitutional interpretation.

The nationalist approach assumes that the Constitution is designed to allow the people, through their elected representatives, to achieve social goals and objectives. This approach centers on the power that the Constitution gives to the national government—relative to the states—to provide for the common defense and the general welfare of the nation. It emphasizes the purposeful nature of the Constitution to solve contemporary problems and achieve public ends (pp. 34-39). The Constitution is seen to create an instrument that satisfies the general public will. This approach underlies contemporary arguments regarding the inability of the federal government to act in a unified manner, either domestically or internationally, to achieve national ends.

The textualist approach conceives the Constitution as a contractual agreement or compact, born out of compromise between the states and ratified by the people as the legal charter of the land. This approach emphasizes the written text of the constitutional document. From this view, if the Constitution no longer reflects accepted political theory or if it no longer helps the people achieve their goals and objectives, then its written text should be changed to allow for the legal alteration of governmental institutions. Throughout American history, this third approach has dominated Constitutional interpretation (pp. 39-48). Indeed, current critics generally have the third, textualist conception in mind when they question the relevance of the U.S. Constitution. How can compacts and words frozen in time from the eighteenth century be expected to address contemporary realities and issues?

The textualist conception of the Constitution is too narrow, however. The Constitution consists of more than just the duly ratified, printed words frozen in time. As the very existence—and the current embodiments—of the theoretical and the nationalist approaches to constitutional interpretation attest, there is also an "unwritten Constitution" (Price 1983). Together, the written and the unwritten Constitutions form a larger, rhetorical constitutional tradition. With this tradition, the written text merely provides a statement of the institutional context and the necessary conditions under which discussion should proceed about foundational political values and norms (derived from current political theories and philosophies) and the proper ends of government (what the people want to achieve). At any given moment, the rhetorical Constitution represents the conversation, debate, and common understandings and agreements about what political norms and values one generation should pass down to the next, as well as what ends government should seek. Those critics who implicitly or unwittingly adopt the textualist conception of the Constitution close themselves off to the immanent possibilities for political openness and social change that the larger "rhetorical Constitution" provides. In a complex, technological age, the relevance of the U.S. Constitution rests with its rhetorical uses of social pluralism and human interdependence to facilitate political dialogue and discussion.

EMPHASIS ON DIALOGUE IN CONTEMPORARY POLITICAL THOUGHT

A significant feature of political thought and philosophy in the late twentieth century is the recognition of the importance of human dialogue and communication. This recognition and its emphasis derive from the realization that at a practical level, public policies and decisions necessarily reflect normative judgments—political, legal, and moral (J.D. White 1990). At this level, decisionmaking involves "practical discourse," that is, "discussion, debate, deliberation, and argumentation over what is true or false, good or bad, right or wrong, and what should be desired" (p. 132).

A variety of philosophers, historians, and political scientists have rediscovered the rhetorical roots of contemporary life. Contemporary political philosophers such as Bernstein (1988), Gadamer (1988), Jonsen and Toulmin (1988), Rorty (1979), Schrag (1986), and Vickers (1988) now emphasize that rhetoric and dialogue must become the renewed focus for anyone wishing to restore a sense of community and individual meaning to the contemporary world. The works of these philosophers reflect the profound effect that pluralism as a permanent feature of human experience has had on modern thought. As one philosopher argues, "the most significant philosophical discovery of the present century" has been that "of pluralism, that the truth admits of more than one valid formulation" (Watson 1985, xi). For philosophy,

> it is becoming increasingly apparent that the attempt to establish the one true philosophy by refuting all other philosophies is not destined to succeed, for the refutation of all other philosophies depends on interpreting them in the terms of one's own philosophy, and this exposes one to the danger of the fallacy known as *ignoratio elenchi*, or ignorance of what refutation is, that is, refuting what has not been asserted. (p. xi)

This discovery has led to the view that truth derives from dialogue and conversation. As Schrag (1986) explains,

> Truth is disclosure eventuated in the describing, arguing, explaining, and showing that goes on in our speaking, writing, and acting. Description and redescription, understanding and explanation, argumentation and showing are themselves displays of communicative praxis, involving an actual or a potential hearer and reader. This comprises the rhetorical conversation of mankind, setting forth and making manifest to the hearer and reader multiple perspectives of world, self, and other. (p. 190)

Similar insights have influenced historians such as Muller (1952), Lottinville (1976), Pocock (1987 and 1989), and Kellner (1989), each of whom emphasizes the importance of language and argument in shaping the prevailing views of past realities. Kellner argues, for example, that while people make sense of their past through narratives and stories, these historical accounts are always skewed or crooked. "Neither human activity nor the existing records of such activity," he offers, "take the form of narrative, which is the product of complex cultural forms and deep-seated linguistic conventions deriving from choices that have traditionally been called rhetorical" (p. vii).

The historical accounts that one generation gives of past ages always reflect the prevailing language and rhetoric of that generation. As Kellner suggests, "historical understanding is a vital cultural enterprise, and the historical imagination an important, if neglected, human faculty." "Because the sources of history include in a primary sense the fundamental human practice of rhetoric," he argues, "we cannot forget that our ways of making sense of history must emphasize the *making*." This means that "to get the story crooked is to understand that the straightness of any story is a rhetorical invention and the invention of stories is the most important part of human self-understanding and self-creation" (p. xi; emphasis in original).

Making the history of the past occurs in the present. The traditional concern to ground current Constitutional doctrine in the intentions of the framers points to the important role that history plays in American political culture, while the continuing legal debate regarding how to determine "original intent" attests to the inability of constitutional scholars to "get the story straight" (Rehnquist 1976; Bork 1971; Grey 1976, 1978, 1984, and 1988).

Finally, political scientists such as Barry (1965), Fischer (1980), Dunn (1981), and Tulis (1987) emphasize the crucial role that policy argumentation and debate play in the formulation and evaluation of public policy. Each of these scholars points to the importance of examining the rhetorical arguments used to support and defend public policies and decisions. Operating from a "good reasons" approach, for example, Fischer (1980) suggests that in the practical discourse of politicians and citizens, the arguments used to support a public policy become the standards later used to evaluate that policy. He outlines a set of questions designed to probe various levels of political and administrative deliberation so that the underlying policy arguments can be clarified, understood, and discussed or debated. In the same vein, Tulis contends of presidential power that

> rhetorical power is a very special case of executive power because simultaneously it is the means by which an executive can defend the use of force and other executive powers and it is a power itself. Rhetorical power is thus not only a form of "communication," it is also a way of constituting the people to whom it is addressed by furnishing them with the very equipment they need to assess its use—the metaphors, categories, and concepts of political discourse. (1987, 203)

Generally, contemporary thought in political philosophy, history, and political science appear to have converged on the importance of practical discourse and dialogue in the establishment of political agreement and action, as well as political evaluation and judgment.

THE AMERICAN RHETORICAL REPUBLIC

On the basis of the contemporary interest in rhetoric and dialogue, some legal and constitutional scholars have begun to suggest a new, rhetorical approach to constitutional interpretation and implementation. The works of these scholars suggest that the Constitution establishes a rhetorical republic.

Some contemporary constitutional scholars, such as Carter and Gilliom (1989), J.B. White (1984), and Fisher (1988), emphasize the importance of language and communication in the preservation of communal relationships. Carter (1988) argues that "the capacity of language to make life livable despite its contradictions depends on the bonds that good communication itself creates" (p. 237). He stresses that "talk itself, despite endless disagreement, cements the friendship" (p. 238). This insight points to an important role that the constitutional system plays in American society.

The Constitution establishes and maintains an institutional framework that allows a national community to emerge on the basis of open communication and ongoing discussion. Pranger (1973) suggests that the Constitution originally established an "open forum at the national level" that allowed "for variation and expression" among diverse groups and interests (p. 116). "For the founding fathers," he contends, "the national center was to operate as a community of citizens rather than as the most powerful hierarchy," and "its distinguishing characteristic was its forum for national community rather than national preemptive organization" (p. 115).

James Boyd White elaborates on the notion of the national forum, arguing that the Constitution sets up "a rhetorical community, working by rhetorical processes that it has established but can no longer control. It establishes a new conversation on a permanent basis" (1984, 246). First of all, White notes, the Constitution must "rely on others to see that its commands are obeyed, for it is not a self-executing document." If a branch of government or a government official violates a constitutional provision, "the omnipotent author of this Constitution will not step down from the sky and force it to do so" (p. 244).

Secondly, the Constitution "creates a set of speakers, defines the occasions for and topics of their speech, and is itself a text that may be referred to as authoritative." Because the authority of the Constitution is contextual, this creates "the occasions and warrants for making a certain set of claims, and in this respect it is like the other constitutions we are always making in our own lives, in the form of contracts and agreements, block-betterment associations, and so on" (p. 245).

Third, the Constitution places speakers into three roles—executive, legislative, and judicial—and provides a way for these speakers (and others) to validate their role. If someone claims to be president, for instance, the document offers a means to validate that claim, providing "the speaker, and others, with materials of argument on the question whether the particular speech is appropriate or inappropriate for him, in form or substance" (p. 245).

Fourth, the Constitution delineates the topics appropriate to the executive, legislative, and judicial roles. For example, by enumerating the powers of Congress, the Constitution provides the catalog of topics for deliberation and action. Fifth, the Constitution sets forth a number of provisions that encourage or require interactive communication and dialogue, oral and written, between the three branches of government. These include such provisions as those requiring the House and the Senate to maintain written journals of their proceedings, and those requiring presidential vetoes to be accompanied by a statement of reasons and objections to proposed statutes.

Overall, J.B. White contends, the text of the Constitution is "addressed . . . to a set of readers, each defined by his role (including the role of one who invokes its language to control the conduct of others)," and each reader "will spend much of his life interpreting the instrument that creates his role and his world" (p. 246).

Other contemporary scholars besides J.B. White have picked up on this dialogical dimension. Fisher, for example, argues "that constitutional law is not a monopoly of the judiciary"; rather, it "is a process in which all three branches converge and interact with their separate interpretations" (1988, 3). He suggests that the rhetorical conception of the Constitution allows for interpretational openness regarding questions about fundamental political principles:

No single institution, including the judiciary, has the final word on constitutional questions. The courts find themselves engaged in a "continuing colloquy" with political institutions and society at large, a process in which constitutional principle is "evolved conversationally and not perfected unilaterally." (p. 273)

The contemporary meaning of the Constitution rests with its status as a communicative model in pluralistic societies, its mediation of complex, interconnected political and social relationships through rhetorical dialogue. Conceived rhetorically, the Constitution embraces what Warren refers to as

radical "openness"—a dialectical openness which preserves the tension between the relative and the absolute, the historical and the
universal, and which prevents a degeneration into the mindless and
vulgar relativism (especially of the moral sort) which can characterize
much of historicist and relativist thought. (1984, 5)

The radical openness of the rhetorical Constitution stresses the limitless
possibilities for the discovery and integration of moral principles and
standards in political life. Indeed, it is this openness that resonates with
the contemporary rediscovery of dialogue and communication. The Constitution is relevant by virtue of its potential to bring people together in a
way that facilitates shared and interconnected relationships, based on
conversation and discussion about mutually sharable moral and ethical
insights.

PUBLIC ADMINISTRATION IN A
RHETORICAL REPUBLIC

If one accepts John Rohr's admonition that "the role of Public Administration is to fulfill the objective of the oath of office," that is, "to uphold
the Constitution of the United States" (1986, 181), what is it exactly that
administrators must uphold when the Constitution is conceived rhetorically?

Rohr hints at an answer to this question when he cites Fisher (1975),
who "convincingly describes a political world in which 'moral understandings' and 'gentlemen's agreements' penetrate the constitutional barriers between the legislative and executive branches." Rohr goes on to state
that

Administrators facilitate these mollifying arrangements and are, at
times, themselves parties to such understandings and agreements.
This is but another way of maintaining the proper constitutional
balance of powers. Rather than choose between the Congress and the
presidency, the Public Administration may at times look for suitable
means to bring them or keep them together. (p. 184).

In the rhetorical republic created by the Constitution, the fundamental
obligation of public administration is to maintain ongoing constitutional
dialogue and conversation within the national government and the larger
society. While space does not permit a full elaboration, a few remarks can
outline the responsibilities that this obligation entails.

Within the national government, as Rohr's remarks suggest, administrative institutions act as facilitators of dialogue and conversation. If the conversation begins to lull or to stall with speakers who have lost their voices, administrative agencies ask questions and make comments that stimulate more discussion or suggest avenues of thought and action that allow new voices to be heard. When an agency tells the Congress or the President about a new social or economic problem, or initiates regulatory actions that lead individuals to express these problems before the Supreme Court, the agency stimulates conversation and dialogue. When an agency seeks to protect the rights of its existing clients or extend the rights of new clients, it is maintaining or giving those clients a voice they otherwise may not be able to generate. As facilitators, the institution of public administration has a responsibility to focus constitutional dialogue on the existing realities of society, in order to point out new situations demanding moral reflection and consideration.

Public administration also has a responsibility, as an institution, to maintain conditions in the general society that facilitate free and open communication and dialogue. Under the Constitution, public administration does not provide public services as ends in themselves, as altruistic expressions of the personal intent of its leaders, or as the benevolent expressions of a sovereign state. After all, hungry people, people without adequate shelter, people in fear of crime and violence, and people who have given up hope of living valuable productive lives very seldom participate in constitutional dialogue or express an interest in constitutional topics. Rather, administrative institutions provide these services to these people so that as citizens they may participate in the dialogue and discussion that ultimately affects their ability to speak and hear moral truths and to live moral lives. In this role, the institution of public administration has a responsibility to remind itself and society that no one person or group possesses the exclusive prerogative either to speak moral truths or to require others to abide by its moral dictates. That is why all citizens must be allowed to participate.

In this complex, pluralistic, multiversalist, and interconnected world, every person has the potential to live a moral, public life. When facilitated in the society at large, constitutional dialogue allows that potential to become a reality through the conversational lines every person is asked to speak and hear. The role of public administration as an institution rests with its anticipation that, if constitutional dialogue is encouraged and if all members of the society are allowed to participate in that dialogue, all individuals may well realize their moral potentials. The conversable world of the Constitution is the multiversalist, interconnected world of moral discourse and experience. In the contemporary age of telecommunications, other nations and other peoples are now beginning to enter this conversable world, and the role of public administrations everywhere must be to help these people become responsible, participating members.

TASK OF PUBLIC ADMINISTRATION THEORY

In any age, determining the ends of government involves conscious recognition of where the society has come from and to where it is going. Without a past, policymaking dissolves into a moral relativism devoid of any underlying ideals because their pursuit appears pointless and counter-productive of immediate pleasures and desires. To force past ideals and aspirations unthinkingly on the future, however, creates a rigid absolutism that makes succeeding generations mere instruments of their past. Thus, the complexity of governmental decisionmaking at any present moment rests with the requirement that public programs and policies live up to the highest ideals and aspirations of past generations and, at the same time, shape future conditions—political, economic, and social—in ways that allow succeeding generations to fulfill ideals and aspirations yet unknown. Since the audience that public officials address includes all citizens of the polity—past, present, and future—any present generation must initiate a rhetorical dialogue with its past and its future. It is these insights that the current emphasis on dialogue and rhetoric brings to the fore.

To fulfill their constitutional role as facilitators of the ongoing dialogue that leads to public policymaking and program development, public administrators must pay special attention to their use of language and to the arguments they create to support current policies and programs. They must become more attentive to the ways in which practical discourse informs their actions. As Jay D. White points out, however, very few understand this.

> Administrators regularly engage in practical discourse. Unfortu-
> nately, they are not guided by an understanding of the type of
> reasoning involved in such discourse or by an understanding of the
> criteria for judging the rationality of practical thought and action. The
> bulk of administrative theory treats practical thought and action as
> being intuitive or subjective, and therefore noncognitive, nondescrib-
> able, or nonrational. Consequently, little attention is paid to the
> process of determining means and ends in the context of practical
> discourse. Little is known about the logic of the normative, political,
> and moral judgments that administrators make. (1990, 133)

As J.D. White's comments suggest, public administration theory must focus on the way in which normative, political judgments are made. To facilitate dialogue, administrators must understand how normative decisions are arrived at through conversational and argumentative deliberation. Public administration theory can encourage this understanding in two ways. First of all, studies such as Fischer's (1980) and J.D. White's (1990) can help to unravel the logic behind deliberative discourse. Secondly, more attention should be paid to the way in which the contemporary understanding of past constitutional rhetoric informs current administrative practice. Here the works of Grey (1976, 1978, 1984, and 1988), Struever (1985), Pocock (1989), and Tulis (1987) stand out.

A certain irony attends this latter task. The renewed interest in finding constitutional legitimations of American public administration stemmed in part from the celebration of the two-hundredth anniversary of the U.S. Constitution. The *Public Administration Review* (Stillman 1987), for example, published a symposium commemorating the bicentennial of the Constitution and the centennial of the American administrative state. In addition, numerous other books and articles on the Constitution appeared in the wake of bicentennial celebrations. Public administration scholars have sought to use the rhetoric of constitutional history to legitimate contemporary administrative institutions and agencies. It remains unclear how successful this attempt has been, however. This ambiguity of results raises a basic question: are the Constitution and the attempts to justify current administrative practice on the basis of constitutional interpretation irrelevant? Or does the apparent irrelevance stem from a basic failure of contemporary thought to address current realities by identifying and articulating those past practices that resonate with present concerns?

8

Knowledge Development and Use in Public Administration: Views from Postpositivism, Poststructuralism, and Postmodernism

Jay D. White

Postpositivism was one of the themes of the first Minnowbrook Conference (Marini 1971). It was expressed as a rejection of the value-free and value-neutral positivist approach to research in the social sciences. Although not all of the participants at the conference may have embraced this position, it was consistent with another theme of the conference: Public administration must become socially relevant, and it must foster social equity. With this as a new direction for public administration, it was difficult to see how research could be value-free and value-neutral. A break with positivism was necessary. Normative theorizing and existential and phenomenological research were called for to deal with the problems of the 1970s and 1980s.[1]

In the years following the conference, a handful of theorists in the field outlined the philosophical alternatives to positivism.[2] They usually include interpretive and critical approaches to inquiry. The alternatives were not discussed extensively at the second Minnowbrook conference. With the exception of Michael M. Harmon's critique of "decisionism" as the basis for research in organization theory, little has yet emerged from Minnowbrook II to guide postpositivist theory development.

In reflecting on Minnowbrook II, Mary Timney Bailey observed that

the world of 1988 appeared to be more complex than did the world
of 1968, when the Minnowbrook conferees and much of society
believed that all problems are solvable in the richest, most advanced
nation in history. Events of the 1970s and 1980s have shaken that
confidence, bringing newer, more intricately complex problems.
(1989, 224)

For Bailey, these intricately complex problems form a web in which
"every solution creates its own new problems" (p. 224). Today, public
administrators face a dynamic and fluid web of interconnected problems
with a feeling of "constrained hopefulness" (Guy 1989) about government's role in solving them. This feeling emerged at Minnowbrook II
because some of the participants were not as optimistic as those of
Minnowbrook I about the ability of public administrators to be effective
agents of change.

Critiques of positivism, interconnected problems, and feelings of constrained hopefulness are manifestations of society's movement into the
postmodern era, an era in which institutions such as science and government are losing their legitimacy. Stories about the power of science and
government to solve problems are no longer universally believed. Society,
science, and government have changed. If anything at all has been learned
in the now twenty-plus years since Minnowbrook I, it is that the stories of
society, science, and government need to be—in fact, are being—rewritten. Those stories must reflect contemporary situations; otherwise, they
remain the basis for unauthentic and ineffective action by theorists and
practitioners alike.

This essay argues for the further development of postpositivist modes
of inquiry to deal appropriately with society's interconnected problems.
The chapter does this by outlining themes from public administration,
postpositivism, poststructuralism, and postmodernism to show how the
logic of knowledge development and use is being reconstructed as storytelling and narration. This leads to a series of implications that the narrative
theory of knowledge holds for research and practice in public administration as it confronts the postmodern era.

PUBLIC ADMINISTRATION AS STORYTELLING

The idea that research in public administration involves storytelling is
not new to the field. Martin Rein introduced it in 1976. He concluded a
lengthy argument about the role of facts and values in policy analysis by
observing that neither the pure nor applied models of science offer the type

of knowledge required to make policy decisions. Both models are concerned with the way things are and the way things might be. Neither addresses the way things ought to be, which is the normative undertaking of policy analysis. For Rein, the distinctive feature of policy analysis is the "giving of advice," which involves storytelling (1976, 261). Advising a decisionmaker always requires the telling of a story that weaves together facts and values. Stories provide "an interpretation of a complex pattern of events with normative implications for action, and not with a universal law" (p. 266). The type of understanding required for public decisionmaking

> depends upon telling relevant stories: that is, deriving from past experience a narrative which interprets the events as they unfold and draws a moral for future actions, suggesting, for example, how the future might unfold if certain steps are taken. (pp. 265-66)

Storytelling is not limited to policy analysis; normative deliberation and giving advice are central to public administration in general.[3]

Rein was troubled by the normative aspect of policy analysis. It was inconsistent with the assumptions of positivist inquiry. Exploring the value side of the dichotomy, he offered three interpretations of the relationship between normative choice and objective inquiry, finding each interpretation unsatisfactory. In the first interpretation, values organize facts, which leads to a distorted perception of facts. In the second interpretation, facts are compatible with different value systems; this leads to competing theories of action with no rules for choosing among them. In the third, facts organize values, which leads to the narrowing of the scope of normative choice (p. 259). Rein did not resolve the conflict between these interpretations; instead he held to a value-critical position that left values open to deliberation in the process of decisionmaking.

Rein also tried to maintain the integrity of objective knowledge in policy analysis. Even though giving advice entails normative choice, he believed it was possible to argue objectively about the relevance of a policy story. This is done by examining the facts of the story in light of the situation it is supposed to describe. In his view, while it is relatively easy to assess the truthfulness of a story by determining what did or did not happen, it is much harder to assess the validity of the explanation of why things happened as they did. Explanations of why things happened are imbued with values and require storytelling. He maintained that the rules for determining the validity of stories are partly logical, partly aesthetic, and not well understood.

Rein worked against the positivist ideal of natural science. Because analysts mix facts and values when giving advice, he wanted to maintain a place for both objective knowledge and normative choice. Yet, his experience did not fit with the logic of positivism. This was the problem he faced: When confronted with two competing value-neutral theories, a rational choice could be made between them by determining which theory more accurately and comprehensively reflects the facts of the situation. When confronted with two stories that mix facts and values, however, the factual aspects can be decided just as described but the value components cannot because values are considered nonrational since they do not have the same objective status as facts. Rein did not have the work of postpositivists to help him resolve the dichotomy between fact and value and the problem of rationally choosing among competing policy stories.

SOME DEVELOPMENTS IN POSTPOSITIVISM

Recent, postpositivist developments in the philosophy of science indicate that the development, dissemination, and use of knowledge in both the natural and social sciences involves narration and storytelling. From these developments, three themes emerge that provide the basis for a narrative theory of knowledge. They are the rejection of the myth of the given, the recognition of practical discourse as the basis for rationally choosing among competing theories, and the humanizing of science.

The myth of the given is a cornerstone of the positivist conception of science. It is the belief that something must exist independent of science itself that serves as the ultimate basis for all claims to knowledge. That "something" is construed as the realm of objective facts. In positivist natural and social science, this elusive realm serves as both the object of inquiry and the basis for accepting one theoretical formulation over another. This leads to the idea that theory is merely an instrument or tool for the objective observation of facts. Theory, in other words, is nothing more than a neutral mirror reflecting nature. According to John Gunnell, however, positivists have failed to "demonstrate that there is any category of primitive, incorrigible, authoritative, and self-justifying perceptions which, when expressed in verbal form, provide a foundation for knowledge and a rational criterion for judging empirical assertions and theories" (1975, 163). Thus, the given is mythical.

A consensus theory of truth, applying to both facts and theories, has replaced this myth of the given. Rather than being independently objective, scientific facts are instead nothing more than well-established concepts that exist only because a community of scientists agrees that they do. Some such concepts are so well established that they are rarely brought into question. Other such concepts, usually at the edge of scientific research, are open to interpretation and reinterpretation. Whether established or new, facts-as-concepts are the closest thing to facts-as-given. Only a leap of faith allows human beings to claim that a fact-concept actually relates to some objective entity independent of themselves. Theories are nothing more than a collection of fact-concepts linked together through a logical relationship. Usually inductive or deductive, that relationship can also be hermeneutic, meaning-circular, or referential.

In this consensus theory of truth, the question of whether or not a scientific theory applies to a specified domain of inquiry is again a matter of agreement among a community of scientists. Like fact-concepts, some theories are well established and rarely questioned; others are newer and in need of testing and interpretation. It is also a matter of faith to say that theories correctly mirror nature or society. In the eyes of some philosophers of science, theories are nothing more than "myths, metaphors, and stories" (Hesse 1980) because facts are a matter of agreement, theories are a matter of agreement, and the relationship between the two is also a matter of agreement.

The consensus theory of truth raises the question of how to choose among competing theories. If there is no objective realm of facts to which to appeal, how can one theory be chosen over another as a better explanation of the phenomenon under study? Richard J. Bernstein (1988) believes that without an answer to this question, science must be a relativistic and irrational undertaking. He offers practical discourse as an appropriate answer to the question.

In short, practical discourse is an ongoing conversation among a group of researchers who more or less share a common understanding of what it is they study. In this conversation, ideas, concepts, theories, and even paradigms are offered up for examination and criticism. They are accepted or rejected on the basis of argumentation, deliberation, persuasion, imagination, interpretation, and the application of open criteria for what constitutes a good theory. Bernstein arrives at this understanding of scientific rationality by showing parallels and similarities among many ideas offered by philosophers of science, most notably Juergen Habermas, Mary Hesse, Thomas S. Kuhn, Richard Rorty, Hans-Georg Gadamer, and Hannah Arendt.

The implications of the practical discourse theory of scientific rationality are more important. Practical discourse stresses the role communication plays in establishing and transforming knowledge. Much of that communication involves argumentation. Theories are not simply announced. To make them acceptable to a community of researchers, reasons must be given for how they fit in with, augment, or even refute existing theories. And persuading someone to accept the power of the better argument cannot be accomplished without narration and storytelling. Giving reasons ultimately involves an appeal to some criteria.

Positivists believe that the criteria for choosing between theories are both standard and universal, thereby making all knowledge claims ultimately determined by fixed criteria that serve as guarantors of truth. This is simply not the case. Criteria do exist, but they are neither universal nor standard. They are nothing more than the values that the particular scientific community holds. According to Thomas S. Kuhn, the most common values are "accuracy, consistency, scope, simplicity, and fruitfulness" (1977, 322). These and other values operate as criteria for theory choice at local levels and in small domains of argument about competing theories.

The values are weighed differently by different scientists, who often come into conflict with one another. The manner in which a theory is presented to a community of scientists necessarily reflects an appeal to some configuration of values. Acceptance of the theory depends upon the scientist's ability to persuade others not only about the evidence or propositions offered by the theory, but also about how the theory satisfies the background values that pertain to theories themselves. For example, is the proposed theory more comprehensive than existing ones? Is it more accurate? Is it simpler? The process of persuading a community of scientists to value one theory over another relies on effective narration and storytelling. The acceptance or rejection of theories in the natural and the social sciences depends upon an ongoing practical discourse, traditionally the domain of argumentation about values.

The third postpositivist theme, the humanizing of science, involves the growing recognition that the logic of the natural sciences, and of the social sciences modeled after them, is remarkably similar to the logic of the cultural sciences, which include such fields as art, history, linguistics, poetics, literary criticism, and cultural criticism. These sciences also include those portions of the fields of cultural anthropology, sociology, and psychology that reject a naturalistic conception of the self and society. Traditionally, the natural sciences have been thought to offer explanations of objective data ("facts") using a precise, exact, and neutral observation language that follows a rigorous and linear inductive or deductive logic. The cultural sciences have been thought to offer interpretations of subjective data using a theoretical language loaded with values and preferences and following a circular logic. Hence, the scientific validity of the cultural sciences was questioned.

Mary Hesse (1980) has shown that this traditional view of the natural sciences is "almost universally discredited" and that in the most important ways the natural sciences are similar, if not identical, to the cultural sciences. Among other things, this means that "data are not detachable from theory," "theories are . . . the way the facts themselves are seen," "the language of natural science is irreducibly metaphorical and inexact," and that science is shot through with theoretical interpretation (p. 172). The logic of the natural sciences, in other words, is remarkably similar to the logic of the cultural sciences.

The humanizing of science is not a critique of the success of science; rather, it is the realization that in many ways the natural sciences operate in the same manner as the cultural sciences. The knowledge offered by the natural sciences does not, therefore, enjoy a superiority over the knowledge offered by the cultural sciences. In fact, the cultural sciences are a rich source of information about how the natural and social sciences work.

The rejection of the myth of the given, the recognition of the role of practical discourse in theory choice, and the humanizing of science offer logical support from within the philosophy of science for a narrative theory of knowledge. This support reflects what Rein saw in policy analysis as the "giving of advice." It also reflects what others have observed about the logic and practice of science. In theoretical physics, for example, storytelling is vital particularly where technology is unavailable to conduct actual experiments. Physicists refer to their stories as "thought experiments" (Prigogine 1984, 43). While they wait for the technology to test their ideas, physicists engage in these thought experiments, composed of facts and values, to explain the behavior of such things as light waves and subatomic particles. Knowledge is acquired and shared among the community of physicists by developing competing thought experiments, or stories. In cultural anthropology, a far cry from theoretical physics, Clifford Geertz (1973) tried for years to abide by the positivist ideal, but then rejected it when he realized that what he did as a scientist was best represented as "thick description." Other labels such as "naturalistic inquiry" have been offered for research that does not strictly follow the orthodox logic of positivism (Lincoln and Guba 1985). Many prominent social scientists have expressed dismay and concern over the failure of positivist social inquiry and have turned to interpretation to represent the logic of what they do (Winkler 1985).

In light of the themes discussed in this section, it should be clear that narration and storytelling are vital in the development, communication, and acceptance of knowledge. It is impossible to conceive of any research report that does not require a story about why the research was undertaken, how the research was conducted, and why the results fit meaningfully within some domain of prevailing theory. Furthermore, research reports are presented against the background of an even-larger narrative: the generally accepted body of knowledge in some field or discipline.

Any remaining positivists, however, might have difficulty in accepting the fact that *all* knowledge—even scientific knowledge—is narrative knowledge. In order to accept this, one must come to understand that science is only one source for the stories that explain why things are the way they are and what might happen if we try to change the way things are. This is precisely the poststructuralist and postmodernist view of knowledge.

POSTSTRUCTURALISM

Several themes from poststructuralism converge on a narrative theory of knowledge. Because poststructuralists are concerned with the philosophical foundations of the cultural sciences, they focus on the interpretation of texts and symbol systems. This section outlines some of the poststructuralist themes that parallel developments in the postpositivist philosophy of science.

Structuralism is a pervasive view of the world. It assumes that all phenomena have invariant structures and that the various components of any particular phenomenon can be explained in terms of the structure of which they are a part. For example, when chemists investigate a molecule, they examine not only the components of the molecule but also the way in which the components are related to one another. The combined relationships between the components make up the structure of the molecule and the behavior of those components are seen as determined by their structure. T. K. Seung (1982) has shown how structural analysis has been central to scientific inquiry since Euclid, Plato, Aristotle, and Descartes. As early as 1945, Ernst Cassirer (1945) noted that structuralism had become prominent in almost all fields of scientific research. Later, Jean Piaget (1970) observed that the concepts of structuralism such as totality, self-regulation, and transformation are commonly found in anthropology, linguistics, mathematics, physics, biology, psychology, and philosophy.

Structuralism is familiar to public administration through the sociology of Talcott Parsons and the use of systems theory to describe and explain organizational phenomena. Although structuralist categories of analysis and systems-theory concepts pervade most current thinking about public organizations, the structuralist perspective is not without its critics. David Silverman (1971) has noted that using the organic metaphor upon which structuralism and systems theory are based fosters a proclivity to reify organizations by attributing to them human powers of thought and action. As a result, there is a tendency to lose sight of the fact that organizations are populated by human beings whose subjective beliefs, values, and intentions are guiding their actions. This is a reality to which the structuralist perspective is blind. Michael M. Harmon and Richard T. Mayer, following Silverman's critique, note that the reification of organizations "ignores the idea that organizational action can be fully understood in terms of meanings and intentions of individual actors" (1986, 180).

That structuralism loses sight of human subjectivity is not an unintentional consequence. Mandan Sarup observed that

> Levi-Strauss, a leading structuralist, called the human subject—the center of being—the "spoilt brat of philosophy." He stated that the ultimate goal of the human sciences is not to constitute man but to dissolve him. This became the slogan of structuralism. (1989, 1)

Much of modern organization theory, as well as much of sociology, psychology, economics, and political science, successfully dissolves human subjectivity.

Subjectivity and language both play central roles in poststructuralist thought. This is evident in the psychoanalysis and linguistics of Jacques Lacan and the linguistics and literary criticism of Jacques Derrida.

Lacan (1978a and 1978b) made a major contribution to psychoanalysis by reconstructing the physiological reductionism in the biological and mechanical foundations of Freudian theory.[4] Lacan does not deny that human beings are biological; rather, he argues that biological existence is always interpreted by the subject through language. There is no real sense of the body before language, even the primitive language that a child speaks. Thus the ability to speak a language separates the subject from the natural world. The inability to speak a language leads to schizophrenia. Language is the precondition for knowledge of both the self and the world, even of one's own biological existence. Since language is the vehicle of culture, culture comes before the body in determining the subject. Culture—not nature—and, ultimately, language become the basis for all knowledge of the world, both social and natural.

Lacan (1977) also reconstructed Ferdinand de Saussure's structuralist theory of language, which shared assumptions similar to those of positivism. Saussure (1974) maintained that language is a collection of signs, with each sign made up of a single signified and single signifier. In a linguistic sign, the signified is a concept, for example, "chair." The signifier is the sound image made by the word "chair." In the structuralist view of language, because the signified dominates and determines the signifier, it is inappropriate to utter the sound image (the signifier) "table" when intending to speak about a chair. When signs are put together to form a language, the structural relationship between signifier and signified supposedly allows for a one-to-one correspondence between propositions and reality. The dominance of the signified over the signifier is consistent with the positivist insistence on an objective realm of facts as the basis for theory. The one-to-one correspondence between propositions and reality is consistent with the more-ancient positivist notion that there can be only one word for each thing in the universe, and that the task of the scientist is to find those words.

Lacan altered the interpretation of the structural relationship of the sign. He speaks of "the incessant sliding of the signified under the signifier" (1977, 154). This means that a signified can take on other signifers and that the process of signification is never complete, resulting in a growing chain of significations. In language, this creates a one-to-many correspondence between reality and propositions. Thus, there can be many propositions about reality, and the interpretation of reality is ongoing.

Derrida's (1973, 1976, and 1978) theory of language is more radical than Lacan's and even more critical of the positivism in the structuralist view. Derrida believes that signifiers and signifieds continually break apart and reattach in new combinations, resulting in no stable meanings for signs. Indeed, the meaning of a sign can change radically, even to the point of having totally different meanings at different points in time. In language, this means that propositions could have a many-to-many correspondence, but it also means that theoretical propositions have no extralinguistic reality at all, a position that is in direct opposition to positivism.

This linguistic theory is the basis for Derrida's deconstructionist approach to literature. As Colin Campbell explains deconstructionism,

To "deconstruct" a text is pretty much what it sounds like—to pick the thing carefully apart, exposing what deconstructors see as the central fact and tragic little secret of Western philosophy—namely, the circular tendency of language to refer to itself. Because the "language" of a text refers mainly to other "languages" and texts—and not to some hard, extratextual reality—the text tends to have several possible meanings, which usually undermine one another. In fact, the "meaning" of a piece of writing—it doesn't matter whether it is a poem or a novel or a philosophic treatise—is indeterminate (1986, 23).

Paul Ricoeur (1971) has argued that situations in which social action take place may be read like texts. I have tried to show how the principles of literary criticism can be applied to the interpretation of social situations in public administration (White 1987). To the extent that social situations can be treated like texts, they are open to deconstruction.

Poststructuralism poses a major threat to positivism. If positivists are willing to learn from the cultural sciences, they may be able to put the logic of science on a more firm footing and correct some of the errors made in the practice of science—particularly social science—especially as it is applied to concerns of public administration.

SOME VIEWS FROM POSTMODERNISM

Postmodernism is a social trend and an intellectual movement in the cultural sciences. While there is no precise date, most scholars agree that the postmodern era emerged after World War II. In general, postmodernism is the recognition that the European Enlightenment's promises of universal truth, beauty, and justice would not be realized in modern society. This section discusses features of postmodernism using the ideas of Jean-Francois Lyotard and Frederic Jameson.

According to Lyotard (1984), knowledge in traditional societies took on a narrative form: stories, myths, fables, legends, or tales. Early on these narratives were transmitted verbally, later in writing. Narratives served several functions. They told people what to believe and how to act. Rules communicated through narratives established social bonds. Narratives gave legitimacy to the institutions that promulgated them (e.g., church, state, and sorcery). Narratives also contained criteria for making statements about truth, justice, and beauty. Not surprisingly, cohesive social groups shared a common narrative.

A major feature of modern society is the growth of scientific knowledge, which was hailed as radically different from the stories, myths, fables, legends, and tales that had guided social practices. Reflecting Ludwig Wittgenstein's influence, Lyotard argues that, on the contrary, science is just another form of narration because all knowledge is fundamentally a matter of playing a language game. While there can be different types of narratives, of which science is just one type, all narratives are fundamentally based on language games. Language games are composed of rules that allow utterances to have meaning to a community of interlocutors. The rules are neither standard nor universal; they are, instead, established by implicit or explicit contract.

For Lyotard, language games are incommensurable, and the rules of each game are different. Scientists play a denotative language game where the rules allow for distinctions between true and false statements. Scientists are not supposed to play a prescriptive language game that distinguishes between just and unjust statements, nor are they supposed to play a technical language game where the rules provide for distinctions between statements about efficiency and inefficiency. Because the rules differ across games, scientists could play prescriptive or technical games, but then they would not be doing science.

Incommensurability means that different types of knowledge can exist; this does not alone, however, support the modern belief that scientific knowledge is superior to other forms of knowledge. Lyotard argues that scientific knowledge must ultimately resort to other forms of narrative knowledge to maintain its legitimacy in society. Popular stories about the power of science, for instance, reinforce the belief that science has a privileged hold on the criteria for truth or that scientific knowledge is just or beautiful. Such beliefs notwithstanding, science is not a superior form of narration; it is just simply one type of knowledge. For Lyotard, a main feature of the postmodern era is that the domains of art, morality, and science have become fully fragmented, separated and autonomous—and each with its own language game.

Another feature of modern society, according to Lyotard, is the existence of grand narratives or "grand *recits* of modernity" that shape belief systems and orient individual and collective action. Western societies have adopted different grand narratives. Some of them include "the dialectics of the Spirit (Hegelianism), the hermeneutics of meaning (French phenomenology and existentialism), the emancipation of the rational or working subject (Marxism), or the creation of wealth (capitalism)." Belief in the power of science to solve natural and social problems is itself a grand narrative, as is Peter L. Berger *et al.*'s (1973) designation of the main features of modernity: technical rationality, the bureaucratic administrative state, and pluralist politics.

For Lyotard, another feature of postmodernism is the breakdown in the legitimating force of grand narratives, leading to a sense of loss and meaninglessness in the lives of the people who once believed in them. The same meaninglessness, without the loss, exists for those who never had the chance to appropriate the grand narrative. All the grand narratives mentioned above have lost their legitimating function—they no longer provide a comprehensive understanding of society and one's place in it.

Lyotard argues that in place of grand narratives, there is only a pluralism of local narratives to guide thought and action. Life can only become meaningful on the local level, and there is always the danger that the local narratives through which people live their lives will clash with one another. The stories are fragile that people create to define both themselves and what they are up to. When those stories break, new ones have to be told for meaning to return to life.

Jameson (1984) draws two parallels to Lyotard's description of the social conditions of postmodernism, relating to the experience of time and personal identity. First, he argues that Westerners have lost their ability to deal with the present or the future. He calls this "pastiche," meaning the imitation of dead styles. One example he uses is the Western fascination with the nostalgia film, suggesting that only the past is meaningful. (Similarly, much of what passes for postmodern architecture seems also to be a form of pastiche in the sense that old styles are grafted onto new designs.)

His second argument starts with Lacan's definition of schizophrenia as the inability to engage fully in speech and language. If the social fragmentation that Lyotard sees at the social level penetrates to the level of language, then the signs break up into disorganized signifiers and signifieds. In this case, language can no longer provide a coherent experience, and schizophrenia is the result. If Lacan, Lyotard, and Jameson are correct, then the postmodern era represents a different future than the one promised by the Enlightenment.

Jameson (1981) is also a proponent for the narrative theory of knowledge. Narration, he believes, is not merely a literary style. It is the most fundamental epistemological category because all experience comes to us as stories. A sense of the world is impossible without weaving a story that can be lived with and through. All experience, both natural and social, makes sense only because it becomes part of an ongoing story about who people are in relation to others, what they might think and believe, what they might hope for, and how they might act. One corrective for the problems of pastiche and schizophrenia is the willingness to engage in telling stories about the past, the present, and the possible future.

IMPLICATIONS FOR PUBLIC ADMINISTRATION

The views outlined above present interesting questions and challenges to public administration. They range from issues of epistemology to questions of methodology, to the role of public administration in society, to the identity of public administration itself, and to the task of solving local interconnected problems.

First, knowledge in public administration is developed and conveyed in many ways, including scientific articles that test hypotheses, case studies, descriptions of administrative or policy events, historical interpretations of the field or parts of it, deductive arguments, philosophical critiques, and personal reflections on administrative experiences. Under Jameson's view that narration is the fundamental epistemological category, then no matter in what form knowledge comes to public administration, it is narrative. Initially, this gives equal status to each way of developing and conveying knowledge. No one form of knowledge should be arbitrarily dismissed in theorybuilding and problemsolving, nor should any one be arbitrarily elevated in status.

Second, much of the knowledge that is developed in the field is intended as advice. As Rein has argued, advice only becomes meaningful if the researcher can weave together a story that has both objective and normative implications. As Jameson has argued, experience of the world comes through stories. While this is more obvious for knowledge conveyed through descriptions of events or logical arguments, it is true even in the case of scientific works that test hypotheses or present statistical analyses. Good researchers do not simply present the results of such research as hard data. Instead, they tell stories, albeit narrow ones, that make the data and findings meaningful and useful to the intended audience. On the other side, readers take the data, findings, and authors' stories and weave them into their own stories about what they should believe and what they might do. Good storytelling and good reading skills are important for all forms of knowledge development and use in public administration.

Third, storytelling as knowledge development serves two important practical purposes: interpretation and critique.[5] Stories help people understand what is going on and why it is going on. Stories allow people to make better sense of their experience and their current situations. Stories also present visions of how things might otherwise be. They offer alternative images of what people's situations might be if they were to act in ways to change them, especially if people find their situations unsatisfactory. Stories can also offer suggestions about what actions would be most effective in changing particular situations. Through storytelling, interpretation and critique enable social change.

Fourth, much of the knowledge in public administration most closely approximates the conventional meaning of a story. On one level, most published articles and dissertations in the field seem to fall into the category of narrative knowledge. They include case studies, descriptions of administrative and political events, logical arguments, and interpretations of the field's history and future (McCurdy and Cleary 1984; Perry and Kraemer 1986; White 1986a). This type of research has been denigrated by positivists as not being scientific, but the poststructuralists and postmodernists give it the same status as scientific research.Ironically, from the latter perspectives, many researchers in public administration are ahead of their time by insisting on developing narrative knowledge. At a deeper level, the postpositivists have shown that even scientific knowledge has a narrative base and that the logic of natural-scientific inquiry needs to be reconstructed in light of recent developments in the cultural sciences.

Fifth, the logic of knowledge development and use as narration deserves articulation. Methodological principles are needed to guide narrative research in the field. Attention must be paid to how to tell a good story and what the consequences of storytelling might be. Discussions of appropriate standards and criteria for narrative knowledge must take place. The rules accepted when playing denotative, prescriptive, and technical language games must be uncovered and examined for their appropriateness for research. Too often, others—namely philosophers—reconstruct the logic of research, and at times, their reconstructions may bear only partial resemblance to what is being done in a field. Philosophers—too busy focusing on traditional disciplines—rarely pay attention to public administration. Public administrationists are the only ones with a real interest in the logic of what they do and the consequences of their actions.

Sixth, the role of public administration in society must be dealt with. The field is responsible for two main features of the modern era: the bureaucratic administrative state and the reliance on technical rationality. Should the field continue to perpetuate these features of society as the postmodern era unfolds? What changes should be made in public administration in light of the postmodern condition? What should be the role of public administration, if any, in dealing with the problems of postmodernism, such as the pastiche and schizophrenia that Jameson fears? If society is really as fragmented as Lyotard claims, what role, if any, does public administration have in bringing it together? Since public administration, through bureaucracy and technical rationality, is responsible for this fragmentation, can the field do anything about it without being radically reconstructed? What would that reconstruction look like?

Seventh, the narratives that guide public administration should be considered in light of postmodernism. The two most prominent narratives that shape beliefs and guide action are the politics-administration dichotomy and the New Public Administration. The technical rationality inherent in the dichotomy between politics and administration clearly supported the development of modern society. To the extent that this narrative is still evident in the field, it is inconsistent with postmodernism. Indeed, modernists and postmodernists alike have been critical of the alienating effect of technical rationality on society such that it results in a disenchantment with science and the administrated state (Foucault 1980).

Some of the themes of the New Public Administration were consistent with the Enlightenment's promise for modernity. There was the optimism that society's problems could be solved in a reasoned and systematic way, as well as the optimism that proactive public administrators—by fostering social equity—could contribute to the creation of a just society. Other themes of the New Public Administration were more in line with some of the demands of postmodernism, especially the theme of postpositivism. Neither the politics-administration dichotomy nor the New Public Administration achieved the status of a grand narrative to legitimate belief and action for all of public administration. As local narratives, they were adopted by some but criticized and rejected by others.

Eighth, as noted in the introduction to this chapter, one theme that emerges from Minnowbrook II is that of the complex web of interconnected problems facing public administrators today. Just one example would be youth gangs. Youth gangs are a problem of public safety and law enforcement, but this problem is connected to others such as poverty, the emergence of a permanent underclass, drug use and trade, inadequate education, lack of economic opportunities, and unaffordable or substandard housing. A problem like youth gangs cannot be approached by a grand theory, for no such theory exists. Efforts to solve the problem must rely on the use of multiple local theories that relate to each of the interconnected problems. The problem of youth gangs may have a more fundamental source in postmodern society. Gang members have not had the opportunity to participate in the narratives that shape the beliefs and actions of the rest of society. They have certainly developed their own local narratives to explain to themselves who they are and what they are up to. Direct interventions to get gang members to think and act differently are fundamentally a matter of convincing them of a story that will give them a different narrative to live with.

Ninth, local knowledge seems appropriate for solving local problems. A local problem is not necessarily one that occurs at the local level of government, but it could. Local problemsolving in the postmodern era will proceed incrementally as small problems are addressed one at a time using local knowledge. For example, a state agency experiencing high rates of turnover is a local problem. It is immediately sensed by managers and workers in the agency, not usually by others outside the agency. The knowledge required to solve the problem will also be local. There are no grand theories of turnover, only local ones. The problem could be a result of job dissatisfaction, or low organizational commitment, or job stress, or work overload, or occupational burnout. The problem could be solved using one or more local theories, or using the experiences of other agencies told in the stories of case studies and administrative descriptions that bear little resemblance to positivist science. Solving the problem of turnover in a single agency is not the type of broad-based problemsolving idealized by some of the conferees at Minnowbrook I; it is, however, more typical of problemsolving today, as suggested by some of the conferees at Minnowbrook II.

The task of public administration is one of developing ongoing local narratives about a multiplicity of local problems to avoid the meaninglessness that comes of social and psychological fragmentation. The interconnectedness of local problems must be identified in order to preserve a greater sense of public administration as a whole. The postmodernists discussed here would deny the possibility of developing a grand narrative for public administration. The development of interconnected, local narratives that cut across the interconnected, local problems of society and that convey meaningful beliefs as a basis for effective action is necessary.

NOTES

1. See Frederickson (1971), LaPorte (1971), and Marini (1971).

2. For example, see Denhardt (1984), Harmon (1981), Hummel (1987), and White (1986a).

3. Herbert A. Simon (1969) has argued that the applied social sciences have a normative element. In his discussion of the design process, central to policy and administration, he notes that the applied-engineering model encompasses normative questions of how things "ought to be in order to attain goals, and to function" (p. 7). But his is a narrow view of the normative dimension of administration and policy analysis. Simon is concerned with normative knowledge and reasoning only to the extent that they achieve given ends and goals. While Rein would agree that normative concerns enter into the achievement of ends and goals, he is more concerned with explicating the logic of the valuational process that leads analysts and decisionmakers to choose among competing ends and goals of public action. That logic involves an interpretive and critical approach to selecting ends and goals. Simon maintains that the design process requires only a "modest adaptation of ordinary declarative logic" (p. 134). Thus, he maintains a positivist stance that Rein finds inadequate for explaining the logic of policy analysis.

4. For an English-language discussion of Lacan's theories, see Benvenuto and Kennedy (1986) and MacCannell (1986).

5. There is a debate between Gadamer and Habermas over the relative importance of interpretation and critique. Gadamer (1975 and 1977, 20-26) sees critique as an element in the never-ending process of interpretation. It is the critical moment when existing interpretations are altered and changed to further enhance understanding. Habermas (1971 and 1977) wants critique to stand on its own as the central ingredient for social change. He feels that interpretation is conservative and tends to preserve the status quo.

In his view, simply understanding why things are the way they are does not help people to change the way things are if they find their situations unsatisfactory. This, in Habermas's view, is the important function of critique that separates it from interpretation.

Epilogue
Dwight Waldo

When asked to write an epilogue for this volume of essays by participants in Minnowbrook II, I readily accepted. The assignment seemed appropriate and easily executed. After all, I had been an observer at both of the Minnowbrooks and, having no talent for creativity, had specialized in "perspectives."

In the event, the assignment presents difficulties. A review and critique of each chapter is not appropriate for a number of reasons. But what can be said, generally, about essays so diverse? What I shall do is offer some observations about the two Minnowbrooks, separately and comparatively, and present for consideration some observations concerning their place in Public Administration[1] during the half-century 1940-90.

Minnowbrook I was centrally a manifestation in Public Administration of the "movement" in the universities and colleges in the sixties and early seventies. To discuss here the origins, dynamics, and results of the movement in general is not possible, but it is also unnecessary—there are accounts, descriptions, and analyses in plenty. I shall speak only to what I regard as the most important matters to and for most Minnowbrook I participants. (Some of those present were passively dissenters.)

One of the slogans of the movement was "You can't trust anyone over thirty." While a majority of the Minnowbrookers were beyond this symbolic divider, all were relatively young because the meeting was designed to reflect relative youth.[2] The youth factor—I judge—operated at several levels, intermingled and (largely) reinforcing. There was a current of anger and rebellion relating centrally to the still-escalating war in Vietnam. There was something of a "crisis" mentality relating to civil and political events and disturbances: assassinations, riots, and their aftermaths. There was a "cultural" rebellion against sociocultural conventions and restrictions, and sympathy for movements toward a youth-inspired counterculture. There was impatience with, and hostility toward, the body of academic status distinctions and conventions associated with history, rank, and age. And there was a feeling that Public Administration lacked respect and relevance: It seemed old, sterile, and irrelevant to pressing contemporary problems.

Regarding this feeling I have three reactions. One, it was justified. Two, it was unjustified. Three, it was easier to see the problems than to identify solutions. A few words to each in turn.

Public Administration in the sixties was hardly the "intellectual wasteland" it was designated by a president of the American Political Science Association. It *was* troubled and unsure of its identity. In the political science departments where it was largely resident, it lacked, on the one hand, the aristocratic aura of the liberal arts tradition and, on the other hand, the prestige of the then-ascendant behavioral movement, which was determined to make the study of political science truly scientific at last.

The essence of the matter is that it had taken on the role of preparing persons for careers in public administration and this central role had imperatives and constraints. Much of what was taught was not "exciting" but was deemed essential to the objective. After all, how exciting is the human musculature to would-be physicians, the law of contracts to would-be lawyers, cost accounting to would-be business persons?

On the other hand, any feeling that Public Administration was a dull and sterile terrain certainly was unwarranted. In the period beginning with World War II, the endeavor had been enlivened and enriched by the contributions of able and varied writers. To illustrate, not to catalog: Paul Appleby, Robert Dahl, Marshall Dimock, James Fesler, Herman Finer, Carl Friedrich, Herbert Kaufman, V. O. Key, Norton Long, Charles Lindblom, Frederick Mosher, Wallace Sayre, Philip Selznick, Herbert Simon, James Thompson, and Victor Thompson. And if it be objected that a number of these were not public administrationists—or even political scientists—the objection makes my point: Public Administration was hardly a stagnant backwater, whatever its problems of identity and prestige.

Turning to the third point, that it was easier for the Minnowbrookers to see problems than to identify solutions, this is hardly a novel situation. One can quickly construct a list of contemporary societal problems for which there is no recognized solution or even agreed ameliorative remedy. But the attendees were dissatisfied and impatient, eager to make Public Administration and the government administration on which it focused effective and respected. They wanted a *new* Public Administration, one more or less freed from instrumentalist constraints arising from history, law, and ideology, one more active, ameliorative, humane, and creative.

Certainly Minnowbrook II had important elements of continuity with Minnowbrook I. The objective was much the same: to assess contemporary Public Administration, improve it, and move it toward a brighter future. George Frederickson, an active member of the organizing committee for Minnowbrook I, was the prime organizer of Minnowbrook II.

But the differences also were great. This was no gathering of angry young men. The national political-emotional climate was much more relaxed—however great the problems "out there." There was a conscious attempt to bridge between the first and the second meeting, with a 1960s representation and a 1980s representation. The average age of participants, as this indicates, was higher. The tone and conduct of the meeting was more nearly in accord with normal procedures and mores. (Rather symbolically, the large lodge where Minnowbrook I centered had been destroyed by fire, and meetings now took place in adequate but quite different facilities.) A very great difference in the two gatherings related to gender: no women were participants in Minnowbrook I, but nearly a quarter of the participants in Minnowbrook II were women—a fact prominently reflected in this volume.

I turn now to an attempt to relate the two Minnowbrooks to the half century of Public Administration beginning with 1940. The date 1940 is rather arbitrary and is meant only to indicate that World War II was important, one way and another, for Public Administration.[3]

In the nearly three decades between 1940 and Minnowbrook I some of the main events and developments included World War II, its aftermath of reconstruction and decolonization (the membership of the United Nations trebling), the East-West polarization, militarization and Cold War, the Korean War and the Vietnam War, general economic stability and growth, and a developing drive toward economic and racial equity.

Clearly, World War II was influential, broadening and deepening Public Administration through its massive impact on organization and administration and through the lives and work of those who studied and wrote about Public Administration. The so-called politics-administration dichotomy, questioned in the thirties, was now subjected to devastating criticism, though its replacement was not and still is not clear and agreed upon. The postwar reconstruction, decolonization, and nationbuilding, together with new intellectual currents in and out of political science, gave rise in Public Administration to the somewhat joined but also somewhat separate enterprises of development administration and comparative administration. Regarding East-West polarization and militarization, it is difficult to discern much direct effect beyond the attempt to extend some budgeting techniques borrowed from business but developed in the U.S. Department of Defense and government generally.

While it is difficult, also, to discern much effect of the Korean War in Public Administration, the Vietnam War has had significant but largely indirect or subtle effects. One of these was to attenuate still further the connection between military-defense administration and "other" administration. The movements toward greater equality in the sixties, for which the phrase "Great Society" became the slogan, were highly influential. They spawned new programs, indeed big, bold experiments, in government attempts at socioeconomic change. They presented a new world for experimentation and analysis, and their relationship to the concurrently developing wave of policy analysis is obvious.

Seeking to site Minnowbrook I in its historical context and speak to its nature and results, what can be said? I venture the following. There was little or no connection with some of the major historical events of the post-war period. The study of comparative and development administration were then vigorous, engaging a substantial number of those identified with Public Administration. But such interests were far from the minds of most Minnowbrookers. What was front and center—intermingled with other motifs and emotions of the student movement—was the idealism of Great Society objectives posed against the extravagant horror of a war seen as without cause and legitimacy.

The result, in my assessment, was two main thrusts. One was to assert the legitimacy of the public administrationist and the practicing administrator in taking moral action, that is, action aimed at reducing or preventing human suffering or, more broadly, seeking to increase the Good as defined by history and philosophy. This was a bold movement into the politics side of the politics-administration dichotomy: the administrator was to become a political-moral agent. The move was too bold for some public administrationists, and one accused the Minnowbrookers of "a brazen attempt to 'steal' the public sovereignty" (Thompson, 1975, 66).

Great Society objectives of ending racial discrimination, ending poverty, and related causes became encapsulated in the phrase "social equity." Of the Minnowbrook I participants, H. George Frederickson has probably been the major figure seeking to advance the Minnowbrook agenda, and the social equity theme has been central in his efforts.

Turning to the last two decades, what events and movements can be identified that are relevant to, that might be presumed to provide context or themes for, Minnowbrook II?

First of all, it is appropriate to observe that while concern for equity hardly vanished from our national political conscience and consciousness, events in the seventies greatly diminished its prominence. As the seventies unfolded there was a perceived or alleged failure of government programs that had social equity as objective. The result was a retreat in such government activity, and an increase in denigration of government and its agents. "Bureaucrat bashing" was part of the successful campaigns of both President Carter and President Reagan.

But the change in mood and agenda resulted also from other causes. Prominently, the petroleum cartel's success in diminishing the supply and increasing the price of petroleum was a shock of major proportions. Centrally, it turned attention from Great Society concerns to another set of problems focused upon the basis and the consequences of our economic system.

Reflecting on the last two decades I conclude that there are too many developments and influences to try to discuss them in the present context. I shall merely call attention to some of the prominent ones—most or all of which receive some recognition in the preceding chapters. So, quickly and without serious discussion, the following.

Feminism as a consciousness and a movement of course long antedated the half-century, but was a prominent and increasing presence during the past two decades. Environmentalism also has roots in earlier times, but grew prominently as a consciousness and sociopolitical force in the recent period. The seventies saw the rise of futurism—an ambition to foresee and control the future—to the status of fad if not industry; and while the movement has declined in prominence, futurism remains important as an activity and as an ingredient of current thinking. "Yuppieism" may perhaps be used as a term to indicate the rise of a complex of activities and values—in many ways the reverse of the "movement" of the sixties—associated with the late seventies and eighties and its manifestation in politics, economics, and life in general.

A growing environmentalism of course has presented problems in several dimensions, but other problem areas that engaged public consciousness should be noted. Among those prominently perceived were education, seen as troubled and deteriorating from kindergarten to graduate school; drugs and drug-related crime, corruption and ill health; deteriorating international competitiveness in economic areas in which we had enjoyed supremacy; a complex of problems in the area of family and sexual behavior. And to be sure, racial—more generally ethnic—problems continued as an important item on the agenda of public problems; generally they simmered, but occasionally rose to a boil.

The advances in communications technology during the two decades, building on already great advances, has been extraordinary. While the known results, in one sphere after another are already astounding, the presumed or anticipated transformations in the human condition, from individual consciousness to global interrelations, can only be described as revolutionary.

The foregoing phenomena are hardly devoid of accompanying ideas and theories, but in the area of philosophy—both strictly and loosely construed—there were developments relevant to Minnowbrook II. In general, I judge it correct to say, a retreat from positivism already under way by mid-century continued and broadened as the years passed. But there was by no means a return to grand pre-positivist systems. Perhaps the main thrust could be characterized as a revival of traditional philosophical pursuits, epistemology and ethics prominently, now pursued on a naturalistic level. So it might be appropriate to say that positivism was not so much repudiated as redefined and variously developed.

To this sketch of the milieu in which Minnowbrook II took place it is appropriate to add another factor: grand interpretations of history and of the present and future human condition. These of course we have at all times, and the past fifty years have seen the exposition and popularity of various of them. The most notable ones, for our purpose, are those that find the clues to trends and events in technology and its interactions with psychology, consciousness, and culture generally. Our half century has given us many books in this area, some of which are, well, Big.

My sketch of the context of Minnowbrook II is, of course, simple, impressionistic. But let me now try to see its relationship to the gathering itself.

I begin with an attempt to capture in a phrase the animating spirit of each of the Minnowbrooks. For Minnowbrook I: revolt and reconstruction. For Minnowbrook II: ambition and exploration.

I hasten to add that the ambition was not personal (though some of this is always present) but for Public Administration. Public administration as a function and activity was viewed as badly treated and unfairly maligned; Public Administration as a self-aware enterprise was viewed as in need of further development and new sources of strength. So, inquiry: for foundations, interconnections, dynamics, new roads forward.

Patently, the essays between these covers and other essays that are the product of Minnowbrook II display important relationships to the course of events and the currents of ideas since Minnowbrook I. They address concept after concept, theme after theme, cause after cause prominent in the score of years. Of course, they do not address all important matters present in the milieu. Economic-budgetary-financial matters, racial-ethnic problems, environmental developments—these and some other important subjects are touched upon lightly if at all. But of course it would be unrealistic to expect from such gatherings an encyclopedic treatment of the public world.

The chapters in general and some of them in particular speak to a world seen as "post" what has formed and defined the world of the past few centuries, a world created and moved by new forces, a world having dimensions and dynamics quite without precedent. They see a New World, one partly in existence but not recognized and acknowledged by those whose consciousness was formed and fixed in old mechanistic modes. They see a world that will emerge and replace the old, one in which administrative technology appropriate to the needs of recent centuries is no more appropriate than the technology of the world of steam power is appropriate for an electronic-communications complex.

I now pose a question. As it happened, immediately after reading these chapters I turned my attention to some "practical" Public Administration literature. I read a piece on "The Current State of the Public Service" in *PA Times*[4] and I returned to the Report of the National Commission on the Public Service and its accompanying task force reports. It goes too far to say that this was entering a quite different world, real as against fanciful. There are, after all, some common themes. For example, one goal stated in the report is "Decentralize Government Management," another "Increase the Representation of Minorities." But most of the recommendations—for example, "Provide Competitive Pay and Demand Competitive Performance"—seem far removed from the conceptions and concerns of the various essays.

Are we, then, to classify the depictions and projections of a new world and its appropriate administrative technology as a species of science fiction, "Public Administration fiction"?

On this as on so many things I am of two minds. This work is but one of a spate of works, recently or soon-to-be published, that pushes past what has been regarded as the perimeter of the world of Public Administration. Often my first response is: Please, Get Real. Don't try so hard. Go back and identify a real problem and work on it, and stop wasting your time and mine. You have overreacted to the charge that Public Administration is dull and irrelevant. Facts, not fiction, please.

My second response is often quite different. I am proud to be associated with an enterprise so lively, forward looking, and multifaceted. Yes, we do need work, more and better work, on the very real problems close to the traditional interests of Public Administration. But we also need experimentation, vision, imagination, projection. And while the engine of change is often identified as something material or something technical (bronze, steel, steam power, internal combustion, whatever) that is seen as the real substructure of society, it is often—or also—words: ideas, concepts, visions. Who would deny the causative, creative power of the books and documents that led to modern democracy?

The pace and scale of change are now incredible, disorienting. Time will tell how close is the "fit" with some of the projected administrative technology.

NOTES

1. There is a troublesome ambiguity in the term "public administration." Economics, the doctrines or discipline, is clearly not the economy; sociology, the doctrines or discipline, is clearly not society; and of course no one would mistake political science for politics. But public administration is used in referring both to the doctrines and discipline and to the activities of government administration. I sometimes deal with this ambiguity by using the style Public Administration to refer to the self-aware enterprise, the doctrines and discipline; and the style public administration to refer to the activities of government administration. This usage does not solve all problems, but I use it in this Epilogue.

2. I was an "ancient" in my mid-fifties, but I was present solely as sponsor and observer. I have recorded some of the history and my impressions in Brown and Stillman (1986, 105-8).

3. Whether to emphasize continuity or change is in large part a matter of taste and purpose. I sometimes visualize Public Administration as a fabric with a warp—continuous strands indicating continuous concerns—and a woof of changing materials and colors. But then—I remind myself—strands in the warp can also change.

4. J. Robert Schaetzel, May 1, 1990, p. 2 ff.

Bibliography

Agassi, Judith B. *Comparing the Work Attitudes of Women and Men*. Lexington, Mass.: D.C. Heath, 1979.

Ahn, Kenneth K., and Saint-Germain, Michelle A. "Public Administration Education and the Status of Women." *American Review of Public Administration* 18(1988): 3:297-307.

Apgar, William C., and Brown, H. James. *Microeconomics and Public Policy*. Glenview, Ill.: Scott, Foresman, 1987.

Appleby, Paul H. *Policy and Administration*. Tuscaloosa, Ala.: University of Alabama Press, 1949.

Argyris, Chris, and Schon, Donald. *Organizational Learning: A Theory of Action Perspective*. Reading, Mass.: Addison-Wesley, 1978.

Attfield, Robin. *The Ethics of Environmental Concern*. New York: Columbia University Press, 1983.

Bailey, Julie. "Jobs for Women in the Nineties." *Ms*. 17:1(July 1988):74-79.

Bailey, Mary Timney. "Minnowbrook II: An End or a New Beginning?" In Frederickson and Mayer (1989, 224-25).

Barnes, Lesley. "The Work Force of the Future." *Government Executive* (November 1988):56-57.

Barrett, William. *The Illusion of Technique*. Garden City, N.Y.: Doubleday, Anchor Books, 1979.

Barry, Brian. *Political Argument*. London: Routledge & Kegan Paul, 1965.

Bass, Bernard. "Leadership: Good, Better, Best." *Organizational Dynamics* (Winter 1985):26-40.

Bayes, Jane. "Do Female Managers in Public Bureaucracies Manage With a Different Voice?" Paper presented at the Third International Congress on Women, Trinity College, Dublin, 1987.

Beauvoir, Simone de. *The Second Sex*. New York: Alfred A. Knopf, 1957.

Belenky, M.F.; Clinchy, B.M.; Goldberger, N.R.; and Tarule, J.M. *Women's Ways of Knowing*. New York: Basic Books, 1986.

Bennis, Warren, and Nanus, Burt. *Leaders: The Strategies for Taking Charge*. New York: Harper and Row, 1985.

Benvenuto, Bice, and Kennedy, Roger. *The Works of Jacques Lacan: An Introduction*. London: Free Association Books, 1986.

Berger, Peter L.; Berger, Brigitte; and Kellner, Hasnfried. *The Homeless Mind*. New York: Vintage Books, 1973.

Bernstein, Richard. *Beyond Objectivism and Relativism: Science, Hermeneutics, and Praxis*. Philadelphia: University of Pennsylvania Press, 1988.

Bianchi, Suzanne M., and Spain, Daphne. *American Women: Three Decades of Change.* Washington, D.C.: U.S. Bureau of the Census, Special Demographic Analyses, CDS-80-8., U.S. Government PrintingOffice, June 1984.

Blair, Diane D., and Stanley, Jeanie R. "Male and Female Legislators: Perceptions of Power." Paper presented at the annual meeting of the Southern Political Science Association, Nashville, 1989.

Bledstein, Burton. *The Culture of Professionalism: The Middle Class and the Development of Higher Education in America.* New York: Norton, 1976.

Bloom, David E., and Steen, Todd P. "Why Childcare Is Good for Business." *American Demographics* 10(1988):8:22-27, 58-59.

Bocher, R.B. "Does Tradition Affect Affirmative Action Results? How Pennsylvania Achieved Changes at the Middle-Management Level." *Public Administration Review* 42:5(Sep./Oct. 1982):475-8.

Boorstin, Daniel J. *The Discoverers.* New York: Random House, 1983.

Bordo, Susan. "The Cartesian Masculinization of Thought." In Sandra Harding and Jean F. O'Barr, eds. *Sex and Scientific Inquiry,* pp. 247-64. Chicago: University of Chicago Press, 1987.

Bork, Robert H. "Neutral Principles and Some First Amendment Problems." *Indiana Law Journal* 47:1(Fall 1971):1-35.

Botkin, J.W. *et al. No Limits to Learning: Bridging the Human Gap.* New York: Pergamon Press, 1979.

Bowman, Garda W.; Worthy, N. Beatrice; and Greyser, Stephen A. "Are Women Executives People?" *Harvard Business Review* 43(1965):4:14-28, 164-78.

Brenner, O.C."Relationship of Education to Sex, Managerial Status, and the Managerial Stereotype." *Journal of Applied Psychology* 67(1982):3:380-3.

Brown, Brack, and Stillman, Richard J., II. *A Search for Public Administration: The Ideas and Career of Dwight Waldo.* College Station, Tex.: Texas A&M University Press, 1986.

Brown, Wendy. *Manhood and Politics: A Feminist Reading in Political Theory.* Totowa, N.J.: Rowman and Littlefield, 1988.

Bryson, John, and Einsweiller, Robert. *Shared Power.* University Press of America, 1991.

Burney, Derek. "Canada and the United States in Global Context: Acid Rain." *Vital Speeches of the Day* (Nov. 1, 1989):43-45.

Burrell, Barbara. "Gender and the Use of Modern Campaign Technologies in State Legislative Races: The Case of Massachusetts." Paper presented at the annual meeting of the American Political Science Association, Atlanta, 1989.

Campbell, Colin. "The Tyranny of the Yale Critics." *The New York Times Magazine* (Feb. 9, 1986):23.

Carter, Lief H. *Reason in Law,* 3rd ed. Boston: Scott, Foresman, 1988.

—— and Gilliom, John. "From Foundation to Discourse: Trends in Contemporary Constitutional Philosophy." In Michael W. McCann and Gerald L. Houseman, eds. *Judging the Constitution,* pp. 13-48. Glenview, Ill.: Scott, Foresman, 1989.

Cassirer, Ernst. "Structuralism in Modern Linguistics." *Word* 1(1945):120.

Castillejo, Irene Claremont de. *Knowing Woman: A Feminine Psychology.* Boston: Shambhala, 1990.

Center for the American Woman and Politics. *Women in Elective Office, 1989.* New Brunswick, N.J.: Eagleton Institute of Politics, Rutgers University, May 1, 1989.

Chandler, Alfred D., Jr. *The Visible Hand: The Managerial Revolution in American Business.* Cambridge: Belknap, Harvard University Press, 1977.

Chodorow, Nancy. *The Reproduction of Mothering*. Berkeley, Calif.: University of California Press, 1978.

Chubb, John E., and Peterson, Paul E., eds. *Can the Government Govern?* Washington, D.C.: Brookings Institution, 1989.

Ciabattari, Jane. "The Biggest Mistake Top Managers Make." *Working Woman* (October 1986):47-55.

Cochran, Nancy. "Society as Emergent and More Than Rational." *Policy Sciences* 12(1980):2:453-67.

Code, Lorraine. "Second Persons." In Marsha Hanen and Kai Nielsen, eds. *Science, Morality and Feminist Theory. Canadian Journal of Philosophy*, supp. (1987): 357-82.

Cohen, Sherry Suib. *Tender Power: A Revolutionary Approach to Work and Intimacy*. Reading, Mass.: Addison-Wesley, 1989.

Colwill, Nina L., and Erhart, Marilyn. "Have Women Changed the Workplace?" *Business Quarterly* 50(1985):1:27-31.

Cooney, Rosemary S., Clague, Alice S., and Salvo,Joseph J. "Multiple Dimensions of Sexual Inequality in the Labor Force: 1970-1977." *Review of Public Data Use* 8:(October 1980):279-93.

Cooper, Cary L. "Corporate Policies and Working Couples." *Journal of General Management* 12(1987):3:52-57.

Cooper, Terry. *The Responsible Administrator*. Port Washington, N.Y.: Kennikat Press, 1982.

Crocker, Jennifer. "Introduction." *American Behavioral Scientist* 27(1984):3:285-86.

—— and Kathleen McGraw. "What's Good for the Goose Is Not Good for the Gander." *American Behavioral Scientist* 27(1984):3:357-70.

CSPA (Council of State Policy and Planning Agencies). "Global Interdependence and American States." Working paper for the 1989 Annual CSPA Conference.

Davis, Elizabeth. *Women's Intuition*. Berkeley, Calif.: Celestial Arts, 1989.

Denhardt, Robert B. *In the Shadow of Organization*. Lawrence, Kan.: University Press of Kansas, 1981.

——. *Theories of Public Organization*. Monterey, Calif.: Brooks/Cole, 1984.

—— and Denhardt, Kathryn. 1979. "Public Administration and the Critique of Domination." *Administration and Society* 11:107-120.

Derrida, Jacques. *Speech and Phenomena, and Other Essays on Husserl's Theory of Signs*. Evanston, Ill.: Northwestern University Press, 1973.

——. *Of Grammatology*. Baltimore: Johns Hopkins University Press, 1976.

——. *Writing and Difference*. London: Routledge & Kegan Paul, 1978.

Dillon, C. Douglas. "The Challenge of Modern Governance." In Donald L. Robinson, ed. *Reforming American Government*, pp. 24-29. Boulder, Col.: Westview Press, 1985.

Dinnerstein, Dorothy. *The Mermaid and the Minotaur: Sexual Arrangements and Human Malaise*. New York: Harper and Row, 1976.

DiPrete, Thomas A. "The Professionalization of Administration and Equal Employment Opportunity in the U.S. Federal Government." *American Journal of Sociology*. 93(1987):1:119-40.

Doig, Jameson W. "Leadership and Innovation in the Administrative State." Paper presented at Minnowbrook II Conference, Minnowbrook Conference Center, N.Y., September 1988.

Dometrius, N.C. "Minorities and Women Among State Agency Leaders." *Social Science Quarterly* 65(1984):127-37.

Drucker, Peter. *Managing in Turbulent Times.* New York: Harper and Row, 1980.

Dunn, William N.. *Public Policy Analysis: An Introduction.* Englewood Cliffs, N.J.: Prentice-Hall, 1981.

Dye, Thomas R. *Understanding Public Policy,* 4th ed. Englewood Cliffs, N.J.: Prentice-Hall, 1981.

Ellul, Jacques. *The Technological Society.* John Wilkinson, trans. New York: Vintage, Random House, 1964.

Etzioni, Amitai. *The Moral Dimension: Toward a New Economics.* New York: The Free Press, 1988.

Ezell, Hazel F.; Odewahn, Charles A.; and Sherman, J. Daniel. "Perceived Competence of Women Managers in Public Human Services Organizations: A Comparative View." *Journal of Management* 6(1980):2:135-44.

———. "Women Entering Management Differences in Perceptions of Factors Influencing Integration." *Group & Organization Studies* 7(1982):2:243-53.

Ferguson, Ann. "A Feminist Aspect Theory of the Self." In Marsha Hanen and Kai Nielsen, eds. *Science, Morality and Feminist Theory. Canadian Journal of Philosophy,* supp. (1987):339-56.

Ferguson, Kathy E. *The Feminist Case Against Bureaucracy.* Philadelphia: Temple University Press, 1984.

Fischer, Frank. *Politics, Values, and Public Policy: The Problem of Methodology.* Boulder, Col.: Westview Press, 1980.

Fisher, Louis. *Presidential Spending Power.* Princeton, N.J.: Princeton University Press, 1975.

———. *Constitutional Dialogues: Interpretation as Political Process.* Princeton, N.J.: Princeton University Press, 1988.

Fitzgerald, Louise F. and Sandra L. Shullman. "The Myths and Realities of Women in Organizations." *Training and Development Journal* (April 1984):65-70.

Flax, Jane. "The Conflict between Nurturance and Autonomy in Mother-Daughter Relationships and Within Feminism." *Feminist Studies* (June 1978).

Follett, Mary Parker. *The New State: Group Organization the Solution of Popular Government.* Gloucester, Mass: Peter Smith, 1965; originally published in 1918.

———. "Leader and Expert." In Elliot M. Fox and L. Urwick, eds. *Dynamic Administration,* pp. 203-36. New York: Pitman, 1973; originally published in 1920.

———. *Creative Experience.* New York: Peter Smith, 1951; originally published in 1924.

Forbes, J. Benjamin, and Piercy, James E. "Rising to the Top: Executive Women in 1983 and Beyond." *Business Horizons* 26(1983):5:38-47.

Foucault, Michael. *Power/Knowledge, Selected Interviews and Other Writings 1972-1977.* London: Harvester Press, 1980.

Fox, S.F. "Rights and Obligations: Critical Feminist Theory, the Public Bureaucracy, and Policies for Mother-Only Families." *Public Administration Review* 47:5(Sep./Oct. 1987):436-40.

Franklin, D.W., and Sweeney, J.L. "Women and Corporate Power." In E. Boneparth and E. Stoper, eds. *Women, Power and Policy,* pp. 48-65. New York: Pergamon Press, 1988.

Frederickson, H. George. "Toward A New Public Administration." In Marini (1971, 309-31).

——. "The Lineage of New Public Administration." *Administration and Society* 8(1976): 2:149-75.

——. "The Recovery of Civism in Public Administration." *Public Administration Review*. 42:6(Nov./Dec. 1982):501-8.

—— and Mayer, Richard T., symposium eds., "Minnowbrook II: Changing Epochs of Public Administration." *Public Administration Review* 49:2(March/April 1989)

Freedman, Sara M., and Phillips, James S. "The Changing Nature of Research on Women at Work." *Journal of Management* 14(1988):2:231-51.

French, J.R.P., and Raven, B. "The Bases of Social Power." In Cartwright and Zander, eds. *Group Dynamics*. New York: Harper & Row, 1968.

French, Marilyn. "Self-Respect: A Female Perspective." *The Humanist* (Nov./Dec. 1986):18-23.

Friere, P. *Pedagogy of the Oppressed*. New York: Seabury Press, 1968.

Fullerton, Howard N., Jr. "The 1995 Labor Force: BLS' Latest Projections." *Monthly Labor Review* 108(1985):11:17-25.

Gadamer, Hans-Georg. *Truth and Method*. New York: Seabury Press, 1975.

——. *Philosophical Hermeneutics*. Berkeley, Calif.: University of California Press, 1977.

——.*Truth and Method*. New York: Crossroad Publishing, 1988.

Gawthrop, Louis C. "Minnowbrook: The Search for a New Reality." In Frederickson and Mayer (1989, 194-95).

Gay, Peter. *The Bourgeois Experience: Victoria to Freud*. Vol. 1, *The Education of the Senses*. New York: Oxford University Press, 1984.

Geertz, Clifford. *The Interpretation of Culture*. New York: Basic Books, 1973.

Geis, Florence L., Boston, Marth B., and Hoffman, Nadine. "Sex of Authority Role Models and Achievement By Men and Women: Leadership Performance and Recognition." *Journal of Personality and Social Psychology* 49(1985):3:636-53.

Gilligan, Carol. *In a Different Voice*. Cambridge: Harvard University Press, 1982.

Golembiewski, Robert. *Approaches to Planned Change: Part 1*. New York Marcel Dekker, 1971.

Gomez-Mejia, L.R. "Sex Differences During Occupational Socialization." *Academy of Management Journal* 26(1983):3:492-99.

Gould, Carol C. "Private Rights and Public Virtues: Women, the Family and Democracy." In Gould, ed. *Beyond Domination: New Perspectives on Women and Philosophy*, pp. 3-20. Totowa, N.J.: Rowman and Allanheld, 1983.

Government Executive. "Day Care Update." 21:4(April 1989):7-8.

Grant, Jan. "Women as Managers: What They Can Offer to Organizations." *Organizational Dynamics* (Winter 1988):56-63.

Grey, Thomas C. "Do We Have an Unwritten Constitution?" *Stanford Law Review* 27(Feb. 1976):703-18.

——. "Origins of the Unwritten Constitution: Fundamental Law in American Revolutionary Thought." *Stanford Law Review* 30(May 1978):843-93.

——. "The Constitution as Scripture." *Stanford Law Review* 37 (November 1984):1-25.

——. "The Uses of an Unwritten Constitution. *Chicago-Kent Law Review* 64(1988):211-38.

Grossman, Harry. "The Equal Employment Opportunity Act of 1972, Its Implications for the State and Local Government Manager." *Public Personnel Management* 2(1973):5:370-79.

Gulick, Luther. "The Metaphors of Public Administration." *Public Administration Quar-*
       terly (Fall 1984).
Gunnell, John G. *Philosophy, Science, and Political Inquiry*. Morristown, N.J.: General
       Learning Press, 1975.
Guy, Mary Ellen. "Passages Through the Organization: Old Dogs and New Tricks."
       Group & Organization Studies 9(1984):4:467-79.
——. *Professionals in Organizations: Debunking a Myth*. Westport, Conn.: Praeger,
       1985.
——. "Minnowbrook II: Conclusions." In Frederickson and Mayer (1989, 219-20).
Habermas, Juergen. *Knowledge and Human Interests*. Jeremy Shapiro, trans. Boston:
       Beacon Press, 1971.
——. *Theory and Practice*. Boston: Beacon Press, 1973.
——. "A Review of Gadamer's *Truth and Method*." In Fred R. Dallmayr and Thomas A.
       McCarthy, eds. *Understanding and Social Inquiry*, pp. 353-63. Notre Dame,
       Ind.: University of Notre Dame Press, 1977.
Hale, Mary M., and Kelly, Rita Mae, eds. *Gender, Bureaucracy, & Democracy*. Westport,
       Conn.: Greenwood Press, 1989.
Harding, Sandra. *The Science Question in Feminism*. Ithaca, N.Y.: Cornell University
       Press, 1986.
Harmon, Michael M. "Normative Theory and Public Administration: Some Suggestions
       for a Redefiniation of Administrative Responsibility." In Marini (1971, 172-85).
——. *Action Theory for Public Administration*. New York: Longman, 1981.
——. "'Decision' and 'Action' As Conflicting Perspectives in Organization Theory." In
       Frederickson and Mayer (1989, 144-53).
—— and Mayer, Richard T. *Organization Theory for Public Administration*. Glenview,
       Ill.: Scott, Foresman, 1986.
Heclo, Hugh. "Issue Networks and the Executive Establishment." In Richard J. Stillman,
       II, ed. *Public Administration: Cases and Concepts,* 3rd ed., pp. 416-25. Boston:
       Houghton-Miflin, 1983
Heilbroner, Robert. "Reflections: Hard Times." *The New Yorker* (Sept. 14, 1987):108-10.
Hesse, Mary. *Revolutions and Reconstructions in the Philosophy of Science*. Brighton,
       England: Harvester Press, 1980.
——. "Aristotle's Shadow: Models, Metaphors, and Myth's." In "Does Ideology Stop at
       the Laboratory Door? A Debate on Science and the Real World." *The New York
       Times* (Oct. 22, 1989):24E.
Holsti, Ole R., and Rosenau, James N. "The Foreign Policy Beliefs of Women in
       Leadership Positions." *Journal of Politics* 43(1981):2:326-47.
Hood, C. *The Tools of Government*. Chatham, N.J.: Chatham House, 1983.
Huber, George P. *Managerial Decision Making*. Glenview, Ill.: Scott, Foresman, 1980.
Hudson Institute. *Workforce 2000: Work and Workers for the 21st Century*. Washington,
       D.C.: U.S. Government Printing Office, June 1987.
——. *Civil Service 2000*. Washington, D.C.: U.S. Government Printing Office, June
       1988.
Huerta, Faye C., and Lane, Thomas A. "Participation of Women in Centers of Power."
       The Social Science Journal 18(April 1981):71-86.
Hummel, Ralph P. *The Bureaucratic Experience*, 3rd ed. New York: St. Martins, 1987.
Jameson, Frederic. *The Political Unconsciousness: Narrative as a Socially Symbolic Act.*
       Ithaca, N.Y.: Cornell University Press, 1981.

———. "Postmodernism and the Cultural Logic of Capital." *New Left Review* 146(July/Aug. 1984).

Janeway, Elizabeth. "Women and the Uses of Power." In Hester Eisenstein and Alice Jardine, eds. *The Future of Difference*. New Brunswick, N.J.: Rutgers University Press, 1987.

Jaques, Elliott. *A Theory of Bureaucracy*. London: Halstead Press, 1976.

———. *Requisite Organization*. New York: Cason Hall, 1989.

Johnson, Alicia. "Discrimination: Roots and Remedies." *Management Review* (Dec. 1987):38-43.

Johnston, Denis F. "Education of Workers: Projections to 1990." *Monthly Labor Review* 96(1973):11:22-31.

Jonas, Hans. *The Imperative of Responsibility*. Chicago: University of Chicago Press, 1984.

Jonsen, Albert R., and Toulmin, Stephen. *The Abuse of Casuistry*. Berkeley, Calif.: University of California Press, 1988.

Josephowitz, Natasha. "Management Men and Women: Closed vs. Open Doors." *Harvard Business Review* (Sep./Oct. 1980):57-62.

Kagan, Julie. "Cracks in the Glass Ceiling." *Working Woman* (October 1986):107-9.

Kammen, Michael. *A Machine That Would Go of Itself*. New York: Vintage Books, 1986.

Kanter, Rosabeth Moss. "Presentation VI, Part 2." *Signs* 1(1976):3:282-91.

———. *Men and Women of the Corporation*. New York: Basic Books, 1977.

———. "Place and Power: Men and Women of the Corporation Revisited." *The World* 3(1989a):2:8-9.

———. "The New Managerial Work." *Harvard Business Review* 89(1989b):6:85-92.

Kaplan, H. Roy, and Tausky, Curt. "Humanism in Organizations: A Critical Appraisal." *Public Administration Review* 37:2(March/April 1977):171-79.

Kaplan, Paul A. "Affirmative Employment Statistics for Executive Branch (Non-Postal) Agencies as of September 30, 1986." In *Employment and Trends as of . . .* Washington, D.C.: U.S. Office of Personnel Management, May 1987, pp. 69-75.

Karl, Barry. "The American Bureaucrat: A History of a Sheep in Wolves' Clothing." *Public Administration Review* 47:1(Jan./Feb. 1987):26-34.

Keller, Catherine. *From a Broken Web: Separation, Sexism and Self*. Boston: Beacon Press, 1986.

Keller, Evelyn Fox. *A Feeling for the Organism: The Life and Work of Barbara McClintock*. New York: W. H. Freeman, 1983.

———. *Reflections on Gender and Science*. New Haven, Conn.: Yale University Press, 1985.

Kellner, Hans. *Language and Historical Representation: Getting the Story Crooked*. Madison, Wis.: University of Wisconsin Press, 1989.

Keohane, Robert, and Nye, J. S. *Power and Interdependence*. Boston: Little, Brown, 1977.

Kirkpatrick, David. "Environmentalism: The New Crusade." *Fortune* (Feb. 12, 1990).

Kirlin, John. "Adapting the Intergovernmental Fiscal System to the Demands of an Advanced Economy." *Urban Affairs Quarterly* 16(1979):123-48.

Kosterlitz, Julie. "Family Cries." *National Journal* 20:16(April 16, 1988):994-99.

Kuhn, Thomas S. *The Essential Tension: Selected Studies in Scientific Tradition and Change*. Chicago: University of Chicago Press, 1977.

LaBier, Douglas. *Modern Madness: The Emotional Fallout of Success*. Reading, Mass.: Addison-Wesley, 1986.

Lacan, Jacques. *Ecrits: A Selection*. London: Tavistock, 1977.
——. *The Language of the Self: The Function of Language in Psychoanalysis*. Baltimore: Johns Hopkins University Press, 1978a.
——. *The Four Fundamental Concepts of Psychoanalysis*. London: Hogarth Press, 1978b.
Landes, Joan B. *Women and the Public Sphere in the Age of the French Revolution*. Ithaca, N.Y.: Cornell University Press, 1988.
LaPorte, Todd R. "The Recovery of Relevance in the Study of Public Administration." In Marini (1971, 17-48).
Lau, James B., and Shani, Rami. *Behavior in Organizations: An Experiential Approach*, 4th ed. Homewood, Ill.: Irwin, 1988.
Lee, James A. "Changes in Managerial Values, 1965-1986." *Business Horizons* 31(1988): 4:29-37.
Lenz, Elinor, and Meyerhoff, Barbara. *The Feminization of America*. Los Angeles: Jeremy P. Tarcher, 1985.
Leopold, Aldo. *A Sand County Almanac and Sketches Here and There*. New York: Oxford University Press, 1949.
Lewis, Gregory B. "Men and Women in Federal Employment: Placements, Promotions, and Occupations." *Dissertation Abstracts International* 45(1985):11:3447-A.
——. "Equal Employment Opportunity and the Early Career in Federal Employment." *Review of Public Personnel Administration* 6(1986):3:1-18.
——. "Progress Toward Racial and Sexual Equality in the Federal Civil Service?" *Public Administration Review* 48:3(May/June 1988):700-7.
——. "Men and Women Toward the Top." Paper presented at the annual conference of the American Society for Public Administration, Los Angeles, 1990.
—— and Park, Kyungho. "Turnover Rates in Federal White-Collar Employment: Are Women More Likely to Quit Than Men?" *American Review of Public Administration* 19(1989):1:13-28.
Lichter, Daniel T., and Costanzo, Janice A. "How Do Demographic Changes Affect Labor-Force Participation of Women?" *Monthly Labor Review* 110(1987): 11:23-25.
Lincoln, Yvonna S., and Guba, Egon G. *Naturalistic Inquiry*. Beverly Hills, Calif.: Sage Publications, 1985.
Lipman-Blumen, Jean. "Female Leadership in Formal Organizations: Must the Female Leader Go Formal?" In Matina Horner, ed. *Challenge of Change*. New York: Plenum, 1982.
Lipset, Seymour Martin, and Schneider, William. *The Confidence Gap: Business, Labor, and Government in the Public Mind*, rev. ed. Baltimore: Johns Hopkins University Press, 1987.
Loden, Marilyn. *Feminine Leadership: Or How to Succeed in Business Without Being One of the Boys*. New York: Times Books, 1985.
Long, Norton. "The S.E.S. and the Public Interest." *Public Administration Review* 41:3(May/June 1981):305-12.
Longman, P. *Born to Pay: The New Politics of Aging in America*. Boston: Houghton Mifflin, 1987.
Lottinville, Savoie. *The Rhetoric of History*. Norman, Okla.: University of Oklahoma Press, 1976.
Lowi, Theodore J. *The End of Liberalism: The Second Republic of the United States*, 2nd ed. New York: W. W. Norton, 1979.

Luke, Jeff S. "Local Governments in the 1990's." *State and Local Government Review* (1986a).

——. "Managing Interconnectedness: The Need for Catalytic Leadership." *Futures Research Quarterly* 2(1986b):4.

——. "Ethics in an Interconnected Web." In J. Bowman, ed. *The New Frontier in Ethics*. San Francisco: Jossey-Bass, 1991.

—— and Caiden, Gerald E. "Coping With Global Interdependence." In Perry (1989), pp. 83-93.

——; Ventriss, Curtis; Reed, B.J.; and Reed, Christine. *Managing Economic Development: State and Local Leadership Strategies.* San Francisco: Jossey Bass, 1988.

Lynn, Naomi B., and Vaden, Richard E. "Toward a Non-Sexist Personnel Opportunity Structure: The Federal Executive Bureaucracy." *Public Personnel Management* (July/Aug. 1979):209-15.

Lyotard, Jean-Francois. *The Postmodern Condition: A Report on Knowledge*. Manchester, England: Manchester University Press, 1984.

MacCannell, Juliet Flower. *Figuring Lacan: Criticism and the Cultural Unconsciousness*. London: Croom Helm, 1986.

Maccoby, Michael. *The Leader*. New York: Simon and Schuster, 1981.

Magnus, Margaret. "Eldercare: Corporate Awareness, But Little Action." *Personnel Journal* 67(1988):6:19-23.

Marini, Frank, ed. *Toward a New Public Administration*. Scranton, Pa.: Chandler, 1971.

——. "The Minnowbrook Perspective and the Future of Public Administration Education." In Marini (1971, 349).

Markham, William T., and Corder, Judy. "Social Structure and Intergroup Interaction: Men and Women of the Federal Bureaucracy." *American Sociological Review* 47(October 1982):587-99.

Martin, Daniel W. "The Fading Legacy of Woodrow Wilson." *Public Administration Review* 48:2(March/April 1988):631-6.

Marx, Karl. *Capital*, vol. 1. In Robert C. Tucker, ed., *The Marx-Engels Reader*, 2nd ed. (New York: Norton, 1978).

Matzer, John, Jr., ed. *Practical Financial Management: New Techniques for Local Government*. Washington, D.C.: International City Management Association, 1984.

Mayer, Richard T. "The Operant Social Theory: Implementing Power for Public Purposes." *Journal of Managment Science and Policy Analysis* 6:1(Fall 1988):14-26.

——. "Technological Modes of Thinking-and-Acting: Theory and Practice in the American Administrative State, 1960-1980." DPA diss., George Washington University, 1989.

McCluhan, Marshall. *Understanding Media*. New York: New American Library, 1964.

McCurdy, Howard, and Cleary, Robert. "Why Can't We Resolve the Research Issue in Public Administration?" *Public Administration Review* 44:1(Jan./Feb. 1984): 49-55.

McGregor, Douglas M. *The Human Side of Enterprise*. New York: McGraw-Hill, 1960.

Merchant, Carolyn. *The Death of Nature: Women, Ecology, and the Scientific Revolution*. New York: Harper and Row, 1980.

Mikesell, John L. *Fiscal Administration: Analysis and Applications for the Public Sector*, 2nd ed. Chicago: Dorsey Press, 1986.

Mitroff, Ian, and Kilmann, Ralph. *Corporate Tragedies*. Praeger Publishing, 1984.

Morgan, Gareth, ed. *Beyond Method: Strategies for Social Research.* Beverly Hills, Calif.: Sage Publications, 1983.

Morgenthaler, Eric. "Under Pressure, Firms Try Upgrade Status of Women Employees." *Wall Street Journal* (March 20, 1972):1,17.

Morrison, Ann M.; White, Randall P.; Van Velsor, Ellen; and Center for Creative Leadership. *Breaking the Glass Ceiling.* Reading, Mass: Addison-Wesley, 1987.

Morrison, Peter A. "Changing Demographics: What to Watch for." *Business Economics* 22(1987):3:5-8.

Mosher, Frederick C. "The Changing Responsibilities and Tactics of the Federal Government. " *Public Administration Review* 40:6(Nov./Dec. 1980):541-48.

Moss, Carolyn J. "Opportunities Expand for Women and Minorities." *Newsletter of the Virginia Council on the Status of Women* 3(1988):4:1-2.

Moynihan, Daniel P. *Maximum Feasible Misunderstanding: Community Action in the War on Poverty.* New York: Free Press, Macmillan, 1969.

Muldrow, Tressie W., and Bayton, James A. "Men and Women Executives and Processes Related to Decision Accuracy." *Journal of Applied Psychology* 64(1979):2:99-106.

Muller, Herbert J. *The Uses of the Past.* New York: New American Library, 1952.

Mumford, Lewis. *The Myth of the Machine: Technics and Human Development.* New York: Harcourt Brace Jovanovich, 1967.

——. *The Myth of the Machine: The Pentagon of Power.* New York: Harcourt Brace Jovanovich, 1970.

National Committee on Pay Equity. "Briefing Paper #1: The Wage Gap." Washington, D.C.:Government Printing Office, 1989.

Nelson, B.J. "Women's Poverty and Women's Citizenship: Some Political Consequences of Economic Marginality." *Signs* 10(1984):2;209-31.

Neugarten, Bernice, and Neugarten, David. "Policy Issues in an Aging Society." In Storandt and VandenBos, eds. *The Adult Years: Continuity and Change.* Washington, D.C.: American Psychological Association, 1989.

Neustadt, Richard, and May, Ernest. *Thinking in Time: The Uses of History for Decision Makers.* New York: Free Press, 1986.

Newland, Kathleen. *Women, Men and Division of Labor.* Worldwatch Paper 37. Washington, D.C.: Worldwatch Institute, May 1980.

O'Brien, Mary. *The Politics of Reproduction.* London: Routledge, 1981.

PA Times. "Women Take on City Governance: Their Ranks Double in One Decade." 12:12(September 1, 1989):12.

Parasuraman, Saroj; Greenhaus, Jeffrey H.; Rabinowitz, Samuel; Bedeian, Arthur G.; and Mossholder, Kevin W. "Work and Family Variables As Mediators of the Relationship Between Wives' Employment and Husbands' Well-Being." *Academy of Management Journal* 32(1989):1:185-201.

Passmore, John. *Man's Responsibility for Nature.* London: Duckworth, 1974.

Patton, Carl V., and Sawicki, David S. *Basic Methods of Policy Analysis and Planning.* Englewood Cliffs, N.J.: Prentice-Hall, 1986.

Perry, James L., ed. *Handbook of Public Administration.* San Francisco: Jossey Bass, 1989.

—— and Kraemer, Kenneth L. "Research Methodology in the Public Administration Review, 1975-84." *Public Administration Review* 46:3(May/June 1986):215-27.

Peters, Thomas, and Waterman, Robert. *In Search of Excellence*. New York: Warner Books, 1985.

Peterson, Norma. "How do Women Manage?" *American Way* (May 1984):45-49.

Pfiffner, John M. *Public Administration*, rev. ed. New York: Ronald Press, 1946.

Piaget, Jean. *Structuralism*. New York: Basic Books,1970.

Pocock, J.G.A. *The Ancient Constitution and the Feudal Law*. Cambridge: Cambridge University Press, 1987; originally published in 1957.

——. *Politics, Language, and Time: Essays on Political Thought and History*. Chicago: University of Chicago Press, 1989.

Powell, Gary N. *Women and Men in Organizations*. Newbury Park, Calif.: Sage Publications, 1988.

Powell, H. Jefferson. "How Does the Constitution Structure Government?: The Founders' Views." In Burke Marshall, ed., *A Workable Government? The Constitution After 200 Years*, pp. 13-48. New York: W.W. Norton, 1987.

Pranger, Robert J. "The Decline of the American National Government." *Publius* 3:2(Fall 1973):97-127.

Price, Don K. *America's Unwritten Constitution*. Baton Rouge, La.: Louisiana State University Press, 1983.

Prigogine, Ilya. *Order Out of Chaos: Man's New Dialogue With Nature*. New York: Bantam Books, 1984.

Radin, Beryl A., and Cooper, Terry L. "From Public Action to Public Administration: Where Does It Lead?" In Frederickson and Mayer (1989, 167-9).

Reagen, Michael V. "Shifting Demographic and Social Realities." In Perry (1989), pp. 68-82).

Rehfuss, J.A. "A Representative Bureaucracy? Women and Minority Executives in California's Career Service." *Public Administration Review* 46:5(Sep./Oct. 1986):454-60.

Rehnquist, William H. "The Notion of a Living Constitution." *Texas Law Review* 54:4(May 1976):693-706.

Rein, Martin. *Social Science and Public Policy*. New York: Penguin Books, 1976.

Ricoeur, Paul. "The Model of the Text: Meaningful Action Considered as a Text." *Social Research* 38(1971).

Riger, S., and Galligan, P. "Women in Management: An Exploration of Competing Paradigms." *American Psychologist* 35:(1980)10:902-10.

Rizzo, Ann-Marie, and Mendez, Carmen. "Making Things Happen in Organizations: Does Gender Make a Difference?" *Public Personnel Management* (Spring 1988):9-18.

Robinson, Donald L. ed. *Reforming American Government*. Boulder, Col.: Westview Press, 1985.

Rohr, John A. *To Run A Constitution*. Lawrence, Kan.: University of Kansas Press, 1986.

Rorty, Richard. *Philosophy and the Mirror of Nature*. Princeton, N.J.: Princeton University Press, 1979.

Rosenau, James. *The Study of Global Interdependence*. New York: Nicholes Publishing, 1980.

Rosenbloom, David H. "Public Administrators and the Judiciary: The 'New Partnership.'" *Public Administration Review* 47:1(Jan./Feb. 1987):75-83.

Routley, Richard, and Routley, Val. "Nuclear Energy and Obligations to the Future." *Inquiry* 21(1978):133-79.

Ruckelshaus, William. "Toward a Sustainable World." *Scientific American* (Sept. 1989).

Sarap, Mandan. *An Introductory Guide to Poststructuralism and Postmodernism.* Athens, Ga.: University of Georgia Press, 1989.

Saussure, Ferdinand de. *Course in General Linguistics.* London: Fontana, 1974.

Schein, V.E. "The Relationship Between Sex-Role Stereotypes and Requisite Management Characteristics. *Journal of Applied Psychology* 57(1973):2:95-100.

———. "Relationships Between Sex-Role Stereotypes and Requisite Management Characteristics Among Female Managers." *Journal of Applied Psychology* 60(1975): 3:340-44.

Schick, Allen. *Perspectives on Budgeting.* Washington, D.C.: American Society for Public Administration, 1980.

Schon, Donald. "Generative Metaphor." In A. Ortony, ed. *Metaphor in Thought.* New York: Cambridge University Press, 1979.

———. *The Reflective Practitioner.* New York: Basic Books, 1983.

Schrag, Calvin O. *Communicative Praxis and the Space of Subjectivity.* Bloomington, Ind.: Indiana University Press, 1986.

Schwartz, Felice N. "Management Women and the New Facts of Life." *Harvard Business Review* 67(1989):1:65-76.

Scott, Andrew. *The Dynamics of Interdependence.* Chapel Hill, N.C.: University of North Carolina Press, 1982.

Sealander, Judith. *As Minority Becomes Majority.* Westport, Conn.: Greenwood Press, 1983.

Seung, T. K. *Structuralism and Hermeneutics.* New York: Columbia University Press, 1982.

Silverman, David. *The Theory of Organizations.* New York: Basic Books, 1971.

Silvestri, George T., and Lukasiewicz, John M. "A Look at Occupational Employment Trends to the Year 2000." *Monthly Labor Review* 110(1987):9:46-63.

Simon, Herbert A. *The Sciences of the Artificial.* Cambridge, Mass.: MIT Press, 1969.

———. *Reason in Human Affairs.* Palo Alto, Calif.: Stanford University Press, 1983.

Smith, James P., and Ward, Michael P. *Women's Wages and Work in the Twentieth Century.* Santa Monica, Cal: Rand Corporation, R-3119-NICHD, October 1984.

Smith, R.L. "Representative Bureaucracy: A Research Note on Demographic Representation in State Bureaucracies." *Review of Public Personnel Administration* 1(1980):1:1-13.

South, Scott J.; Bonjean, Charles M.; Corder, Judy; and Markham, William T. "Sex and Power in the Federal Bureaucracy." *Work and Occupations* 9(1982):2:233-54.

Stanley, J.R. "Gender Differences in Texas Public Administration." Paper presented at the meeting of the American Political Science Association, Chicago, 1987.

Stanley, Manfred. *The Technological Conscience: Survival and Dignity in an Age of Expertise.* New York: Free Press, 1978.

Steinberg, Rhona, and Shapiro, Stanley. "Sex Differences in Personality Traits of Female and Male Master of Business Administration Students." *Journal of Applied Psychology* 67(1982):3:306-10.

Stewart, Debra W. "Gender and Management Ethics: A Preliminary Inquiry." Presented at the annual meeting of the American Society for Public Administration, Indianapolis, 1985.

——— and Garson, G. David. *Organization Behavior and Public Management.* New York: Marcel Dekker, 1983.

Stillman, Richard J., II., ed. "The American Constitution and the Administrative State: A Symposium." *Public Administration Review* 47:1(Jan./Feb. 1987).

Stone, C. "Efficiency Versus Social Learning: A Reconsideration of the Implementation Process." *Policy Studies Review 4(1985):484-96.*

Stone, Nan. "Mother's work." *Harvard Business Review* 89(1985):5:50-56.

Struever, Nancy S. "The Conversable World: Eighteenth-Century Transformations of the Relations of Rhetoric and Truth." In *Rhetoric and the Pursuit of Truth: Language Change in the Seventeenth and Eighteenth Centuries,* pp. 77-119. Los Angeles: William Andrews Clark Memorial Library, University of California, Los Angeles, 1985.

Thayer, Frederick C. *An End to Hierarchy & Competition: Administration in the Post-Affluent World,* 2nd ed. New York: Franklin Watts, 1981.

Thompson, James D. "Society's Frontiers for Organizing Activities." *Public Administration Review* 33:4(July/Aug. 1973):327-35.

Thompson, Victor A. *Without Sympathy or Enthusiasm: The Problem of Administrative Compassion.* University, Ala.: University of Alabama Press, 1975.

Tulis, Jeffrey K. *The Rhetorical Presidency.* Princeton, N.J.: Princeton University Press, 1987

USDOL (U.S. Department of Labor). *Eleventh Annual Report of the Commissioner of Labor 1895-6: Work and Wages of Men, Women and Children.* Washington, D.C.: U.S. Government Printing Office, 1977.

———. *Employment in Perspective: Women in the Labor Force.* Report 738, Bureau of Labor Statistics, Washington, D.C., 1986a.

———. "20 Facts on Women Workers." Fact Sheet No. 86-1. Washington, D.C.: Office of the Secretary, 1986b.

———. "Over Half of Mothers With Children One-Year-Old or Under in Labor Force in March 1987." Press release, USDOL 87-345, August 12, 1987a.

———. *Facts on U.S. Working Women.* Washington, D.C.: U.S. Government Printing Office, 1987b.

U.S. News & World Report. "Top Women Bureaucrats Talk About Jobs, Bias and Their Changing Roles." (September 5, 1977):38-40.

Van Riper, Paul P. *History of the United States Civil Service.* Westport, Conn.: Greenwood Press, 1976.

Ventriss, Curtis. "Toward a Public Philosophy of Public Administration: A Civic Perspective of the Public." In Frederickson and Mayer (1989, 173-9).

——— and Luke, Jeff. "Organizational Learning and Public Policy: Towards a Substantive Perspective." *American Review of Public Administration* 18:4(Dec. 1988).

Vertz, Laura L. Women, Occupational Advancement, and Mentoring: An Analysis of One Public Organization. *Public Administration Review* 45:3 (May/June 1985):415-23.

Vickers, Brian. *In Defense of Rhetoric.* Oxford: Clarendon Press, 1988.

Wajahn, Ellen. "Why There Aren't More Women in this Magazine." *Inc.* (July 1986):45-48.

Wakeman, Frederick, Jr. "Transnational and Comparative Research." *Social Science Research Council: Items* 42:4(Dec. 1988).

Waldo, Dwight. *Public Administration in a Time of Turbulence.* San Francisco: Chandler, 1971.

Wall Street Journal. "More Women Conquer Business World's Bias, Fill Management Jobs." (February 25, 1963):1,16.

Wamsley, Gary L. "The Public Organization as Agency and the Public Administrator as Agential Leader." In Wamsley, Charles T. Goodsell, John A. Rohr, Philip S.

Kronenberg, Orion F. White, James F. Wolf, Camilla M. Stivers, and Robert N. Bacher, *Refounding Public Administration*, pp. 114-62. Beverly Hills, Calif.: Sage Publications, 1990.

Warren, Scott. *The Emergence of Dialectical Theory*. Chicago: University of Chicago Press, 1984.

Watson, Walter. *The Architectonics of Meaning: Foundations of the New Pluralism*. Albany, N.Y.: State University of New York Press, 1985.

Welch, Susan; Karnig, Albert K.; and Eribes, Richard A. "Correlates of Women's Employment in Local Governments." *Urban Affairs Quarterly* 18(1983):4:551-64.

Westin, Alan F. "Technological Change and the Constitution: Preserving the Framers' Balance in a Computer Age." In Burke Marshall, ed. *A Workable Government? The Constitution After 200 Years*, pp. 189-207. New York: W.W. Norton, 1987.

Whitbeck, Caroline. "A Different Reality: Feminist Ontology." In Carol C. Gould, ed. *Beyond Domination: New Perspectives on Women and Philosophy*, pp. 64-88. Totowa N.J.: Rowman and Allanheld, 1983.

White, James Boyd. *When Words Lose Their Meaning*. Chicago: University of Chicago Press, 1984.

White, Jay D. "On the Growth of Knowledge in Public Administration." *Public Administration Review* 46:1(Jan./Feb. 1986a):15-24.

———. "Dissertations and Publications in Public Administration." *Public Administration Review* 46:3(May/June 1986b):227-34.

———. "Action Theory and Literary Interpretation." *Administration and Society* 19:3(Nov. 1987):346-66.

———. "Images of Administrative Reason and Rationality: The Recovery of Practical Discourse." In Henry D. Kass and Bayard L. Catron, eds. *Images and Identities in Public Administration*, pp. 132-50. Newbury Park, Calif.: Sage Publications, 1990.

Wiebe, Robert H. *The Search for Order 1877-1920*. New York: Hill and Wang, 1967.

Wildavsky, Aaron. *Speaking Truth to Power—The Art and Craft of Policy Analysis*. Boston: Little, Brown, 1979.

Wilson, Woodrow. "The Study of Administration." *Political Science Quarterly* 2:2(June 1887):197-220.

Winkler, Karen. "Questioning the Science in Social Science: Scholars Signal a Turn to Interpretation." *The Chronicle of Higher Education* (June 26, 1985):5-6.

Young-Bruehl, Elizabeth. *Mind and the Body Politic*. New York: Routledge, 1989.

Index

About the Editors and Contributors

MARY TIMNEY BAILEY is associate professor of political science and Director of the Master of Public Administration Program at the University of Cincinnati. Her research focuses on public administration theory and environmental policy. Her work has appeared in *Public Administration Review*, *Public Productivity Review*, and *New Directions in Public Administration Research*.

CAROL J. EDLUND is assistant professor at San Diego State University.

MARY E. GUY is professor of political science and public affairs at University of Alabama at Birmingham. She teaches management courses in the Master's of Public Administration Program and conducts research in decision processes and organization behavior. She has written extensively on managerial issues; her books include *Ethical Decision Making in Everyday Work Situations*, *From Organizational Decline to Organizational Renewal: The Phoenix Syndrome*, and *Professionals in Organizations: Debunking a Myth*.

JEFF S. LUKE is associate professor of planning, public policy, and management, and assistant to the vice president for research, at the University of Oregon. He is coauthor and coeditor of three books on management training, strategic planning, and public policy. In addition, he has been a trainer for the World Bank, the U.S. Office of Personnel Management, and a wide variety of state and local agencies.

FRANK MARINI is professor of urban studies and of political science at the University of Akron. He has served as Associate Dean and Director of Public Administration Programs of the Maxwell School. He was managing editor of *Public Administration Review* from 1967 through 1977 and was the editor of *Toward a New Public Administration: The Minnowbrook Perspective*.

RICHARD T. MAYER is visiting professor of public affairs at George Mason University and managing editor of the *Journal of Public Administration Research and Theory*. He edited, with H. George Frederickson, the symposium "Minnowbrook II: Changing Epochs of Public Administration" in *Public Administration Review* and is coauthor, with Michael M. Harmon, of *Organization Theory for Public Administration*.

CAMILLA STIVERS is member of the faculty, Graduate Program in Public Administration, The Evergreen College, Olympia, Washington. She is coauthor of *Refounding Public Administration* (Beverly Hills, Calif.: Sage, 1990), and her work has appeared in several collections and scholarly journals. She was associate study director for the Institute of Medicine report, *The Future of Public Health*.

DWIGHT WALDO is Albert Schweitzer Professor in the Humanities, Emeritus, at Syracuse University. Beginning in the 1940s, he has published many books and articles dealing with historical and theoretical aspects of public administration. For eleven years, he was editor-in-chief of the *Public Administration Review*.

JAY D. WHITE is professor of public administration at the University of Nebraska at Omaha, where he teaches graduate courses in public management, organization behavior and development, personnel, management information systems, and quantitative methods. His research, which appears in such journals as the *Public Administration Review*, *Administration and Society*, and the *Public Administration Quarterly*, focuses on the philosophical foundations of policy and administrative research.

ROBERT C. ZINKE is assistant professor of public administration at Eastern Washington University. He has published in the areas of cost-benefit analysis and administrative rulemaking, administrative ethics, and technology and public policy. His recent research centers on the influence of technologically based rhetoric on legal, moral, political, and organizational discourse.